Indian Country

Indian Country
Inside Another Canada

Larry Krotz

M&S

Canadian Cataloguing in Publication Data

Krotz, Larry, 1948-
  Indian country

ISBN 0-7710-4547-6

1. Indians of North America – Canada – Reservations.
2. Indians of North America – Canada – Politics and
government.   3. Indians of North America – Canada –
Government relations.   I. Title.

E92.K76 1990   323.1'197071   C90-093319-4

Printed and bound in Canada

McClelland & Stewart Inc.
The Canadian Publishers
481 University Avenue
Toronto, Ontario
M5G 2E9

Contents

Acknowledgements

My heartfelt thanks to the people, the communities, and the families who shared their ideas and their lives with me as I travelled across the country. You will encounter them all in the book. Their passionate sense of vision continually inspired me. The stories in *Indian Country* are theirs; I had but to write them down.

I also want to thank Doug Gibson, publisher at McClelland & Stewart, whose encouragement initiated the project, and Dinah Forbes, whose patience and editing skills carried it through to completion.

Without the generous assistance of the Canada Council, research for this book would have been difficult indeed.

1   Visiting the Indians

The splash of the September sun makes the landscape, thick
stands of white pine, black spruce, rock, and the ever-present
water, look like something framed in a postcard or a calendar
picture or a travel brochure. Which is what it is; tourist country
northwestern Ontario, Lake of the Woods, some of the most
consistently splendid natural scenery in the world. When Pickerel jump, the reverberations of their leap break the mirror
surface of the clear, deep cold of the lake; loons laugh through the
smoke of the early morning mists, moose hide in the bays,
wading languidly through the lily-pad shallows. This is the land
of the Ojibway.

The Indians are still there. Not the Indians of our mythology,
perhaps; for the most part they have been relegated to the caricatures and trinkets that fill the gift shops that line Highway 71
on its 200 kilometre route between Fort Frances down on the
U.S. border and Kenora, the trading and administrative heart of
northwestern Ontario. Or they are memorialized in the lodges
where tourists and fishermen from Chicago and Iowa and Mis-
souri are lured by visions of Ernest Hemingway.

Fishing camps around Sioux Narrows and Nestor Falls have
such names as "Red Indian Lodge" and "Totem Lodge." In the
commerce of tourism and souvenirs the Red Man still has
currency. The Trading Post, a combination grocery store, gas
station, tackle and gun shop, and souvenir stand in Sioux Nar-

rows has a cartoon Indian brave on the sign perched on its roof. The Red Indian Lodge has the image of a dignified chief in full head-dress on its marquee. The idea planted in the mind of the tourist, no doubt, is of moving into a cowboy-and-Indian movie or a wilderness movie where adventure and danger lurk, but in a way that is titillating and exciting, not downright threatening. In truth, the comical looking tomahawk-wielding brave atop the Trading Post store is no more menacing to the good families come boating and fishing than is the stuffed brown bear dressed in overalls and red neckerchief who stands upright beside the doorway to the gift shop just up the highway.

The real Indians stay at a distance, rarely if ever encountered in the over-priced boutiques or dining rooms. A tourist might meet an Indian as his fishing guide, as a chambermaid at a lodge, or at the Sunset Place IGA grocery and liquor store in Nestor Falls. But that would be it; the Indians stay quietly in the background, minding their own business, wishing who knows what on the tourist season that sifts past them for three months of every summer. Their reserves are out of sight, off the highway, at the ends of long roads that most tourists never drive, like the Indians of Whitefish Bay. The souvenir-stand caricatures will be more familiar to most North Americans than the real faces and homes of people like the Ojibway of Onigaming, who live in the patch of brightly coloured houses at the sharp curve of the highway.

I turn in off the highway at Onigaming. A half-dozen men are seated atop the roof of the day care centre. They have torn the roof half off and are at work reshingling it, nailing down black tarpaper. At the baseball diamond another small crew works at making some repairs to the fence, hammering broken boards back on. A group of young boys make life difficult for the workers, they swing their bats and tag grounders into the infield and pitch balls against the broken fence. I follow the road further into the reserve until I reach a dead end at a big wooden building that turns out to be the fish plant and faces onto a deep, blue bay. Along the way I have passed a couple of houses, their yards full of topsy turvy furniture, piles of insulation, lumber, and a couple of other houses neat as a pin. One has a worn baseball mitt hanging from a nail by its door, the other has a humming-bird feeder attached in front of a window. I have passed a man dressed in black from his black leather jacket down to his black cowboy boots, an adolescent girl on a bicycle, and three dogs.

In the course of a year and a half I am going to be on this reserve and many others. I am going to drive down many highways, get on and off airplanes, in and out of boats, all in a quest to meet Indians. They will not have invited me to come and see them. They will not ask me to walk around their reserves taking notes, asking questions, asking directions as to which house it is I need to go to see such and such a person, making a nuisance of myself. I will arrive brashly having invited myself; writing a letter to a chief, making a phone call to someone I know vaguely from some previous time, some other event. But they will accommodate me and put up with me. They will humour me. No one will say, "stay away, don't come; we don't want to see you." Unfailingly courteous, they will give me time and they will show me around. They will let me poke around and they will try to answer my questions; try, with touching patience, to explain what their life is like, who they are, what their community is like, what they would like for the future. A few people will be enormously hospitable. In places where I lack the means of transportation, people will pick me up in their cars and drive me places. Families will offer me a place to stay in their homes, they will give me a bed in the basement, a cot in a room with their children, a couch in the living room. They will give me meals and invite me along to family gatherings and community gatherings where I will be fed again. One family will take me along for a five-day trip on their fishing boat. I will not attempt to speculate on their motives beyond a simple one of a natural hospitality and kindness. Though I introduced myself as a writer, I think the hospitality would have been there for any tourist who showed up with some demonstrable sincerity, sincerity to meet someone and learn something and understand something.

Twice, I was given what appeared to be warnings. They were from people, a community, that had been "burned" by journalists in the past. They didn't want it to happen again, they didn't want to be made fun of, they didn't want to be "stereotyped," they didn't want to be used as an illustration of everything that has gone wrong in the world. In short, they didn't want to be reduced to one-dimension. I took the warning as an admonition to make sure I took the time, the trouble, to look carefully and understand things. If you are going to try to do this kind of job, they were saying, don't hit and run, don't take a few notes and leave, do it right. Stay long enough, look hard enough, take the time to meet enough of us and you'll learn something. If there was a discernable motive on the part of the people of the five communities I went to visit, it was a motive that took on almost plaintive qualities. "Understand us" they seemed palpably to cry out. "We are not cardboard cutouts, we are not statistics, we are not stereotypes, we are not caricatures, we are not one-dimensional, we are not problems. We are complex. We get up in the morning and live through the day and try to do things and want things. We have ancestors and we have memories, we have children and we have hopes. If you have theories, put them aside for a moment; shut up, watch and listen, and perhaps something will become apparent to you."

I am rarely so demoralized as when I encounter something in the media about Indians. Invariably a story in a newspaper or on television that has anything to do with Indian people will be like a flare going up that tells us yet again how bad things are. A new study will come out citing more dismal statistics. Or some truly disastrous event will happen, a fire in some flimsy house, a multiple murder, an episode of gasoline sniffing among adolescents, and the cameras will be right there on the spot. Yes, the article or the documentary wants to tell us, things really are that bad.

In the data-gathering mania that has become our culture, almost all the reliable indices of health, happiness, economic well-being, and progress set off alarms when applied to Indian people. Suicide, infant mortality, alcoholism, educational failure, violent death, health problems, crime, incarceration, unemployment, poverty, family breakdown, single-parent families, business failures; in a month's reading of any major Canadian newspaper you can encounter dismal and depressing news stories about native people on all these fronts, with statistics from earnest sociologists to back them up. But is this an accurate picture of Indian life? And if so, what is to be done? If you believe the media reports, you are encouraged in hopelessness. You read things like this: "The Canadian taxpayer has paid and continues to pay to correct an historic wrong against Canada's original people. And in return the status quo has barely been maintained." Or this: "Instead of power, Indians have become the administrators of their own misery..." (both from the *Winnipeg Free Press*) Where can you go with that kind of information?

Indians in recent years have not been shy about using the media to their own ends, especially if it helps them point out hypocrisies on the part of the Canadian government. A couple of years ago, when the public statements of the Canadian government in condemnation of the apartheid system in South Africa were at their height, a Manitoba Indian chief invited South Africa's ambassador to Canada to pay a visit to his reserve. After a tour of the reserve, the ambassador pronounced it to be not dissimilar to a segregated South African township. The media reported his statement and the government was embarrassed. The comparison is provocative, in some respects apt. What mattered though, was that the chief had pulled off a PR play in grand style.

Lots of arguments can be made that an Indian reserve in Canada is not like a South African segregated township. Unlike South African blacks, Indians are free to vote. But when they vote, they vote for a choice of mainline political parties, not one of which is any better than another when it comes to understanding and dealing creatively and generously with Indian people's

13

special issues. And moreover, while they can make the gesture of voting for members of Canada's Parliament or provincial legislatures, their hands are virtually tied when it comes to running the simple matters of their own communities.

Unlike South African blacks, Indians in Canada are not prevented from leaving their reserves. For a time, in fact, and still in subtle ways today, they are encouraged to leave. But they leave to encounter what many describe as an alien, forbidding world beyond the reserves, a world many say they are not prepared for and have difficulty coping with both socially and economically. Also, while Indian people may leave the reserves, non-Indian people cannot come and live on the reserves, so it is de facto if not always de jure segregation.

What Indian people have also said, with an increasingly loud voice over the past twenty years, is different from what black South Africans are saying. Black South Africans are the majority who are prevented from having a say in the running of their country. Indians in Canada are a minority who, by contrast, have stubbornly resisted assimilation and say increasingly that what they want is the dignity of their traditional culture, the integrity of their territories, and the right to manage their own affairs.

What beckoned me to this journey onto these reserves, though, was an urge to venture into a world that has seemed always to hover at the fringe of the mainstream (whatever that may mean) of North American life and existence. I think there is at the back of the mind of every North American of European ancestry a niggling discomfort, a guilt, a perplexity, a curiosity about the people who were here first, before our forebears arrived and took over everything.

My own ancestors have been in North America, in both the United States and Canada, for four generations. They came from central Europe as peasants. They came to escape warlords who conscripted them into their armies, feudal lords who rigidly regulated their use of the land, political lords who taxed them to death, religious tyrants who dictated how they should think and behave. As farmers, it was the land that was most dear to them. Land in Europe was scarce, overpopulated, and freehold was tenuous; land in America seemed limitless. Having lost land and been shunted about, one might suppose my grandfathers and great grandfathers to share an implicit sympathy with the Indians who likewise lost land and were shunted about. Whether or not they did, I have no idea. It was the waves of immigrants, from Europe first and then from all over the globe that shunted, pushed, marginalized the people whose peoples for several thousands of years up to then had inhabited and worked the plains and the woods, the coasts and the waterways of this continent. And ever since I had seen Tonto on television and Chief Donnacona in the history books I had had, as I believe almost every blue-eyed immigrant child among my countrymen must have had, a kind of abstract curiosity combined with abstract guilt about original peoples, about Indians.

I say abstract, because how many of us know any Indians? I mean, really know; as a co-worker or as a best friend? And if we do, we are as likely as not to say, "Oh yes but he or she is not a *real* Indian. He or she, this person I know personally from my work or from next door or from the gymnasium or wherever, is just a . . . person. An Indian is something else. Meaning, what?

I was twelve years old before I'd ever seen a real Indian, that is, a person or persons I peered at through the safety of the windows of my parents' car as we drove over a bumpy rock-strewn road past a string of high-perched plywood houses on a reserve in eastern Ontario. And then, suddenly, we were gone again, back into the familiar landscape of farms and villages and countryside that seemed "normal." It had taken fifteen minutes to drive the stretch of road that cut through the corner of the reserve, and to my twelve-year-old eyes it was as if we had entered and then emerged from the movies. I never forgot the faces I thought I saw peering from the smudged windows of the houses. I never forgot the feeling of dreamlike forlorness that overwhelmed me, the disorienting feeling of being in another world and of being superbly isolated from it.

When I was seventeen I had a summer job in the far north of Ontario, and one of the other boys working on the job and living in our bunkhouse was an Indian from Moosonee. He was a Cree, to be precise, but at that time I hadn't learned yet that there were distinctions. We became friends of sorts and even wrote letters to one another a few times after the summer was over. And though I have no idea what was going through his mind, certainly an undercurrent in my mind during the time of our acquaintance was a recurring realization: "Mark is a real Indian." The realization left me almost in awe. It was as if I'd been reading too many books and here I was, suddenly and abruptly, right in the pages of one of them. Mark was just another teenaged boy doing a summer job, but in my mind he represented something other than just himself.

Years later I worked on a construction crew in the bush in northern Ontario. Every Wednesday evening we played softball games against an Indian team at a baseball diamond on a reserve. We played with quite a jovial, although occasionally sharp-edged, rivalry until one night, in a tavern where we would drink after our games, a fight broke out, for reasons of which I am still not certain. It pitted the Indians on one side and the white construction workers on the other. By the time it was over and the chairs and furniture and glass lay broken on the floor and a half-dozen fellows on both sides were wiping the blood from their noses, we had forfeited both our future welcome at the tavern and the goodwill and camaraderie that had marked our weekly baseball games. We never played one another again.

When I went to live in Winnipeg I found there were lots of Indians. They were on the street, on skid row; but they were also in the university and in the government. Some worked in the Indian Affairs bureaucracy in a tall building on Portage Avenue; others could regularly be seen protesting there, parading on the street in front of its doors with placards. My curiosity was piqued. These Indians were strong and purposeful; they had a mission. They said they represented people and they wanted things changed. They wanted rights, education, land, economic opportunity, respect for their culture, self-government.

Behind everything, of course, was an inescapable, burning, conclusion. We, the whites, had behaved badly; that was our guilt. And we were still, it seemed, behaving badly; that was our confusion. We, or those who represented us, had behaved badly toward people, groups, communities; far too many of each. And something would have to be done to right those wrongs.

But there is something as equally disturbing as the unrighted wrongs. The simple existence of the Indians and the stubborn way in which they refuse to accept assimilation into our culture elicits an uneasiness that persists in all of us immigrants and children of immigrants. The Indians, simply by their existence, serve to remind us of our collective inability to come to terms with something: nature perhaps, or the vast wilderness of the new world in its original state, or the environment. Whatever it is it engenders a profound unease and we try clumsily and for the most part ineffectually to come to terms with it.

Over the centuries non-Indians have often responded in inappropriate or exaggerated ways to Indians and to the idea of "Indians." We have lionized them with images of the "noble savage." At other times we have taken away the word "noble" and seen only the "savage," and we have reviled and despised their lack of civilization, as we understood it. We have tried to change them, working diligently to put white shirts on their backs, learning in their heads, Christianity in their hearts, and discipline in their habits. We have ignored them and shunted them to the furthest corners of our geography where they would be out of sight and, with luck, out of mind. We have tried to make them conform to our image of them and continue to do so now.

When we see Indians as "noble savages" we believe that they embody all that is intelligent and wise in their relationship with the natural environment. Certainly Indian people have lived with nature for millennia and have worked out their philosophic connections and their unique methods of conservation. An Ojibway Chief in northwestern Ontario explained to me the ritual his father had instilled in him for his behaviour toward an animal after the kill; an apology to the bear, the tacking of a piece of hair from the beard of a moose to a tree as an offering of thanksgiving. On the coast of British Columbia the Haida people with daring and imagination and considerable courage blockaded logging roads to make the point about the rapacious nature of industry's desire to cut and log the ancient forests. Bringing to bear the moral authority of their dignified ancestors, Indian people might yet persuade us to approach the natural world and our natural resources with some sense. Believing this, however, we fear to criticize practices we might otherwise disapprove of: the slaughter of deer on nighttime back roads with high powered repeater rifles from the backs of moving trucks with spotlights that stun the animals into motionlessness. And we fear to criticize once more when we encounter the sea of Pampers and empty Coca Cola cans that surround the landscape of many a pristine lake or river-fronted northern reserve. We think that to criticize will make us racists. If they are noble savages, they must be incapable of wrong.

We seem to want Indian people to represent something abstract that is important for *our* sake, not for theirs. It might be our collective other or dark side. Whatever the reason, this need to make icons of them, the failure to see them as they really are, is monumentally unfair and, I would say, is one of the things that paralyzes the potential for a real relationship between our cultures.

In Nestor Falls, on Highway 71 in northwestern Ontario on a fine July summer's evening, I go to a restaurant at Green's Camp. An old log building painted school-bus yellow on the outside, it is one of those good old places that hasn't been taken over with formica tables and colour coordination. Musty heads of whitetailed deer and dried-out Northern Pike trophies adorn the walls.

A whole row of moth-eaten stuffed ducks line up on the mantel of the stone fireplace. The ceiling lights are nestled in cupped deer antlers from some long-ago kill. Camps like this one, dating back to the 1920s, still operate up and down the length of Lake of the Woods; open and busy in the summer, quiet and still in the winter. They are a throwback to some colonial time; whites run the businesses, Indians are the hired help.

The supper crowd at Green's Camp is fishermen, sunburned men mostly from the Midwest of America. Three Indian fishing guides are having supper at a table near the centre of the room. One by one the visiting fishermen stop at their table for a joke, a chat, some homage to those who know where to find the big ones, some advice. The Americans talk on and on in their dinner conversation about walleyes. They can't catch enough of those walleyes. A well-built girl in a short skirt, her hair banked high on her head and wearing dangly earrings takes my order and recommends the walleye. At the next table a family are having dinner with Tequila Sunrises and Amaretto Sours and iced tea to begin. They are a man and a woman in their fifties, a younger man, their son, and a young woman and a baby. The older man opens a conversation by apologizing for the baby who is squalling and squirming a bit. He tells me they are on a holiday, then tells me where they are staying and how many fish they have been catching. When he asks me what I am doing, I say I am going that evening to visit the chief at the Indian reserve up the highway.

"How are they doing up there?" he asks.

"Are they depressed?" asks the son.

I must look puzzled. The father jumps in to keep the conversation going. "You know," he volunteers, "I've been to Indian reservations all over the United States and Canada and I've come to the conclusion that there's only one solution. I'm afraid it's a cruel one, but someone, sometime, is going to have to go in there and say, 'We won, you lost. So no more of this nonsense, no more treaty, no more reserves. Get out there and integrate. Fit in.' "

19

He finishes and looks at his drink. I can hear the burble of conversation from a couple of other tables across the room. I can hear the hum of the fan from the kitchen. We sit in silence because there doesn't seem to be much any of us can or needs to say. The Indian problem has just been solved.

As I travelled across the country visiting Indian reserves, government offices, politicians, sleeping in people's living rooms, on their boats, in cabins and little-used motels, I became aware of something that is a fundamental difference in the way Indian people and non-Indian people look at history and the difficulties between them. When they look at the history, the white people I talked to invariably wanted "solutions." The Indian people never used the word solution. They consistently asked for something quite different. The word that they kept using was "justice."

2   Norway House, Manitoba

Nelson Scribe is a fisherman and a trapper. In the early June
morning he stands outside his house pulling his nets from their
boxes. His hands work quickly and methodically on the nets,
cleaning bits of weed and debris from them, and then lifting
them and looping them on pegs that jut from the side of his house
so that they will dry. In northern Manitoba it is fishing season.
The weather is warm and bright, and there was a good rain the
night before. Mosquitoes swarm in the wet grass; bulldog flies
roam lazily in the sun. Scribe has been fishing all week and this is
his day to regroup. I approach him warily, I have been warned
that he is crusty, not friendly to strangers. "Don't go to see him,"
some people have told me, "he's often in a bad mood." I go
anyway and I find him quite welcoming. He looks dapper in a
checkered western-style shirt with pearl buttons, and he sports a
gleaming white Panama hat.

Scribe is sixty-three and in the past he has twice been chief of
the Norway House Indian band. He is currently president of the
140-member Registered Trappers Association. It is apparent
within the first two minutes of our conversation, however, that
he does not like the way things are going, both in the community
he used to lead, and in the world in general. The philosophies
and values by which people now live don't agree with him.

Nelson Scribe is a proud, independent, and resourceful man,
but he feels he lives in a time and a place that do not value those
qualities. In the 1930s, he tells me, his father, who is now ninety,

refused to ask for relief or welfare. " 'We have meat and potatoes,' he said. 'And there's tons more meat in the bush.' " As
Nelson describes it, the Scribes had their own homestead along
the riverbank. They fished, trapped, planted large gardens, and
always kept a few head of cattle. Nelson himself gets up now
every morning before the sun. Depending on the season, he
either heads out to Playgreen Lake to set his nets, or in winter
goes to his trapline eight miles from town. In between he attends
to his gardens.

But these are tough times for Nelson Scribe. His trapline is in
the flood area, a large tract of land adjacent to Norway House
that has been devastated by Manitoba Hydro's water-level regulations. Because the water continually floods and ebbs as levels
are altered by Hydro's control dams, the ice never forms properly, things never freeze up properly and this makes life on the
trapline hazardous for him. Woodland caribou no longer cross a
highway to come into his hunting area. Damage from slush has
cost him six snowmobiles in as many years. The fur trappers will
be compensated by the government but he is unhappy both with
the pay-off they will likely receive, and with the way he suspects
the band will administer it. He is upset by current politics. The
number of functionaries employed by the band galls him. The
fact that the Indian band pays $60,000 a year to someone who
coordinates an office it maintains in Winnipeg, while he earns
maybe $10,000 in a good year from trapping and fishing, makes
him almost speechless with anger. He feels that his way of life is
not valued and he is like a stubborn anachronism both in the
world and at home. In Europe, the markets where his furs are
sold are besieged by anti-fur and animal rights lobbies; at home,
where he says people would rather live either on welfare hand-
outs or on the take from their political positioning, he has been
advised in a letter that fur trapping should no longer be considered an authentic economic activity.

Norway House is almost the north. At 450 air kilometres north
of Winnipeg, it is just out of reach of the backwards and for-

wards, east-west motion of transportation, communications, and economic activity in this country. It is still south of Thompson, and south of a handful of other mining and pulp-mill towns in Manitoba, and with hydro electric power developments happening all along the Nelson River between its emergence from Lake Winnipeg and its arrival at Hudson Bay, Norway House sees some traffic from people like hydro engineers. But its situation is most definitely in the hinterland, on the frontier. This is even more so than it was a century ago; for Norway House was once very much in the thick of things.

There are several ways to get to Norway House. One is to travel by water as the explorers, voyageurs, missionaries, traders, fishermen, and Indians always did. You start at Winnipeg and go north on the Red River, cross Lake Winnipeg, and exit on the Nelson River through Playgreen Lake. Nobody, however, with the exception of the odd pleasure craft, or barge hauling heavy freight or picking up fish, comes to Norway House by boat anymore. The waterways are still important for fishermen and are used for local traffic; outboards zip from riverbank houses around to the store to shop or to the band office for a meeting. But it has been twenty years since a three-day trip over the lake was necessary to get local people down to Winnipeg, to bring in visitors or tourists, new teachers or nurses, and loads of dry goods, canned goods, flour, tea, sugar, salt, lard, boat motors, radios, or mail. Now an hour on a Perimeter Airlines sixteen-seat Fairchild Metroliner will bring you in from Winnipeg or take you out again. If you prefer a longer and more solitary journey, you can set out in a car and drive north into the black spruce forests. The drive will take you ten hours. The first seven are on a smooth, straight, well-maintained highway that slices through a seemingly endless carpet of bush, punctuated only by a half-dozen lonely gas stations. The last three hours are over a rutted and dusty logging and hydro road which, if it hasn't been graded lately, can jolt you from your seat.

Whether you fly or drive, it is impossible to ignore the water. If you have a window seat on the airplane flight, you'll spend fifty minutes looking down at the blue, or in winter the ice, of Lake Winnipeg, 5,500 feet below. If you drive, two substantial moments on that last two hundred kilometres of potholed dusty road will be your passage by Jenpeg – the giant Manitoba Hydro station built in 1979, whose dam regulates the flow of all water out of Lake Winnipeg – and your trip on the Nelson River ferry. The Nelson River is a half-mile wide at the ferry, about thirty five kilometres north of Norway House. It is pleasant somehow, still, to be forced to wait and do something special before making your final entry into a community. Cameron York, a large, lumbering man with a toothbrush moustache and dark glasses was running the ferry the morning I arrived and said he transports about fifty cars and trucks a day and that Wednesday is usually his busiest day.

The Nelson River doesn't so much flow out of the north of Lake Winnipeg as spill out. The river at that point is wide as a lake, and dotted with islands. In the days of the fur trade, when the Hudson's Bay Company was at the apex of its power, the Norway House site, a combination of shoreline and island at a point where the Jack River and the Gunisao River join with the Nelson, was chosen by the giant fur trading company for one of its most important depots. The location was critical. By travelling north along the Nelson you could reach York Factory and Hudson Bay. Then you could travel up to Churchill or go all the way to England. South from Norway House you could travel the length of Lake Winnipeg and reach Red River. A little bit to the south and the west was Grand Rapids, where the Saskatchewan River enters Lake Winnipeg. Down the Saskatchewan came furs from as far west as Fort Edmonton and the foothills of the mountains. The site for Norway House was in the middle of everything, the thick of things, the junction of every crossroads.

The post was built by Norwegian carpenters, hence its name. For the early and middle years of the 1800s Norway House was a leading colonial, almost cosmopolitan centre. The Cree Indians from the surrounding territory brought in their furs. Many of them entered into the employ of the Hudson's Bay Company, some as workers at the post, some as freighters, running canoes or rowing the big York boats that hauled furs out and supplies in. Middle management of the Hudson's Bay Company arrived from England and Scotland to take up residence at Norway House, and quite a little society developed. Their names are left behind, both on the weathered gravestones in the cemetery that still faces the river across from the old fort, and in the surnames – Sinclair, Ross, McKay – of the people, some treaty, some mix blood or Métis, who live on at Norway House. A hospital was built, the Methodists and later the Roman Catholics started missions and schools. In 1840 the Rev. James Evans, working for the Methodist Wesleyan Missionary Society, arrived at Norway House, learned the Cree language, and invented a system of phonetic syllabics so that it could be written down. In this way the Bible was translated and published in Cree.

As animal species were trapped out and the fur trade declined, activity at Norway House also ebbed. The community continued for a time to have a residual role as a northern distribution point. But the sense now is that its heyday is over. There are still two Hudson's Bay stores at Norway House. The archway warehouse built in 1848, with its white plastered walls and its shiny red roof peeks out from behind one of the new stores. But the Hudson's Bay Company no longer runs the stores; they are operated, as are all the stores in the north now, by independent merchants. The hospital is still there, but it functions not so much as a regional but as a local hospital; serious cases are flown out to Winnipeg. The churches are still there, but they no longer run the school system, and attendance is spotty. There are two elementary schools and a high school, but the kids don't know what to do when they graduate: Will they find a life in Norway House, or should they leave? If they stay, do they really need an education?

There are a couple of hotels, but with the exception of a few fishermen, tourist traffic is minimal. Hotel guests are mostly government functionaries or consultants at the service of the band or one of its agencies or the schools or the hospital. There are seasons of good fishing in the waters adjacent to Norway House and then the refrigerated semi-transports haul the catch out daily to the processing plants in Winnipeg. But trapping has taken a beating both from hydro-electric developments that have upset the ecosystem and from the turn of tastes and fashions in the world.

Twenty-five hundred treaty Indians live at Norway House on the reserve, and another thousand non-status and Métis people live off the reserve in the town of Norway House. Most of these people are not steadily employed, and many have to depend on welfare for much of the year in order to subsist. In a way, all these people are waiting; waiting for something to happen, waiting for something that they are not sure of yet to become evident. Norway House's past is past. Its future is not yet clear.

Water governed Norway House's past. In ways that no one expected, the water also controls its future. One of the first people I meet when I arrive in Norway House is an engineer whose company, for the next three years, will be supervising the installation of a sewage system in the community. This white man from the south is the project manager, and is in the employ of a firm of consulting engineers from Toronto who have a Winnipeg office. Last summer they built a water-treatment plant, and this summer they are constructing a sewage lagoon. Before it is all over, every house on the Norway House Indian Reserve will be equipped with a bathroom to replace the outhouses most have now. The whole system will be connected either by pipe, or by truck haul for the more remote houses, to the sewage lagoon and treatment plant. It will cost, explains the engineer, $18 million. A quick calculation in my head brings this out to $6,000 for every man, woman, and child in this community of three thousand. The money will come from the Northern Flood Agreement.

The story of the Northern Flood Agreement is a long and complex one which comes up regularly in the life and politics of Norway House. Put simply, it is a comprehensive compensation agreement that was formulated in the mid 1970s when Manitoba

Hydro embarked on its massive scheme of Nelson River power development. Party to the agreement are five northern Manitoba Indian bands: Norway House, Nelson House, Split Lake, Cross Lake, York Factory, the governments of Canada and Manitoba, and the Crown power corporation, Manitoba Hydro. The hydro development has enforced a lengthy and complicated relationship between the Indian bands, the governments, and the hydro utility that shows no sign of easy resolution. When I am at Norway House I am told that the fishermen have just completed a ten-year marathon of negotiations culminating in a $2 million settlement in compensation for hydro project damages. The trappers are still in negotiations. Norway House politics and development would be impossible to understand without an understanding of the role played by the Northern Flood Agreement. Chief Alan Ross of the Norway House Indian Band and others refer constantly to its tenets as if they were an order of service to some ritual.

The agreement concerning compensation is so comprehensive that some aspect of it seems to figure regularly into the community's plans and affairs. The $18 million water and sewer system, for instance, comes from the simple promise in article six of the agreement of a guarantee of clean, potable water. The cost of supplying this to the five Indian reserves could conceivably come to $90 million. There is broad speculation about the cost of the flood agreement in its entirety. Thirty million dollars might have been a reasonable estimate for a total settlement in 1975; in 1989 the guesstimates run to $500 million. As Indian bands and their lawyers learn how to use the agreement and explore the power that it gives them over the governments, the hydro utility, and by implication the Manitoba public, it becomes more and more clear what a wonderful boon it has been. The Cree of northern Manitoba, like the Cree of northern Quebec and the native peoples of Alaska, when confronted with the inevitability of industrial development pushed by the southern energy seekers, at least tried to make the best of what negotiating position they had. They couldn't bring back the pristine waters and stable shorelines of pre-hydro days, but neither would they be left entirely out in the cold after a hit-and-run development.

There is a certain absurd quality to what is going on. A provincial government employee lamented to me that the water system project is installing toilets at a cost of many millions of dollars into houses, a good many of which are ramshackle and falling down and desperately in need of other kinds of repair. "First-rate bathrooms for third-rate houses" was how he put it. But this is what happens when an economy is tied to government funding and then fragmented amongst a variety of different programs and agreements. The houses of Norway House might be in need of all manner of repair and rehabilitation, toilets being the least of their worries, but this year and in this program the money is for water and toilets, so water and toilets is what they get.

Yet one thing Norway House understands very well according to the visiting engineer, is the value in every development project of getting employment and training for their local people. In the sewer and water job the band's construction company, Playgreen Development Corporation, is working with a Winnipeg-based contractor. Seventy-five per cent, or fifty to one hundred jobs by the final phase of construction, will go to Norway House people. The engineer gives the Norway House band high marks for the seriousness with which they adhere to this. Many bands, he says, are either cynical or easily manipulated concerning such provisions. "The contractor is forced to hire local guys by the nature of the contract. He pays them but doesn't give them anything to do. And they seem satisfied with that. That would never happen at Norway House; they would never get away with operating that way."

"Development," when applied to a place like Norway House, is a word that has many powers. For Norway House, like most Indian reserves, is the Third World residing in Canada. The people of Norway House would not like it if you used that term about them and their community. Neither do the politicians of Canada like to hear that term applied so close to home. But that doesn't change the fact that the most useful way to understand the economy and the society and the struggle of Indian reserves in Canada is through the terminology and the models of the Third World.

"Third World" is a highly charged term; it implies judgements that we take for granted without necessarily examining them. The terms "Third World society" and "Third World economy" can refer to a tribal society and a subsistence economy that has undergone a period of colonization by another power. The Third World nation might be exploited or bullied out of its resource base or its traditional livelihood, as Norway House believes it was when Hydro disrupted the hunting, trapping, and fishing grounds in order to create power projects. Because of contact with the First World society and economy, wants and expectations rise so that the economy of subsistence on local products, in this case the fish, furs, animals, roots, berries of northern Manitoba, no longer seems adequate. And because there is either not enough surplus product, or it is not enough valued, or the local people are by-passed in its production, the Third World people are not in a strong position to trade on an equal footing for the highly prized First World goods they now desire: cars, televisions, factory-made clothing and foods, urban style houses, schools. Since they are unable to trade equally to get them, they must go into debt. Were Norway House or almost any other Indian reserve in Canada an independent country, the money that tumbles in under the auspices of the Canadian government would be considered debt. So when the bankers would tally up the international debt lists, there alongside Peru and Honduras, Kenya and Bangladesh, would be Norway House.

The pressures of change, the stresses of contact, and the seduction of new sets of values take their toll on the society's traditional structures; family and tribe. People become confused about the values and the customs of their forebears, and there is inter-generational strife. Parents fear there is nothing they have that they can teach their children, and children believe there is nothing for them to accept from their parents. Family life collapses. This happens over and over in Norway House, and is a major cause of complaint for both the elder and the younger generations. "The young people don't respect us," complain the old people. "The old people's ways of doing things are irrelevant," say the young people.

Struggling in the middle of this is the notion of "development." It might mean development to be self-sufficient; development to create a base of wealth that would provide a surplus for trading; development that would provide the basis for an existence of dignity and usefulness and contribution to the community for all its members.

One night when I sit with Chief Alan Ross, he acknowledges that there are three thousand people in his band, counting members who live off the reserve. In considering the potential for the reserve, he calculates that it has a land base of 18,577 acres and an outstanding land entitlement, according to band calculations, of approximately 56,900 acres more. It has access to water on several fronts. But when he itemizes the resources available to the community's future economy – forestry, fishing, local small industry – he confesses that it is beyond him how they can ever find a way to support with usefulness, self-sufficiency, and dignity a community of three thousand people.

I have been to Norway House numerous times, and I always look forward to running into Byron Apetagon. Byron is in his mid-thirties and has been a teacher for the last ten years. He has a keen interest in his community's heritage, and from that has carved out an interesting and somewhat unorthodox role for himself: he has become Norway House's resident historian. For half of his time Byron teaches Cree in the two elementary schools. The other half of the time the school board allows him to pursue his interest in community history. When I see him at his office at the school he hands me half a dozen fat binders that he has compiled over the past couple of years. I open them to find neatly typed pages recording the recollections of virtually every old person in Norway House. In every spare moment, Byron has been going to visit the elders of the community and has coaxed out and patiently written down their stories, most of which he must translate from Cree.

The stories are mostly of what life used to be like when the speakers were children or young adults, what it was like out on the trapline or in the fishing camp, what it was like at residential school. There are anecdotes of adventures: the first time a moose was shot, nights in the bush, or long trips endured. There are stories of hard work and resourcefulness: skinning muskrats, setting rabbit snares, using muskeg moss for diapers. There are descriptions of remedies and medicines. Those who are old enough remember the flu epidemic of 1918 in which 160 people at Norway House died. Others remember the nights of important fires: the hospital burned down in 1922 and again in 1952, the boarding school burned down in 1946, the Roman Catholic mission school burned in 1973. The reminiscences also provide an informal community and family history: recollections of who was married to whom, who brought brides in from other communities, who remarried whom after the death of a spouse, which children were adopted and raised by which families. A recurring reference is to young sons or young husbands dying suddenly and unexpectedly "from overwork and exhaustion."

Byron hopes to get all this published some day. He says that every time an elder dies he is reminded of how critical this work of gathering the stories is. He laughs that each time he completes an interview with an elder they have a standard joking comment for him: "I guess that's enough lies for now." But Byron's research also underlines the generational gulf in Norway House. It is as if there are not just years between the generations, there are worlds and lifetimes. It makes him feel sad and frustrated. An elder will sometimes flare up and say about young people: "What's the use to talk to them, they don't listen. When we were young we listened, we worked hard, we went to bed with the sun . . ." He fears that the old people are too pessimistic about the future and about the young. A passage from the story of a woman named Mary Farmer reads:

The children are very stubborn today. They are very disobedient. They have no respect for parents and other people. They run around at all hours of the night. There are too many negative things exposed to them. These things motivate the young people to become disobedient and disrespectful. The children are not punished any more. They get away with many things, even with the RCMP. The young people do not want to work; they do not help their families get their needs. They would rather go from house to house to find a place to eat and sleep. When we were children if I did any of those things, I was severely punished and disciplined. I could not go outdoors after sunset; I was told to relax and rest. Next morning I was told to get up early and most times it was before the sun rose. There was much work to be done . . .

Byron Apetagon says he was invited to run for the band council in the last election but declined, telling people he liked the work he was already doing. But his wife, Vicki, ran and now is in charge of the social welfare portfolio for the band government. It is an onerous task, she says, in a community where at times 90 per cent of the families may be on social assistance. There are six band councillors, which is a small council for a community of three thousand. The job is considered full-time and is given a salary. Vicki interrupted the teacher's training course she was taking through a program at Brandon University in order to take the council job. She says she did it out of a desire to help her people, "because there are so many things that need to be done."

Part of the interest that Byron and Vicki Apetagon take in the community and its future is because of their four children, boys ranging from James, ten, down through Norval and Toban to one-year-old Johnson, a hefty baby who is just taking his first steps. Byron and Vicki with the four boys have just moved into a newly built "bi-level" house which they have been waiting several years for. A frame house, stained light brown, it sits proudly in a grove of trees high on a knoll on the opposite side of the road from the river. There is a pond filled with frogs and muskrats at the bottom of the hill, and when I drive up the older boys and some cousins are busy at batting practice, whacking stones from the driveway into the pond.

The Apetagons' old house, in a low area on the other side of the road, is so broken-down it was condemned. Byron has agreed with the band that he will tear it down but he doesn't know when he will do that. Even with twenty new houses built every year, there is a housing shortage. Currently Vicki's brother and his wife and children are living in the old house because they have no other place to live.

It is easy to look around Norway House today and see that in the past the place must have had considerable charm. Some of that still exists simply in the layout of the community: in the confluence of its waterways and the gentle way the smooth granite rock, interspersed with islands of grass, runs from the front steps of the houses down to the shores of the water; the way that the houses built along the river surprise you, each like an isolated cabin with the woods around it, laundry flapping on the line, smoke curling from the chimney, a boat tied to a makeshift log dock. In the last twenty years, though, an influential development has changed the face of Norway House forever: the construction of roads.

The original Norway House was built to face the water. Travel was all by boat, and houses were built on the shores of four large islands and a couple of extended stretches of mainland shoreline. All houses faced the water, and all had small docks to tie up canoes or, later, outboard powered runabouts or fishing canoes. The Hudson's Bay store had a wharf, the band office had a wharf, the Indian Affairs office had a wharf, the churches had wharves. The centre of the community was the big wharf near the HBC store and the hospital, where the big boat, the *Chickama*, docked every week with its load of freight, Norway House passengers, and visiting tourists.

Then, in the 1960s and 1970s, roads started to be built inland on the islands, behind the houses. And it was as if all life was forced to do a 180-degree turn and start looking in the other direction. People still used their boats and loved the water, but real life and real transit seemed to happen in the clouds of dust as road vehicles took over. The first school bus was used in 1971; the bridge over the Jack River connecting Rossville and Mission Island was opened in the summer of 1971. Now big rickety automobiles, cars quickly aged by the bolt-jolting roughness of the gravel roads, are everywhere.

In 1977 the all-weather road out across the Nelson River ferry, past Jenpeg and on to Thompson and Winnipeg was opened, and the freight that had been brought in by water for a couple of hundred years started to roll in daily by semi-trailer. A convergence of roads and a big iron girder bridge spanning across to West Island sliced up the once regal grounds of the Hudson's Bay Company complex with its nineteenth-century red roofed white buildings, archway warehouse, and jail. The roads and bridge, combined with the addition of a new Hudson's Bay store, constructed from corrugated steel, and a trailer housing the post office, made the former centrepiece of the community look like a badly planned strip mall on an eminently forgettable urban truck route. Whole subdivisions of new houses are now built in Norway House on little roads carved right into the centre of the bush with no aesthetic notion whatsoever of the presence of water.

Looking back at old photos of the scenes and landscapes of Norway House can fill one with nostalgia for a time when things were built with craftsmanship and in proportion to their natural surroundings. Rossville, one of the communities that make up Norway House, used to have trees; now this collection of a couple of hundred houses is as bald as the desert. The basic style of building these days, whether it is a band office building, a housing subdivision, a motel, or a new school, begins with a wide clearance by bulldozer followed by pre-fab construction. The new construction, because of government budget constrictions or the practicalities deemed necessary by contractors building in the north, is visually appalling and is of such flimsy quality that if a building is not assiduously maintained in short order it begins first to look shabby, and then to fall apart. Before too long these slapped-up buildings give the community the scarred and tawdry qualities of bombed-out Beirut. When one of the band council members pointed out that the Catholic Church was thinking of erecting a new and larger building, I shuddered to think of that charming, steepled, white-and-blue frame structure coming down, and what might replace it.

Leonard McKay is a former band manager, the highest ranking civil servant job in the Norway House band government; now he holds the position of "project officer." He is a relaxed, affable man in his mid to late forties. If anyone can claim to have an extensive knowledge of the affairs of the Norway House band, the make-up and the history of the community, it is Leonard. When we sit down to chat he begins by offering the standard historical overview.

"Forty and fifty years ago the people here were self-sufficient," he explains. "Taking the children away for school purposes broke up the family economic unit. The people left their traplines and fish camps and moved in order to be near to the schools." After that everything changed; the people were really on a reserve. The government and its institutions made the reserves. But the reserves, in McKay's opinion, are what have kept the Indians Indians . He smiles and says, "It is an irony, but without the reserve system Canada would have long ago achieved the assimilation of Indian people, even with the treaties. It's the designated territories, the reserves, that have kept Indians distinct and created the unnatural bonding between Indian people and the government." He pauses, as if to emphasize the words, "unnatural bonding."

McKay goes on to describe a relationship between governments and Indian bands that is so complex one really needs a roadmap to understand it. In the case of Norway House, the political hierarchy includes the band; the non-reserve community, which also has a council; the provincial government, which has a Department of Northern Affairs; and the Indian Affairs department of the federal government, as well as a handful of other federal departments and agencies. Of the future, McKay says he is basically optimistic. "The next twenty years will see more autonomy and more local self-determination in health care, child care, education. There will be an improvement of the infrastructure of roads and housing, and there will be better access to training and skills development." The local economy, McKay says, will improve. Fishing will be stabilized and will include the development of fish farms. Forestry, he predicts, will become another substantial aspect of the local economy.

Then he becomes reflective. Nobody, he says, can ignore the fact that the last twenty, thirty, or forty years have been a time of terrible rootlessness for many reserves, including Norway House. It has been an unsettled time of changes and pressures and uncertainty. "There have been terrible personal costs in the last forty years," says McKay, "mostly with alcoholism. We have to get the people back on track." One way of doing this, he believes, will be through culture. The people must do what they can to preserve and value the Cree language, for instance. But other aspects of a traditional culture are so far lost that he questions if they can be rediscovered. "Of things like the dances and religion, I just don't know what our ancestral culture actually was before it was diluted by the Europeans. Except for the people of the St. Lawrence valley, we were the first to have contact with the Europeans. Way back, I don't know if our people had a dance or if they were too busy trying to survive."

Despair and the disruption of alcohol are still around. On a Saturday afternoon I give an elderly man a ride from the main road up to his house. I assume he is elderly though he is really of indeterminate age; he might be eighty or he might be fifty. He is a debilitated individual with long scraggly hair escaping in all directions from under a greasy baseball cap. One eye, behind horn-rimmed glasses, is taped shut with white tape. He tells me that bootleggers are busy and can command fifty dollars for a bottle of rye whiskey. He says he has been to the RCMP, whose barracks are just around the corner fiom his house, several times to suggest that they allow the opening of a liquor store.

At night I observe the alcoholic entertainment at the Playgreen Inn hotel. The reserve proper is theoretically dry, but the Playgreen is off-reserve and appears to do a whopping business. The place has a Chicken Chef restaurant and is licensed for beer, which it serves in copious amounts. Good times at the Playgreen are definitely rugged. I had been there once before, on another visit, when people were flush with cash from selling their T4s to an income tax discounter, one of the "services" that arrive in town seasonally from the outside. A table companion estimated that the bar would have done $25,000 worth of business that night.

This night, a hot Saturday in June, has the same busy flavour as that March income-tax night. A dozen or so men who've run out of money and credit reel around the parking lot trying to bum cigarettes. The cover charge is $2.00 and beer sells at $2.60 a bottle. A band plays old Creedence Clearwater Revival and Hank Williams songs, and a dozen people attempt to dance. Two hundred more drink as loudly and as busily as at any place I've ever been. Later someone tells me about the old man with the patched-up eye. He lost it on such a night as this when, drunk, he was set upon by a bunch of kids from nearby Rossville who beat him with sticks and stones.

Norway House is unquestionably unique in northern Manitoba for the way in which its whites and Indians, southerners, outsiders, and locals interact and are able to work together. This openness is part of the long history of the place, starting with the fur trade when it was cosmopolitan, open to the outside, open to strangers and to the flow of new ideas. If there is a serious wedge in the community, it is the internal and artificial one created by the issue of Indian status.

The community of Norway House is only part reserve. A jagged line runs through the two large islands that form the community and passes back and forth on the shoreline a couple of times, tracing the boundary between what is reserve and what is not reserve. Of the population at Norway House, 2,500 people are band members while 700 are non-status and Métis people who live off the reserve. There are, as well, a couple of hundred "transient" people who are in the community for a limited period of time to work at the hospital, the schools, the store, or for the RCMP. But it is the division between the treaty and the non-treaty people that is most poignant.

"We're all the same people," Bill Arthurson tells me as we sit one afternoon in his office in the school division building. "We're from the same families." Indeed Bill Arthurson's situation is one that illustrates the absurdity of the divisions. Bill was born and has lived most of his life at Norway House as a Métis. But at fifty-five, under the provisions of Bill C-31, the federal legislation that was passed to right the historic wrong of Indian women and their children who lost their Indian status, he and his wife have just become Indians, members of the Norway House Indian band.

When the federal Indian Act came into effect in 1876, one of the many things it did was define who legally was an Indian. For the next 109 years, until 1985, by the definitions of Canadian law, "Indianness" became something that was defined by the male line. If an Indian man married a non-Indian woman she would, for the purposes of the Indian Act, legally become an Indian, as would their children. A woman born Indian would remain an Indian if she remained single or married a status Indian man. Should she marry a non-Indian or a non-status man, however, she would lose her status and their children would have no status.

Bill's mother was a treaty Indian but lost her status when she married his father, a white man. Bill's wife was also treaty but lost her status by marrying Bill. Under the provisions of C-31, Bill, his nine brothers and sisters, and his five children are eligible, if they choose, to gain Indian status. Bill has done it, he says, for reasons of both sentiment and economics. He jokes with someone who comes by the office of the Frontier School Division, where he has worked for the last nine years, that he has "gone across to the other side," the other side in Norway House's we/they situation.

The economic factors are hardly to be discounted. As a status Indian, and not a Métis, Bill Arthurson will be exempt from income tax for money earned on the reserve. He will be exempt from provincial sales tax for anything consumed on the reserve. He will be eligible for Indian Affairs health benefits (although the provincial Manitoba medical system has no premiums in any case). And he will be exempt from property taxes and, when he gets his house on the reserve, he will be required to make a one-time-only contribution of $200 instead of the $200 a month he pays CMHC for his mortgage now.

Arthurson will be an Indian and not a Métis. But he will still be at Norway House, and although he claims he will be content with his new status, he says he is in Norway House in the first place against his better judgement. He left the community when he was sixteen and worked until he was twenty on lake boats on Lake Winnipeg, on farms, and in lumber camps and mines. He came back to get married and is still here thirty years later. He has always had jobs but says he won't encourage his children to stay. Four of them have not taken his advice. One works for the local radio station, one works for the community council, one is welfare administrator for the band, and one is a housewife. "They should go out and take their chances in the bigger world," says Bill.

The Roman Catholic church at Norway House is near the south end of the reserve at Jack River. The United church, James Evans Memorial Church, is ten kilometres away at the north end of the reserve in Rossville. There is also an Anglican mission on

Towers Island and a second Catholic church in Rossville, though it is boarded up. Pentecostal groups, or what some people locally refer to as "Holy Rollers," also meet at various places in the community.

The Christian missionaries came so early and with such determination to Norway House that any notion of a traditional religion of the Crees seems long gone. The religious history of Norway House is one of a long and vigorous competition among the Christian churches for Cree souls.

The Catholic church was established in 1906. The present compound includes a small white frame church with bright-blue trim and a silver steeple, a grey frame house on the river shore for the priest, and a larger building, which used to be a school but is now the home for three Sisters of Jesus-Mary, nuns who help the priest and work in the school. The school that had been run for years by the Catholics has now been rebuilt and is called Jack River Elementary School. It and a collection of bungalow-style houses for the teachers sit at the north end of the Catholic compound's driveway. To the immediate south of the church is a graveyard shaded by huge spruce trees and filled with an army of simple, stark, white crosses, which make it look like an armed forces cemetary.

On a fine Sunday morning I go to the church, not expecting much; I have been advised that Christianity's days on Indian reserves are pretty much over. To my surprise, I find the place packed. A little black-eyed girl in a pink dress standing outside on the sidewalk tells me it's too late to get in, but I push my way in anyway. There are perhaps seventy people inside, young and old and teenagers alike, and the mass has started.

The priest is a visitor from Cross Lake and has a heavy French accent. A big home-made sign wishes everybody a "Happy Father's Day." On the altar are half a dozen bouquets of plastic flowers. The paintings on the walls are of the fourteen stations of the cross, and at the front of the church, under a cheerful bright-blue ceiling, are three huge paintings of a very white-skinned Christ. Three local men get up in turn to read the Scriptures and the priest gives a short homily about the storms of life based on the story of Job.

The history of the United Church in Norway House goes back further than that of the other religious institutions. James Evans was one of the stars of the Wesleyan Methodists. He built the first church at Norway House in 1840 on a point of land just at the end of what is now Rossville. In his brief six-year stay he learned the Cree language and invented the Cree syllabic alphabet so that the language could be written down and Scriptures and hymns translated and published in Cree. The present United church was built in 1960 on Evans's original site with the same spectacular view up the river. It is a charming building, but not as well maintained on the outside as the Catholic church. The inside is well kept and on display are historic plaques commemorating Evans, John Semmens (another missionary), and various war dead from Norway House, including men with names like St. James Whiskey.

The Methodist/United church was always seen as the church of record in Norway House, perhaps because of the contributions made by Evans. In 1987 I happened to be present when a local boy, Grant Queskekapow, was ordained as a minister. On that day the church was bursting at the seams with people, and they put on quite a ceremony, right down to the chief showing up in his blue blazer with gold braid, and red striped trousers, the costume given years back for chiefs to wear on Treaty Days.

In the week-to-week sense, though, I get the impression that it is the Catholics, or probably even the Holy Rollers, who now have the momentum, especially with the younger people. The United church service this Sunday afternoon is at two o'clock and I arrive to find an old man sitting on an aged wooden chair outside waiting for somebody to open up the doors. A brisk wind blows up waves below the point, and we can hardly carry on a conversation because of the thunder of the river and the wind. Behind us, around a ten-foot-high stone cairn erected to the memory of James Evans, a half-dozen horses, two lovely, rangy white ones and four chestnuts are grazing away, wandering free.

Presently twenty or so people show up, and when we enter the building, ten of them head straight for the platform. They will be the choir and the conductors of the service. As with the Catholics, the minister is away this week. He is a local man named John Crate; the United Church has been working hard to get local ministers in its northern Indian churches. In his absence a couple of elders, John Thomas and Susanna Mcdonald, will lead the service. It is all in Cree and goes on for almost two hours. I don't understand a word but I get a sense of great solemnity and devoutness, particularly among the old people. There are a couple of teenage kids present but during the service they leave, then return, then leave again.

The best part for me is the singing, also in Cree, old gospel songs sung in a slow, slower than syrup Cree wail. The hymn books are printed in English and Cree. I try to follow along in Cree, which is actually quite easy with long lines like Manito Kikawiiwiicewik (God be with you till we meet again). Or, Kiskinohtahin Manito (Guide me O thou great Jehovah). All the singing is accompanied by a guitar and an accordion, played slowly. At one point the accordion player, a man named Bert Poker, opens a window and three vases of artificial flowers are promptly blown over by the wind. I look out the window at the other side of the church where the horses are chomping away contentedly right up against the church hall.

Nelson Scribe has asked that I come back to see him on Tuesday evening at seven o'clock sharp: "Don't go by Indian time," he ordered. I meet him at the Trappers Association building across the road from his house. For the next two hours he gives me a private seminar on fur trapping. Scribe, at sixty-three, is still a strong, erect man with a strong face and large, flat hands. He has been a trapper since he was fourteen years old, except for a few years between 1965 and 1974 when he worked for the natural resources department of the provincial government conducting trapper education. Tonight he is going to educate me. The Trappers Association building is a bit like a clubhouse. Scribe shows me into a large room that still smells of the paint and varnish of new construction. A long table and a couple of kitchen chairs sit at one end under three sets of deer and caribou antlers and a bilingual No Smoking sign – in English and in Cree. On the walls are posters from the Fur Institute of Canada exhorting us to have respect for animals, for people, and for the environment. There is also a large wall map where Norway House's forty registered traplines are drawn, like political boundaries imposed on a topographical map; or like a huge cake cut into squares.

Outside the building are the signs of Scribe's plans. He has a dream to make this a centre for trapping education and information that is the best in all the north, a sort of living museum of trapping. He shows me a pile of logs with which he wants to build an authentic trapper's cabin, and there is a tipi-like construction of long spruce poles, debarked, which he says will be used to reconstruct a wigwam of the sort used in the bush by his trapping ancestors. At the other end of the hall, accessible through a different outside door, his wife, Lillian, is at work on some handicrafts. She has three pairs of elaborately beaded moosehide moccasins made by herself and a couple of other women in the community. With all the beadwork on them – fancy red flowers stitched on a white background – they are heavy, weighing a couple of pounds each. Scribe says if they were to calculate the women's work at $5 an hour, they'd have to sell the three pairs of moccasins for $1,300 to break even.

He goes to a wooden box in the corner and lifts out two powerful-looking steel gadgets, each of them two squares of steel rod about the size of first base, with heavy, round, steel springs at the sides. These are Conibear traps, the larger one for beaver, the slightly smaller one for muskrat or mink. He shows me how to set them and anchor them with a stick of wood, and then lets them snap, which they do with a startling clatter. An animal, caught, has the life squeezed out of it instantly. Nelson says he was converted to humane trapping at middle age and would never return to any other method. Leg-hold traps, of which there are also a pile in the box, are still legal but they are not considered humane. They hold the animal in their jaws until either it freezes to death or the trapper arrives to kill it. The stories of animals chewing their legs off in desperate attempts to escape are not farfetched.

Nelson then shows me a chart that delineates the prime times for the catching of various furs, indicating the time of the year when each fur is at its best and likely to bring top price. Beaver is good from mid-January to the end of March; muskrat, March and early April; lynx in January, February and the first half of March; mink for only a brief period between late November and Christmas. Trapping is a conservationist business; there is no point in taking an animal other than when it is prime. "You are wasting the animal's life and you are wasting your time. Have patience and wait for the right time to trap each animal."

"I could train you to be a trapper in six months," he says. "It's routine work. I would have to teach you how to look for the signs of how the animals live, then I'd have to teach you how to skin an animal and look after the fur. Then I'd have to teach you how to look after yourself in the bush." I start to imagine myself plugging along on bright mornings when it is cold as a bell, trudging through three feet of snow. "The main thing," Nelson tells me, "is to keep your matches dry."

Nelson started his own trapping when he was a boy, after his mother died. And he has taken his own sons, now young men, trapping. One is pretty good, he says, "but they only like it when they catch something. Otherwise it's boring, tedious, and cold." But Scribe is ambivalent and worried about the future of trapping. There are lots of animals; a nearby lake is "lousy with beaver." "And I guess there will be trapping as long as people want to buy fur coats." But he is worried about the campaign in Europe against fur. He says he wishes people from Greenpeace would come to Norway House, he'd like to have a serious conversation with them. He believes they could see one another's point of view. Then he becomes depressed; "It's pretty shaky," he says, "to say that trapping will exist a hundred years from now." He looks out the window into the purple of the late evening sky. "It's sad to see the way of life you have lived come to an end. The life you spend in the bush is the best life there is."

Even more significant than anti-fur lobbies to the end of trapping are cultural changes in his own people. To explain this he offers a quick thumbnail sketch, similar to Leonard McKay's, of how life has changed over sixty years. And the analysis is the same as McKay's.

Sixty years ago, Scribe explains, people had free access to the land and essentially lived off the land. The whole family would move out to the trapline for the winter, children and grandparents included, and everyone had his role in making the enterprise work. In summer the family would move in from the bush and set up camp at its fishing spot on the lakeshore. Following World War II, though, education of the children became more and more of a priority. Taking children and putting them away in school broke down a vital element of the traditional family labour unit required on the trapline. Soon families as a whole did not go trapping; men went out by themselves while the rest of the family – women, grandparents, children – stayed in the community, close to the school. Then came social assistance and family allowance benefits, and suddenly survival did not depend on enduring the hard work and precarious life of the trapline.

The next change for the people of Norway House came with the opening of other natural resources in northern Manitoba. A nickel mine opened in nearby Thompson in the late 1950s, and Manitoba Hydro began construction on major hydro-electric power developments. Big money in construction and in the mines seduced more men away from their traplines into a wage economy. Indian leadership started to see fur trapping as a part of their past, not their future. Nelson reaches into his leather briefcase to show me what to him is the final insult. Last winter the Trappers Association applied to the Canada Employment Commission for a job development training grant to provide trapper training to "individuals who do not possess the necessary qualifications and experience in the field of trapping." They

45

were turned down with the explanation that "trapping is not a recognized occupation (no one hires trappers) therefore they could not fund training in this field."

The assaults on his profession have been almost too much for Nelson Scribe. Anything that represents the "real economy" has disappeared. His trapping income for the last ten years has totalled $25,000, which equals his expenses, so he has had no profit and no payment for his labour. If he makes money from trapping, it will be when Hydro and various governments ante-up an anticipated $300,000 to Norway House trappers as compensation for the damages of the hydro development. But you can't build an economy on compensation. Trapping as a genuine market activity in Norway House is near the end of its tether.

Norway House believes itself to be perpetually under study, and there is ample evidence to back up this supposition. On an Indian reserve there is always somebody from the "outside" poking around: an anthropologist working on a graduate paper, a government or health department or school board official doing a study, a journalist. These people, even when they try to blend in, dressing "native," wearing all-weather rain gear and rubber boots just like the locals, tend to stand out like flagpoles. They can't help but do so; they are outsiders, strangers. The outsiders are there either out of their own curiosity, or representing the curiosity of the organization that sent them. They either want to learn something new, or they want to gather data to support a theory, or, if they are from some branch of the government, they want to dig up some information to support either continuing, changing, or perhaps abandoning some program and some expenditure. What can they always be wanting to know? the people on the Indian reserve must wonder.

In the cities or in non-Indian communities, the same information gatherers are out doing their work. In the city you can be subject to a survey arriving at your door or reaching you over the phone or stopping you on the street. There are journalists and government agents and graduate students all labouring away in the city too to gather their minutiae. But in the city or off the reserve these information gatherers are somehow not so obvious, they blend in with the scenery, they don't seem so overtly to be "snooping around." On the Indian reserves people doing studies always seem to be "snooping around." In our own minds, and I have to count myself as one of them, we justify ourselves by our earnestness. We feel that we are seeking some kind of objective truth. We are such products of the Protestant work ethic that we could not just be in a place like Norway House for its own sake, we need some project in order to justify our being there, going all that distance. The project, however thin its rationale, serves to make us feel useful and justified and we busily scurry about the community trying to fill in the blanks. The Indians must think we are crazy. Can you imagine the Cree of Norway House coming to Winnipeg or Toronto or Ottawa with research projects in their briefcases and then setting out immediately and busily to interview all the white folks?

For several days while I was at Norway House, a CBC television news crew was also there. While I was busily seeking my information they, also attired in brightly coloured hooded slickers and rubber boots, were seeking theirs. Such, however, is the standard route of information gathering in a place like Norway House that we found ourselves all pursuing the same people. Time after time over the course of a few days I would arrive in an office or at someone's house only to be asked if I was from the CBC. "No, no," I would answer hurriedly, not wanting to be confused with that bunch. "Are you expecting the CBC?" "Yes. They're supposed to be coming this morning." And then, sure enough, just as I was leaving, up would pull the blue van and out would pour the reporter, the cameraman, the lights, the video recorder, the microphones; the CBC had arrived.

The Indians have extraordinary patience with all these pokers-around. Maybe they feel it is something they have no choice but to tolerate, having got used to it by living like colonials for so long. But at some level it must be bothersome; Indian

47

folksinger Winston Wuttunee had a rather bitter song once that he used to sing at folk festivals called "The Anthros Are Coming." It must be bothersome, too, that much, almost all, of the information that comes out of these missions reflects badly on the community, if not on the Indians themselves. The thesis of the news documentary by the CBC was that there were problems with education in Norway House. Sure enough they found information to support the thesis. When they got back to Winnipeg and the piece appeared on the news, there was the all-too-earnest reporter standing on the road by the Jack River bridge facing the camera and proclaiming: "Norway House has the worst high school in Manitoba for attendance . . ."

Sometimes the information and the studies make the Norway House people mad. A couple of years ago a young reporter from the *Winnipeg Free Press* showed up in Norway House and set out to gather information and write a series of articles about alcohol and bootleggers. The articles, written mainly from the viewpoint of the RCMP, were entitled "Where Bootleggers Siphon Food From Babies' Mouths." The people of Norway House were ashamed and furious about the image the articles projected of their community. As with anything there was truth in the articles, but you can say almost anything you want and find some shred of fact to support it. What the Norway House people resent most are the hit-and-run artists who arrive with a preconceived thesis, take a quick look around to grab enough data to support it, and leave, never to be seen again. They complain about and feel powerless against reporters and anthropologists who do not really want to understand them, and worse, have no affection or generosity for them.

Twenty years ago Heather Robertson came through Norway House in the course of writing her famous book *Reservations Are For Indians*. The results for Norway House were devastating, and the people never forgave her. They are still smarting, twenty years later. The people felt criticized for everything, from having their houses face the river to spending time drawing water and carrying it home in pails, as they had to do then. An image used over and over in the description of the community and its river was "slime" or "scum": "the community floats on the surface of the water in suspended animation, as if it had, like green scum, grown out of the river." The council at Norway House described in some detail what they would do should that writer ever return to Norway House. "We don't like being stereotyped as a bunch of drunks," councillor Freddie Muskego said.

When the CBC news documentary criticized education at Norway House, it used statistics to do so. It said that, in spite of a per-student expenditure that was twice the provincial average, all the latest in computers and learning equipment, and a low student-teacher ratio, 45 per cent of the high school students dropped out before graduating. In the elementary schools, the documentary reported, 30 per cent of students were passed on from grade to grade, even though their work was not up to scratch.

These criticisms might as easily have been levied at almost any northern and native community. Education in the three schools of Norway House is administered by Frontier School Division, a far-flung school board that looks after virtually every school in northern Manitoba not under Indian Affairs or Indian band control, or not in a substantial urban area. While the television crew were in Norway House, some personnel of the Frontier School Division seemed apprehensive. The local administrator said he feared the television people were going to "do a number" on them. The school board people feared that the program might even have been set up by the band council to make them look bad.

Even though the school division operates with the agreement of the band council, there are the usual number of power struggles and jealousies. Some in the community have started a movement to have the band council itself take over the administration of education. This would be called "local control." While the superintendent of the school division says he would not oppose local control, still, it represents a threat to his power. As the band council flexes its muscles and grows bigger and more powerful, the anxieties of the school division and its concern to improve education and improve the responsiveness of the school system to local needs also grows. Sure enough, when the news documentary aired, the conclusion of both the CBC reporter and the chief of the Indian band was that local control would be the way to solve the education problems of Norway House.

But would it? The problems facing educators in the north and on Indian reserves are complex. As Norway House is witness, lack of money being spent is not one of them. There are cross-cultural problems that more local input might help address, but the school division similarly appears to bend over backwards to encourage local school committees and has initiated programs to foster Cree language, local history, and local handicrafts as part of the curriculum. Brandon University in southwest Manitoba has a special program to train northerners and natives to be teachers, and the school administration seems to be placing local people as teachers as quickly as that program can turn them out. Still, the school administration is faced with horrendous turn-overs in its staff at the beginning of each school year (a turn-over of one-third to one-half is common). To find non-native staff to fill its rosters it has to go far afield for teachers who are either willing, or feel themselves forced, to take a job in isolated places. And on the other side, the schools must deal with the reluctance of students to put their heart into training for a world that they don't understand, or fear, or don't see around them.

Locally controlled schools would face these same problems. I once had a job making a television program that was designed to encourage northern students to complete high school. The program was to play on local television and was meant to be a pep talk both for the students and for their parents. What I found in researching and producing the program was a poignant mix of desire and fear among both the students and their parents. School, we found, represented a great generational leap. Many parents had successfully completed only grade three, and so to ask them to help their children with grade eleven math home-work was absurd. What the parents expressed was a sort of general goodwill that the best be available for their children, mixed with a fear of what that might turn out to be. The children themselves wanted to do well, but when they looked around their communities and saw the shortage of jobs they wondered what they were preparing themselves for. A mother and daughter in a neighbouring community to Norway House expressed most people's thoughts. "We have a dilemma," said the mother. "I want the best for my child and I want her to have an education. But I know there are no jobs here and if she gets educated she will be dissatisfied here. Then she will move away, to the city. If she becomes educated, we lose her; if she is to be happy with life here, education might only be an impediment."

Norway House and other isolated Indian reserves are trying to find a way through this dilemma. One of Norway House's educational thinkers is Maggie Balfour. A sixty-year-old grandmother and a former chief, she has a reputation for holding strong views and being outspoken. She is also affable and hospitable, and when we meet, her hair is in curlers as she prepares for a night out at yet another community meeting. She chain-smokes Players and offers me a coffee. She asks me what the best course of study would be for her eighteen-year-old granddaughter who has just completed her first year of study at the University of Winnipeg and wants to be a journalist.

Education has been one of Maggie Balfour's great interests over the years, starting from her own frustrations as a young girl. She was sent off to St. Joseph's, an elementary school run by the Oblate Sisters in nearby Cross Lake. Her dream was to become a teacher or a nurse, and after graduation from grade eight she repeatedly bugged the Indian agent, she says, for access to further education. But she was stymied; there was no money for it, she was told. She went to Winnipeg and worked for a few years as a nurse's aide in a senior citizen's home. In 1971, when she was forty, her dream of further education finally seemed close to realization. She was accepted into something called the "Impact Program," a special program at Brandon University to train native teachers. Within four months of entering the course, however, she developed infectious hepatitis and had to drop out. Her regret lingers.

Maggie Balfour's campaign in her community has been to insist that education at Norway House be of the same standard as that offered outside. Given the catch-up that will be required, this is no small task. "Native kids have to work extra hard because their parents aren't always able to help them with their school work, no matter how much they might want them to succeed. Maybe in ten years that will have changed, most of the parents by then will also be high school graduates. Meanwhile the kids complain about their boredom and the lack of challenge."

Maggie Balfour credits the schools with trying to do the right things, but adds, "I believe the kids when they say it's boring." She talked, she says, to a group of high school drop-outs who complained that the work was not challenging, it was too easy, they could do it too quickly. "We need to make more demands on our kids and have more discipline," she says. "If we make it tough, they will really enjoy it."

Though the young people of Norway House may be unsure what exactly they want from their education, they do know that they want to be part of the decisions that get made and the things that get done in their community. There is a youth movement in the band office at Norway House that is encouraged by the chief and the administration. Borrowing from the experience of Indian bands in Oklahoma, the Norway House band in the spring of 1986 sponsored a Youth Conference attended by four hundred band members under the age of thirty. As a result of that event, the young people of the reserve selected a Youth Council and a Young Chief to parallel the senior chief and council of the band. To acknowledge the young was clearly wise politics. The young are a critical sector; half the population of the reserve is under the age of nineteen.

The fellow who was elected Young Chief is a tall, slim twenty-year-old named Brian Cromarty. He speaks well and is handsome in a swaggering kind of way. Although he doesn't receive any pay, he takes his role seriously and attends almost as many meetings as the real chief. In between times he can be found bustling around the band office in acid-wash jeans and sweatshirt. He oversees things like the Youth Summer Employment program, which this year will provide forty jobs, and runs a landscaping business which will employ a further ten. The young people of Norway House have descended on the band office with a vengeance. "The chief wanted the young people to get involved," Cromarty says, "but I think we got more involved than he figured."

Cromarty sees himself as the band council's pipeline to the young people. He is learning a lot about the frustrations of band politics. He goes to all council meetings and recognizes the burden of leadership. "It is frustrating," he says, "to be in the position to have to make a decision and you don't know the answer." He is also a pipeline carrying the ideas of the youth back to the adults of the band council. He sees his job as reminding the adults of the realities of the young people's world, including some of the more disturbing realities. "You have to bring them down to earth sometimes," he says of the adults. "They don't see the kids who are out there sniffing their brains out."

If there are kids in Norway House with problems, the young chief can identify with them. Though at twenty he seems smooth and self-assured, Brian Cromarty has come through a few personal problems of his own. For nine years, starting when he was seven, he was a solvent sniffer; gasoline and glue. For a time he was high on glue and in trouble so much of the time that they ran out of things to do with him. He was shipped out of the reserve to foster homes and ultimately ended up in reform school. He didn't start to get his life together until he was seventeen, and then only after several suicide attempts. He worries about the high suicide rate among native teenagers both in northern Manitoba and across the country, and calls it "an epidemic." He says now, "If we don't pull up our socks as young people today, Indian people in Canada won't have a future. That's what motivates me as an individual. Each of us as individuals has to take personal responsibility for the collective future. That in turn will help us in our personal lives. You have to have pride. Pride and self-worth are the key."

I have a couple of conversations with Brian Cromarty about the youth of Norway House and how he feels they can and must salvage a future for themselves despite the confusions that growing up brings. His stories make me more observant of the other young people I encounter. As I hang around the band office, one thing I can't help noticing are the tattoos on the forearms and hands of a number of the young women working there. They laugh and joke a lot as they hang around the typewriters and the phones at the front desk, enjoying their cans of Coke or coffee in styrofoam cups. But the tattoos make me alert to an undercurrent that is unsettling. They are the kind I have seen in the city on girls who are juvenile delinquents, or girls who are in institutions for wayward teenagers. Small, blue, homemade tattoos inked like spiders' webs into the fingers and tops of hands and on the arms.

I watch and get to know the girls in the band office, and the message I take is a hopeful one. These girls are not juvenile delinquents, but they were. They could have been sucked down into the vortex, but they weren't. They could have died, but they didn't. They made it through. Like Brian Cromarty, the girls are graduates and survivors of a tough, dangerous, chancy adolescence. The tattoos are the scars and badges of that. Now they are employed by the band office, helping in the daily functioning and running of their community. To see that some made it, of course, serves to remind that others, doubtless, did not. But the presence of these young women, tattooed fingers and forearms and all, gathered at the reception desks must be taken as a sign that is profoundly hopeful both about their own lives, and in the life of the community.

At Norway House I spend what seems an inordinate amount of time in the band office. But then so does everybody else. I stop by almost every morning to wait for interviews with the chief, or

Brian Cromarty, or Leonard McKay, or anybody who I feel will help me gain perspective on this place. As I wait I see everybody else who has got anything going at Norway House: the accountant from Winnipeg who is doing the band's books; the engineer from the sewer project; the young man from Indian Affairs who is helping negotiate a new financing arrangement for the band.

As a "nerve centre," the band office is an unlikely building. It is a rickety, pre-fab structure that looks like it might fall apart at any moment. Its sagging partitions, crookedly hung doors, haphazard maze of wiring and electrical connections make it resemble a temporary command post in a field camp at wartime. Yet there is no sense of the building being seen as only a temporary structure either by the community, or the band council, or by the twenty-nine employees who work in it every day. One morning the band fix-it crew arrived in rubber boots and carrying a step ladder to "do something about" a flourescent light fixture in one of the offices that was dripping water. What they did was remove the tube and set it upright against a wall. Then they left.

Band life is an ongoing series of meetings. Almost every morning when I arrive at the office Vicki Apetagon is there ahead of me, lounging on the shaky table next to the reception desk, joking with whoever is playing receptionist, waiting for the start of another meeting.

Norway House is a band with big issues on its plate. It is the largest Indian band in northern Manitoba and its local administration is far-reaching. It also has some substantial problems to confront. Unemployment is high, and a significant number of Norway House's residents do not have full-time jobs; without social assistance or welfare, they have no regular or reliable income. The band has a young population who are far from clear in their own minds what kind of future they want. Do they want a future at home? Or do they want to move to a future in the city, in a northern city like Thompson or the big city of Winnipeg to the south. Most are all too well aware of the perils that life beyond the familiarity of the reserve holds for those who move out. My visit to Norway House coincided with a well-publicized murder trial in The Pas, a northern Manitoba city a couple of hours to the northwest. There, after a delay of seventeen years, four white men had finally been arrested and brought to trial for the brutal rape and murder of an Indian girl, Helen Betty Osborne. In 1971 Osborne had been a nineteen-year-old student attending high school in The Pas because her home community had then no high school of its own. One winter night she was picked up by four white youths, driven to the edge of town, raped, and then stabbed fifty-six times with a screwdriver. Where was Helen Betty Osborne from? Norway House.

Norway House wants to take a substantial step toward greater authority over its affairs. At the time of my visit it was well on its way to negotiating what is called an Alternative Funding Arrangement (AFA) with the federal government's department of Indian Affairs. It had not yet gone over all the hurdles, but assuming it did, at nearly $63 million over five years, it would be the biggest AFA arrangement with an Indian band in the country. If it goes, says Leonard McKay, "it will give the band more autonomy and more flexibility over its own affairs. The band will be able to plan and budget in five-year terms."

For governments to think in five-year terms might seem a perfectly natural thing to do. One of the frustrations of being an Indian band, however, has been the inability to do just that. Indian bands by and large get their money from the federal treasury, but the way they have been getting that money and the way most continue to get that money is through something called Contribution Agreement funding. Under this system, Indian Affairs finances each band program, whether housing construction, welfare, or police, through a separate agreement, negotiated separately, each year. In the government's eyes it is a route well suited to fiscal responsibility. One budget item for one band might screw up; Norway House, for example, might lose or overspend or otherwise fail to meet its police budget, but even so, everything else would still be all right.

The plan gave the government control. In the Indians' eyes it was a huge frustration. It meant that the government didn't trust them, and the negotiating and the securing of an agreement and a budget for every separate item every year sucked up all their administrative energies. Besides, time always ran out. Moneys came late, and they never knew until the last minute or later if they were going to get what they asked for. The band lived and operated continually on a margin of uncertainty. They had no flexibility for the long-term plan, and they had no flexibility within their own administration. If they were under-budget in housing but over-budget in education, they couldn't move money. If they were under-budget one year, they couldn't keep the money for the next year. They were at the mercy of the government, and at the mercy of endless paperwork and waiting.

The AFA, the Norway House band feels, goes some distance to rectify this. No longer obliged to negotiate each program separately, the band will have more room to set its own priorities and more flexibility to move funds from one area to another. The reporting time to government will be yearly rather than monthly. It is not self-government; it is still taxpayers' money coming in from the outside; but it goes a long way toward allowing some autonomy. And it provides the Norway House band with their big challenge: to prove that they can do it, that they can put the management mechanisms into place and show that they deserve the government's trust. "The pressure will be on. If we're not good managers it will show," says Leonard McKay.

For Chief Alan Ross, the AFA is both a huge challenge and a rich opportunity. Ross was not born a treaty Indian; like Bill Arthurson, he came to his status through the benefits of Bill C-31. He was born off the reserve at Norway House. His maternal ancestors were Cree, his paternal ancestors Scottish traders, explaining, no doubt, his fair complexion and sandy coloured hair. He looks so tall, so blond, so white, so professional in his lawyerly glasses, that he repeatedly feels obliged to remind people that he is an Indian.

Alan Ross grew up at Norway House in that mix of reserve and non-reserve back in what he calls "the halcyon days when it was all a remote hamlet." He left in the early 1950s to join the air force. Then he left again to go to law school. Five years ago he returned to run for and be elected chief.

Ross lives, however, in Winnipeg. Regularly, he catches the Perimeter Air flight or makes the long ten-hour drive north to his constituency. The fact that he doesn't live on the reserve and the fact of his opening an office for the band in Winnipeg have engendered resentments among some people, but not enough to prevent him from winning a second term in office with the largest majority ever given by Norway House. In a ploy worthy of the public relations razzmatazz of big-time southern politicians, he once made a videotape of himself giving a sort of fireside chat. His handlers tried to compensate for the chief's frequent absences by making the tape available to anyone in the community who might want to watch and listen to it. But absent or present, the consensus seems to be that Ross has strength, and that that strength comes from his ability as a lawyer and a negotiator. He has consistently been able to deliver the goods: government programs, the benefits from the flood agreement, the AFA.

When he is on the reserve, the chief has breakfast every day at Joe and Virginia Paupanekis's Historic Trails motel restaurant. Even though he has a busy day planned, he seems eager to chat with me. The thing the community most needs, he says, is a chance to develop itself and prove itself. "Over the years the people here have always been under the jurisdiction of and the authority of somebody else. It has affected the confidence that they should have in themselves. They're not sure many times whether they should go ahead and do something. They're not sure if they can do this, if they can do that. A lot of people here need to have greater confidence in themselves. That will come, perhaps, with time, when they do the things that make determinations for themselves and develop ways and means of carrying out their objectives. Perhaps that's the way their confidence will return. Perhaps I won't be around to enjoy seeing the result of this happening, but I'm quite confident it's coming."

Indian people, according to the chief, still feel stymied by regulations. As an example he gives a lengthy account of what it's like to try to get something done on an Indian reserve. At Norway House they would like to have a drug-treatment or solvent-abuse centre. They have made some moves; studies have been conducted and discussions have been held. "The effects of solvent abuse in the community are self-evident," says the chief. "They are so visible and speak so loudly for themselves that there's little question that some kind of treatment centre right here in this community is required." And they've talked, says Ross, to everybody: Indian Affairs, the provincial government, the churches. "We've talked with a lot of people. And while the placement of a solvent-abuse centre here is justified by any- body's criteria, we run constantly into division of jurisdictions. Within the federal government, Indian Affairs says we'd really like to help, but that's a problem for National Health and Wel- fare. Health and Welfare will say, yes, but we have this special arrangement in Thompson where we have cost-sharing in proj- ects such as this. You get tossed around just within the federal bureaucracy. And then you have inter-government things: the province will say yeah, yeah, but Indians are the jurisdiction of Canada. Manitoba Hydro might be brought into the picture because someone will say, my goodness, with the power develop- ments that have been put in place along the rivers, you're having an impact on those people because you're depriving them of their natural lifestyle, and by your manipulation of the waters you're taking away their recreation from the pleasures they used to enjoy.

"So we all get tossed up in this mix, and many times we get lost in the morass. The need is here, it should be done, governments agree it should be done, but they can't agree among themselves who should fund this or who should fund that. Many times we get everything in place and are ready to put ink on the paper and something happens. DRIE [Department of Regional Industrial Expansion], for example, went broke last June. They'd spent their full appropriation by last June so everything was in limbo. Then they may change a regional director in Winnipeg; he's gone so that's disrupted. The regional director will go on holidays so they'll have a temporary replacement. Then we'll hear that a school burns down someplace so the priorities change. We just can't get going."

I must have proven a good listener; the chief comes to see me late in the evening unannounced. It has been a long day. He had driven out on the bumpy dirt road and across the Nelson River ferry and on to neighbouring Cross Lake for meetings with the chief there. He wears a black baseball cap, sits down with a soft drink in his hand, and puts his feet up. "One thing that's been on my mind for a long time," he says, "is this whole thing of leadership and the people on the reserve. This, at one time, was a very healthy community, one of the nicest places to live. I never wanted to leave here and I always wanted to come back. I didn't think there was any place better in the world than this quiet little hamlet way out of sight of the hustle and bustle of the rest of the world. We were as self-sufficient as you could be." He takes a sip of his drink. "Now things are changed; we're no longer that cosy little hamlet. We're exposed to the rest of the world and all these different forces have an influence on us." He talks about television and roads and how one of the things they do is push people to draw comparisons between themselves and others, between their home and other places. "We're now more aware of our relative position with the rest of the world. And because we're conscious of it, we tend to be more depressed than we should be. We've lost a lot of those very important values that we used to have."

"When I was a child," Ross tells me, "one of the first things that was instilled in me was that I had to have respect. I had to have respect for life, I had to have respect for elders. I had to have respect for people who were less fortunate than myself. I had to have respect for the environment; we couldn't abuse anything. I'm not trying to say we were a perfect society or a perfect people, it's just that we grew up with this respect. We didn't molest or destroy or do any of those things. People would leave their homes and they wouldn't have to lock the door. Traplines were the same; the trapper could leave anything. You travelled by boat or canoe and you pulled ashore anywhere. It seemed easy for everybody at that time.

"But now it's different. Children wander around at all hours of the night; parents seem to have lost control over their families. Everybody's personal property is in jeopardy. You can't leave your car or your boat and motor alone too long for fear you'll lose it. It's a different attitude in people."

It was getting late. Outside, the spruce trees stood black against a sky that had the faintest glimmer of northern lights dancing in its distance. The chief returned to the subject of outside influences and lamented that most of them were negative. Or at best they hadn't brought the needed improvements to the lives of the people and the community. "In spite of the fact that we've got roads in and out of here, we've got jet aircraft and everything, twentieth-century life hasn't brought jobs, it hasn't given us greater opportunities, it hasn't improved the quality of education. It hasn't done too many of those things. What it has done, it has created social problems. People watch TV. It's brought drugs in. Because of unemployment people have given up hope in many cases. They seek comfort in alcohol or something else. They neglect their families, and it goes on and on and on. And when they no longer pay attention to their families, when they no longer give the tender loving guidance that parents should give their children, when the children are left to their own devices, the whole thing gives us real problems. There's real breakdown and our values get lost in the shuffle because they're no longer passed on from generation to generation."

This, according to the chief, is where the question of leadership comes in. His leadership. And I got the sense that it sits as a huge burden on him. If he could, he believes, through some extravagant force of will, move everybody to embrace traditional strengths and values, and then bring those qualities to bear on the problems of everyday life, everything would somehow be

61

all right. He would provide the leadership; the community, though, would have to develop a consensus concerning where it wants to go.

The next morning he was going to meet with a group of the community's elders to listen to what they have to say. "Those values I'm talking about as they applied in 1940 or 1840 are still relevent today," he said again. "If we can behave as we did at one time, we'll have a better shot at the world around us because we'll study harder, we'll have more confidence in ourselves, we'll be more respectful of elders, the rest of the world around us and ourselves. We'll be more likely to succeed."

He talked about wanting to get away from crisis management in the affairs of the reserve, and into more long-term visions. He talked, perhaps thinking of his own family, about how the environment and the resources at Norway House could not support all three thousand people; people would have to be prepared to move out into the larger world. But they should do that with their identity intact, secure in knowing they were "still Norway House Cree Indians."

"The important thing begins with ourselves," said the chief. "We can build all the roads, we can build all the docks, we can build all the structures and do all the physical things, make all the physical improvements we want, but we can't ignore the resurrection of ourselves. We have to start with ourselves."

3   Opinions: Thomas Berger
July 14, 1988

"Probably no White Man in Canada has a better understanding of aboriginal people and their fight for survival," *Maclean's* magazine once wrote of Thomas Berger. Nor does anyone, they might have added, possess more sympathy and passion for the issues they are facing.

A former British Columbia Supreme Court Justice, Berger, as a lawyer, represented the Nishga tribe of British Columbia in their landmark land claims case in 1968. Then, as a judge, he was named commissioner of the Mackenzie Valley Pipeline Inquiry in 1974. The series of hearings he undertook across the western Arctic revolutionized the process by which native people made their views known to government, and to the Canadian public. At a critical moment in history, the process reassured people grown fatalistic and cynical of all government motives that they might hope to be heard after all. His report, recommending that Canada settle native claims before even dreaming of proceeding with industrial and resource development schemes in the north, was profoundly unsettling to the Canadian government and its habitual way of doing things. The Mackenzie Valley pipeline was not built.

Berger headed two public inquiry commissions after the Mackenzie Valley Pipeline Inquiry. In 1979 Prime Minister Joe Clark appointed him to look into Indian and Inuit health care programs, and in 1983 he was chosen to head the Alaska Native

Review Commission in Anchorage. This commission was sponsored by two international organizations of aboriginal peoples, the Inuit Circumpolar Conference, and the World Council of Indigenous Peoples. His work, including his books *Fragile Freedoms* and *Northern Frontier, Northern Homeland* and *Village Journey*, argues eloquently and passionately for respect of aboriginal rights and territories, and for a new order in the ways the immigrants and the descendents of the immigrants relate to the original peoples of the Americas.

Chubby faced and looking boyishly studious behind steel-frame glasses, Berger at fifty-seven looks like a man who has spent more time in chambers than in an open canoe on northern rivers. In truth, he has spent about equal time in each. Soon after the end of the pipeline inquiry he left the bench and returned to private law practice, spending a good deal of his time representing native clients and travelling the world to speak and study. His belief is that the broad ownership claim aboriginal peoples have to land has legal as well as moral roots. I met him over breakfast at his hotel in Winnipeg, where he had come to undertake some work for a new client, the Métis of Manitoba.

Berger: We've always had the problem of sorting out this question: If the Indians were here first, governing themselves on their own land, how do we justify the fact that we now have the land and we are now the sovereign power? In the United States, Chief Justice John Marshall grappled with that question in the 1820s, and he said: The Indian tribes are domestic dependent nations, their sovereignty has been limited because European powers now have the ultimate sovereignty over the continent. But, he said, that doesn't alter the character of the Indian tribes, they still possess a measure of sovereignty, that is, of self-government. And that's the notion that we've adopted in Canada. The Indian tribes were here governing themselves before we came, and they are still here. And they still, to a certain extent, govern themselves. The idea of Indian self-government certainly isn't a new one, what is new is the problem of adapting it to a modern context.

Question: Native self-government is not a new notion, but it has taken time for it to become a general notion. How do you feel about the last ten or twenty years; have there been huge conceptual strides during your career?

Berger: I think there have been. All three of our national political parties are now committed in principle to native self-government. Implementing that principle is, of course, what causes the problem, but it's clear that it's going to come. It's coming. Many native bands are administering programs that used to be administered by the Indian Affairs Department. They are establishing their own schools on reserves and their own band school boards. They are establishing health boards; the Nishga tribe in British Columbia set up the first native health board. More and moɾe native people are being equipped to work in institutions of native self-government. We have native Indian teacher training programs all over the country; more and more native lawyers are graduating; they are going to establish programs for native nurses and doctors. You have to have these people if these institutions are going to be in truth run by native people, and not simply institutions with native figureheads at the top and white folks in fact running them.

Question: How important is it that the principle of native self-government be recognized and established by a paragraph in the Constitution of Canada?

Berger: Everyone agrees; the old Liberal government agreed and the present Conservative government agrees that native self-government needs to be entrenched in the Constitution, and to do that you need a constitutional amendment. They met on this and I understand that the native leaders said, "Let's agree to an amendment that enshrines the right of native people to govern themselves within the Canadian confederation." And the federal government and the provinces said, "No, we can't do that, that's too open-ended; let's agree on the specific items that are covered by the idea of native self-government. Define what you mean in

65

detail, then if we can agree on that we'll put that in the Constitution." Well, they couldn't agree on the one approach or the other. And when the Meech Lake accord was reached, native people felt betrayed, I think, because the prime minister and the premiers were able to agree to an amendment to the Constitution that declared Quebec to be a distinct society without any attempt to define what that means. And I think native people felt, "Look, when you white folks decide that it's important to agree to something you don't insist on dotting all the 'i's and crossing all the 't's; it's only when it comes to native people."

And they've got a point. Constitutions, charters of rights, are always written in broad, general language. When you enshrine freedom of speech you don't define all the circumstances in which it is going to apply. But with native people we say, "Oh no, no, no, we've got to make sure we've thought of every possible contingency right from the very outset."

Question: Is the constitutional amendment critical in a practical sense? What in the end does the constitutional amendment signify?

Berger: It's not a condition precedent to progress, but it confers a certain legitimacy. Look at the Charter of Rights, how it has affected the way Canadians think of themselves, and how minorities in Canada whose rights are secured under the Charter think of themselves. People feel, yes, they have rights. They have ground to defend; they don't have to apologize for what they are and what they want to be. The amendment to the Constitution in 1982 that recognized aboriginal rights and treaty rights was very important to native people because they've been able to use that provision to advance those rights. But it also meant that they could say to themselves and to others, "Hey, we don't have to go around apologizing and explaining; we're in the Constitution." So I think there's a symbolic importance to these things that shouldn't be underestimated.

Question: In your work, both on commissions and as a lawyer representing the Nishga and other native groups, it seems that you had a broader notion of what in fact might be owned by native bands than the government or society is prepared to acknowledge.

Berger: Fifteen years ago there were no land claims. There were claims, but the government refused to have anything to do with them. Since the Calder case, the Nishga decision in 1973, a number of land claims have been advanced. The federal government has adopted a formal policy for settling them. In some provinces, like Ontario, Quebec, and Manitoba, the province has tried to work out ways of settling claims. In other provinces they are not interested. The key to land claims is what it says: land. Especially in the more remote regions, people still live off the land. So land, and the hunting, fishing, trapping that go with it, is essential for the people's future self-sufficiency.

The whole history of white settlement has been one of pushing back the native peoples' access to fish and wildlife resources. I think they want to turn that around. In some land claims there have been, and will continue to be, provisions for cash to be used to buy, among other things, more land. Letting the Indians go into the market. In recent land claims settlements in the United States that has been one of the prominent features. In the Northwest Territories the federal government has agreed that the Dene and the Métis should have a share of the revenue from the exploration of sub-surface resources. Well, that's something that will provide a continuous stream of income to native communities.

I think you can have a measure of self-government in urban centres where, clearly, native people can't expect to hold a land base in the way of reserves, or any land at all in a communal sense. In places like Winnipeg and Regina, where there are large urban native populations, we may have native school boards by the end of the century. In that type of situation there may very well be self-government in that form without a land base. You might also, in urban centres, have institutions for the delivery of health services to native people that are administered and supervised by native people. That's another way of establishing self-government in urban centres without a land base. But in the end, I think native people still think of a land base as essential to the continuity of the native communities and the native institutions.

Question: How great is the moral imperative, the moral pressure on the government, to settle the land issues?

Berger: We've come very far in the last fifteen years. In 1969 Prime Minister Trudeau said he would never recognize aboriginal rights, but by 1973 he had changed his mind. I think a consensus has developed among the politicians; they've stopped talking about assimilation. Something like the White Paper of 1969 is just not in the cards today. The intellectual foundations are there. If we truly believe in the rule of law, we have to reach an accommodation with the people who occupied this land and governed themselves here before we came. And we have to rationalize the whole arrangement, and we have to reach a fair accommodation with them.

People say, "Why should native people have rights that I don't have?" The point is, they are the original people, they do have rights. They go back to the origins of the country and they were here first, as communities. My father came from Sweden; he made an individual choice to come to Canada. He couldn't expect that when he got here the Swedes could claim that they would have a land base and a right to self-government. When he came, and other immigrants came, they made individual choices, or choices as families, to live here under the rules that they found here, and that was that. Native people never had that choice, never made that choice. They were here with their own land held communally and their own form of self-government and they've never acknowledged that they should have to surrender those things and become just like us. And I think that's something that we've come to understand at last.

And it isn't something that is ever well and truly over; it's an ongoing part of the Canadian experience. Novelist Hugh Mac-Lennan was asked once about the French Canadian problem and he said: "Talking about the French Canadian problem is like talking about life as a problem. Life isn't a problem, it's an experience." It seems to me that we've started to comprehend that our relations with native people are not so much a problem as one of the vital things about the Canadian experience.

4   Kahnawake, Quebec

When you are down in the town of Kahnawake, in the narrow streets that thread among the jumble of tiny cottages and centuries-old stone houses, when you are on the rain-slicked streets under the rich damp orange of the autumn leaves, you look up, and you see the Mercier Bridge, the Pont Mercier. It looms high above the town: grey girders like some surreal structure, some gawky prehistoric pterodactyl. The sight is symbolic, mythic. The bridge represents the connection between Kahnawake, the reserve of the Mohawks on the south shore of the St. Lawrence just east of Lac St. Louis, and the sprawling city of Montreal. It links Kahnawake, the tiny enclave of English-speaking Indians (English, they like to say, spoken with the Brooklyn accent picked up during lengthy sojourns as construction workers in New York), and Montreal, the bursting, busy, cosmopolitan capital of French-speaking Canada.

The bridge spans not only the St. Lawrence River but also the deep channel of the St. Lawrence Seaway. Thirty years ago the seaway was built to bypass the Lachine Rapids. The rapids were an impediment to ship traffic on the river, but they were also a rich fishing ground used traditionally by the Kahnawake Mohawks. And now the concrete walls of the seaway push right up against Kahnawake, boxing it, squeezing it in.

The iron girders of the bridge are also a reminder that Kahnawake is the home of the famous Mohawk ironworkers. High steel work has at times employed 90 per cent of Kahnawake's available men. In the 1850s when the Grand Trunk Railway was building the Victoria Bridge across the St. Lawrence, one of the engineers looked up and saw the Indians who had been delivering materials to the construction site scampering up and down the girders, trying to learn how they were put together. The engineer, marvelling at their agility, decided to recruit these men. A report by an official of the Dominion Bridge Company described the Mohawks as "agile as goats," and said, "These Indians were very odd in that they had no fear of heights, they would climb up the spans and walk around up there as cool and collected as the toughest of our riveters."

You drive south out of Montreal on Highway 20, over the Pont Mercier, above the turbulent, grey St. Lawrence and the deep murk of the seaway channel. When you are halfway across the bridge you are over the Kahnawake reserve. Until 1981 it was called Caughnawaga, but the name was changed to be closer to a traditional pronunciation. You pull off the highway, turn onto a narrow road, and abruptly you are driving on what amounts to not much more than a path among the pillars that hold up the soaring bridges. Painted on the concrete posts are the first indications that you are now some place different, that you are approaching a place of conflict. Not all is happy Canada here. In broadly brushed letters: "Long live the Warrior's Society"; "Why can't the White Men behave like Human beings?"; "In Washington they call it assimilation! In Ottawa Indian progress! In Quebec Francization! We who are the Victims call it Genocide!" The messages are stencilled in white paint.

These slogans hearken back to the "cigarette wars" and the day in June 1988 when two hundred Royal Canadian Mounted Police, backed by the Quebec Provincial Police, backed by helicopters and riot squads swooped down on the cigarette merchants of Kahnawake in an operation that had all the markings of a military manoeuvre. The Mohawks won't soon forget. Those among their number who weren't already "radicalized"

71

in their attitudes toward white government authority found that this action did the trick. Gene Diabo, a mild mannered fifty-seven-year-old ironworker who later became my escort around the reserve says that for many people for a long time the Mohawk Warrior Society was seen as something peripheral, an arm of the traditional culture that wasn't too relevent. "But when they blockaded that highway and told the RCMP they couldn't come on our land, everyone was behind them." The RCMP came anyway, in force. But that is another story.

You enter Kahnawake from the east by driving through a tunnel under the railroad bridge. This, too, is like a symbolic act, a passage from one world into another. As you emerge from the tunnel the town bursts upon you; curving streets, a jumble of houses. At each end of the town is a ten-metre high iron cross filled with lights, memorials to the Mohawk men who died in the 1907 collapse of the Quebec Bridge, a half-constructed bridge that was to span the St. Lawrence River at Quebec City. Ninety-six men died in the accident, thirty-three of them Mohawk ironworkers from Kahnawake. Following the disaster, the Kahnawake women made the surviving men sign a covenant promising that they would never all work on the same project. The women felt they could ill afford the risk of all becoming widows at once.

Kahnawake is both growing and shrinking. The town of six thousand is growing as its new suburbs spread in every direction, but its land has shrunk. Gene Diabo remembers in his childhood that the people gathered by the banks of the river for their festivals, picnics, to bathe, to wash their clothes. In 1959 the completion of the St. Lawrence Seaway ended the easy access of the people to the banks of the river that had been their life. Instead of the sloped banks, now the sharp concrete channels of the seaway cut past the back of the town. Ships as big as football stadiums with names like the *General Valdez* (Manila), or the *Petka* (Dubrovnik), glide silently past the back doors of the houses. The farmland that once spread out from the reserve, too, is cut back. The Mohawks are Iroquoian people, and thus farmers; traditionally they were growers of corn and squash and

72

potatoes and tobacco. Highway interchanges, shopping centres, gas stations, and no fewer than five golf courses serving the citizens of Montreal are now laid out over land that once was their farms and gardens.

For Earl Cross, the last few centuries of European settlement in North America are but a blip on the great map of history. I meet Cross one brisk October morning in the kitchen of the Mohawk Nation office. The office fills both the upstairs and main floor of an old house in the downtown section of Kahnawake. The bulletin board just inside the front door is jammed with newspaper clippings detailing the actions of the Lubicon Cree in Alberta. Also posted are reports of last summer's skirmishes and battles at Kahnawake, and at other Mohawk reserves at St. Regis and Akwesasne. For most North Americans these are just news items, but for the Mohawks they are episodes in a great war, one they have been caught up in for three hundred years.

Earl Cross is a large, lumbering man who wears his hair pulled back in a long pony-tail. He has a neatly trimmed black beard and dark eyeglasses. He wheezes a bit when he talks, like Orson Welles used to do. The people who work at the Mohawk Nation office represent the Kanienkehaka, or Mohawk people's "other government." In the eyes of the Canadian government they are not legitimate, the Mohawk Nation government does not exist. The Indian Act specifically describes what a band government should look like, what its responsibilities should be, how it should be elected and constituted, how often it should meet. At Kahnawake this band government is in another office, in another building, just up the street. In many Mohawk eyes, though, the Nation is the only true government, its authority is a thousand years old and comes from the longhouse and the Great Law of Peace. The band government, the government constituted by the Indian Act, is for them barely more than a municipal office responsible for the laying of sewer pipes and water mains. As they see it, the role of the band chief and band council is to oversee the ministration of the Canadian government's money; the role of the Nation is to maintain (often by functioning underground, away from the eyes and the attention of the white man's authority) the connection with the Mohawk past, and the Mohawk laws, and the Mohawk tradition. "They're building a town," Earl Cross says. "We're building a country."

The traditional, or Longhouse government, is made up of the hereditary chiefs of the traditional clans: the Turtle, Snipe, Bear, and Wolf, and a series of other marvellously mythical names: Great Name Bearer, Ancient Name Bearer, Great Bear, Ancient Bear, Painted Turtle, Standing Rock, Large Plover, Little Plover, Deer Pigeon, Hawk, Eel, Ball, Opposite Side of the Hand, Wild Potatoes. The Longhouse Society represents the Kahnawake people in the government of the Six Nations Confederacy at its headquarters on the Onondaga reservation near Syracuse, New York. The Confederacy governs all the Six Nations Iroquoian peoples, including those in the Brantford area of southwestern Ontario, and those in the reservations all along the northern territory of Pennsylvania and New York State, south of Lakes Erie and Ontario.

Mohawks who follow the Longhouse have their own perspective on North American history. Earl Cross unrolls a map of the northeastern portion of North America that shows "the Mohawk Nation at its greatest extent." This eighteenth-century view gave the Mohawks nine-and-a-half million acres of territory as far north as the Île de Montréal, and far enough south and west to take in the whole of the Lake Champlain watershed and most of the central and northern part of what is now New York State. The territory of the Kanienkeh, as described in the book *Seven Generations*, a text used in Mohawk schools for social studies courses, "stretched from Montreal Island to the Mohawk River. It included the Green Mountains of Vermont, the Connecticut River valley, the Lake Champlain Valley, and the Adirondacks. Westward the Kanienkehaka were in possession of vast hunting grounds all the way west to Schoharie Creek."

Prior to European contact, the people lived in the southern territory along the Mohawk River where the cities of Utica, Schenectady, and Albany are now. With the arrival of the Europeans, the people whose descendants now inhabit Kahnawake moved north and became middlemen in the French fur trade operating out of Montreal. They fell under the influence of the Jesuit fathers and many became Catholics. But in their view of things, nothing ever happened to change the fundamental fact that they were independent peoples and the aforementioned lands were their territory. North American history, as understood by all of us who went to Canadian or American public schools, is an irrelevant footnote to these Mohawks, the record of squabbling Europeans. "You'll notice," says Earl Cross, pointing to his map, "that the border imposed between Canada and the United States divides our territory."

The border between Canada and the United States is not one traditional Mohawks recognize. For legal support they cite the Jay Treaty of 1794 between Britain and the United States, which they claim exempted Indian people from any duty payments and trans-border trade restrictions imposed on white citizens of the two countries. It guaranteed them, they believe, free transit. The Jay Treaty has been cited and tested in a number of border skirmishes over the years. It was used in 1926 by an ironworker, Paul K. Diabo, to win a case against the U.S. Department of Immigration; Diabo was arrested in Philadelphia and charged with being an illegal alien in the United States. This was considered to be the test case for the free movement of all Mohawk ironworkers back and forth for jobs on either side of the border. The Jay Treaty was invoked again in 1968 when forty-eight people including activist Kahn Tineta Horn, were arrested while blockading the International Bridge at Cornwall Island to protest Canada Customs charging duty on goods purchased by Akwesasne residents at Cornwall. And it is being invoked now in defence of the cigarette trade, in defence of trans-border casino and bingo operations, and in defence of any practice that the Mohawks consider to be none of the white man's or the white government's business.

One of the most sacred agreements in Mohawk history, and the one they believe defines their relationship to all non-Indian North Americans, is the Two Row Wampum Treaty. In 1645,

75

after they defeated the Mohicans, the Kanienkehaka met with the Dutch, who were increasing their activity in the lower Hudson River Valley, at Tawasentha near what is now Albany, and they agreed to respect one another's territory, culture, political systems, and religious beliefs.

The symbol of the treaty was a belt of white wampum with two parallel rows of purple shells along the length representing the two nations who made the treaty. For the Mohawks the making of this treaty was the action of an independent nation, sovereign in every European sense of the word. They believe they are a sovereign nation still, that nothing has changed that crucial fact. Though they have never done so with enough force to make a fundamental difference in the way European North America has laid itself out and behaves, the Mohawks have always tried to remember their nationhood. They refuse to vote in Canadian or American federal, state, or provincial elections. No Mohawk runs as a candidate, no polling booths are set up on their reserves. The Six Nations Confederacy, they believe, has the power of diplomatic relations with other governments and issues its own passports, which many Mohawks carry and which are honoured by Switzerland, Nicaragua, and the Soviet Union. And the whole of their history is one struggle after another with the other powers of North America in efforts to define and govern themselves.

Gene Diabo and his wife Martha live in a neat brick bungalow with a round, above-ground swimming pool in the yard and an Oldsmobile with Quebec plates and a Chevrolet with New York plates parked in the driveway. Gene is a short, stocky, quiet man with a pleasant laugh who spent his life as an ironworker until a back injury last year forced him to stop. He is on Workers' Compensation and goes every week for physiotherapy. It is a traumatic and unsettling time. The doctors have told him he will probably never work again as an ironworker and he should look into retraining. This frightens him. He resists the doctor's diagnosis; he seems unwilling to admit that his days of doing heavy work out of doors might be over. And yet there are times when he can't even lift a garden rake to carry it across the yard.

Ironwork for him, as for many Mohawk men of his generation, has been a good life, his only life. He can't think of anything else he would want to do. For the community, ironwork created an average annual income of $22,000 and placed Kahnawake among the wealthier reserves in the country. When he was young Gene travelled to work in Boston and New York. He worked on the Hilton hotel in New York and the Champlain Bridge and the Bell Canada building in Montreal. When he and Martha started a family, she insisted that he not travel so much, so Gene agreed to take jobs closer to home. He worked on the Olympic Stadium in Montreal. But now, with the bad back, he is unsure what will happen. He plays with his video camera making tapes of his family and grandchildren, watches sporting events on television, and listens to jazz on his stereo, music from years ago, not the new stuff. He likes Oscar Peterson and Billie Holiday.

Martha Diabo is a human dynamo. She is heavily involved in organizing amateur sports in the community, sits on local education committees, and works in the United Church. She is also on some of the church's national committees, including one that trains Indian ministers and is working to set up self-determination for native churches. Martha is passionate about everything, and everything she takes on becomes a hard-fought battle. She recounts story after story of personal confrontations with school principals, school committees, government authorities, and church officials. In each story her role is that of the crusader against a stupid and unbudging world. Though Gene sometimes wonders why she persists in such frustrating crusades, he seems all the while to be quietly supportive of her work.

The walls of the Diabo living room are covered with pictures of children and grandchildren: three grown sons and a daughter, aged twenty-three to thirty-seven; five grandchildren. One grandchild, Stephanie, a tall, blonde, thirteen-year-old (her mother is French Canadian) lives with Gene and Martha and calls Gene "Bub." The Diabo children live close to home: Gene Jr., twenty-three, manages a furniture store on the reserve; the oldest son, David, is manager of the local Boys and Girls recreation club. Martha points to the photos on the wall and goes into lengthy histories of athletic achievements. Kahnawake is a sports-proud community. Olympic medal winner Alwyn Morris, who won both gold and bronze in kayak events at Los Angeles in 1984, is a local hero. Martha says she has shoulder problems that are probably the result of years of spotting gymnasts; son Gene Jr. was once at the Olympic try-outs as a gymnast.

On Sunday morning the Diabo family gathers like a small convention. Martha spreads the dining-room table for what she calls a traditional Indian breakfast: fried steak and heavy-duty cornbread, brick-like loaves made from the flour of white Indian corn and laced with kidney beans like raisins in a raisin loaf. It is tasty but heavy and dry unless soaked with gravy, of which there is plenty. Gene Jr., who they call Gene-gene, shows up and polishes off a mass of the corn bread, as does seven-year-old grandson Joshua who, when I tell him the food is good, says "It's supposed to be good."

At 10:30 the Diabo family gets ready to go to church. I have agreed to go along and drive Stephanie and Joshua while Martha and Gene Jr. go to pick up another grandchild. Gene stays home to listen to jazz.

On Sunday afternoon, with NFL football on the television, the Diabo family collects again. Gene Jr.'s wife of one year, Karen, is there; a slim, pretty, young woman. The women of Kahnawake are very stylish; access to the shops of Montreal has not been wasted on them. The Diabo's daughter Glenna who works in the Kahnawake Credit Union arrives with her husband Martin Jacobs, who works off the reserve for a paper company in Montreal, and their children Lee-Ann and Joshua; David, the oldest son, is there with his wife Kathy and children Greg and Amanda.

Stephanie is there but her father Barry, the second son and a musician, is out of town.

Contrary to the prevailing stereotypes, the dismal stories of family breakdown and chaos that we tend to hear so often through the news media, I have encountered many strong families in my travels, and the Diabos are certainly one of them. This is not to say that social and family problems do not exist in Indian communities, but on the other side of the coin, Indian people are strongly centred around their families, much more so perhaps than people of other cultures especially in these scrambled times when people disperse themselves so easily from one end of the continent to the other. The native families I've met work extremely hard at staying together. And it doesn't seem to cross their minds that it is an effort; family closeness is simply a high priority. The family connections seem to be so important to one's identity and sense of security that the work at maintaining them is not considered work, it is just something you do. Later in the evening Martha explains the matrilineal system of family trees that the Mohawks adhere to. It should not be confused, she stresses, with matriarchal systems of authority and government. But she explains that every child with a Mohawk mother gets a Mohawk name along with the other names. That morning at the church a child had been baptised with the name Megan Debbie Kanonseiosta Diabo. Kanonseiosta, Martha says, should be translated into something that has to do with water. "That will be the Mohawk name that little girl will always keep."

I leave the house mid-afternoon for a walk through the village. The rain has stopped but water is dripping from all the trees. The Mountain Ash on the Diabo's front lawn is loaded with fall berries and in the fading soft light they are a deep, blood red. I am struck, after the other reserves that I am used to, by the general hodge-podge conglomeration that is Kahnawake: winding streets and an immense variety of housing styles, from stone houses with steep, metal-sheathed mansard roofs à la old Quebec to little cottages overgrown with vines and vegetation. Here and there are quite grand, two-storey frame houses of the sort you would find in Vermont, and of course there are the obligatory, recently built, sprawling brick bungalows now ubiquitous in North America. Instead of street numbers, many of the homes have a standard door sign with an Indian chief in full headdress on the left edge and the family name printed on the right: Horn, Montour, Diabo, Jacob. Many family homes also double as businesses; a front room or a built-on extension has been turned into a small confectionary or restaurant, a hairdresser, a video store, and the ever-present cigarette discounters. There are, I have been told, some one hundred and ten such small businesses operating in Kahnawake.

I walk down toward the river and climb the crushed rock dike that separates Kahnawake from the twenty-five-metre-deep seaway channel. The water is a turquoise-cobalt colour, and when a great ship glides by, it is close enough to touch. I walk behind a row of very old stone houses, and then a row of Jesuit-owned buildings until I reach the Catholic church. As I look out on the seaway I am reminded of the conflict its construction is said to have caused. The community was deeply divided between those who wanted to try to stop it altogether and those who felt the best they could do was try for decent compensation. Martha Diabo has described the seaway construction as "the beginning of the end" for the social life of the people of Kahnawake. The prime farm land once ran to the river's edge, and the people fished daily. They would gather at the river and go out to the islands. They would have picnics and pick berries. The cows would wander down to the river's edge to drink and then the horses would come down, too. She paints a lazy picture of an idyllic life. When she was young and Kahnawake was home to only a thousand people, it was almost like a summer resort. Many of the people spent much of the year at work elsewhere: Martha's father worked for the federal government as a customs excise officer in Toronto and Gene's father was an ironworker, off a lot of the time in New York. In the fall the "summer people" would leave Kahnawake to go back to jobs in New York or Detroit or Philadelphia. "Kahnawake was very big once," says Martha, meaning open, spacious. "It didn't look like a city."

I walk around the grey stone building of the Catholic church. Kateri Tekakwitha 1656-1680, its sign says. This is in fact a shrine for Kateri, a Mohawk girl who came to Kahnawake in 1677, led an exemplary Christian life, and died young. A movement is afoot to have her declared a saint. I peek into the massive interior of the church; it smells of plaster, wood, candle wax, and damp air. The high vaulted, frescoed ceiling, the lighted candles, the statuary, including representations of St. Francois Xavier and St. Ignatius of Loyola, are in sharp contrast to the pink simplicity of the United church. A painting inside the nave shows Pope John Paul with his arms around two Indian children.

I leave the church and walk across the street to the war monument. Gene Diabo has told me that Kahnawake people, possibly because so many lived and worked in American cities, often feel more interest in the United States than in Canada. There are, for example, numerous Stars-and-Stripes flags flying in front of homes around the town. On the war monument for Kahnawake residents who died in World War II there are names of four men who died fighting under the U.S. flag, and one who died as a Canadian.

Kahnawake's notions of "nation" are spelled out everywhere. But they are never notions of a Canadian nation or an American nation. Over the cigarette shacks fly versions of the Mohawk flag: a yellow-and-black depiction of an Indian brave in a circle against a bright orange background. Flapping outside a couple of houses and tacked to the wall of one of the restaurants, is a flag I've never seen before: a Mohawk brave, peace pipe clutched across his breast, with the Stars and Stripes in the background.

The Mohawk's independence, sense of self, sense of sovereignty, has a long history. In 1645 there was the Two Row Wampum Treaty with the Dutch. In 1762, after the Mohawks at

Kahnawake assisted the British in their war with the French, Mohawk ownership of their territory was confirmed and they won a court decision against the Jesuits for the land on the south side of the St. Lawrence, where Kahnawake now stands. The court was presided over by British General Thomas Gage, whom the Mohawks had assisted in battle.

It was after Confederation that Mohawk troubles with the Canadian government really started. The Iroquoian people resisted the forms of government imposed on them by the Indian Act and the government of the new Dominion of Canada. They did not want band governments to replace their traditional chiefs. In 1887 and 1888 the Mohawks of Tyendinaga petitioned the Governor General of Canada to be allowed to keep their system of hereditary chiefs and their Council Fire system of government. "We have by large majority," the Indians wrote, "approved of the system of having hereditary chiefs instead of council men. We therefore do not want our Council Fire extinguished because it was the custom and manner of our forefathers ... Our main object is to do away with the way of electing council committees because they are working contrary to the welfare of the Bay of Quinte Six Nations, we have entirely lost confidence in them." The petition did not receive approval. When the government attempted to organize band elections at the St. Regis reserve the people resisted, elections were disrupted, police came to make arrests, and in the resulting skirmish a Mohawk by the name of Jack Ice was shot to death.

Such outbreaks of resistance occurred off and on over the next hundred years. The Mohawks would repeatedly insist on the traditional Iroquoian forms of government to replace the hated colonial administrations of the Indian Act; the Canadian government would regularly resort to force to put the Mohawks back in their place. In 1924 the Mohawks, both at Kahnawake and at Six Nations near Brantford, Ontario, resisted a government push to have them take up Canadian citizenship. Once more the Mohawks refused to institute the Canadian-imposed band government, and again confrontation ensued. In September of that year, RCMP officers arrived at a meeting of the traditional council of chiefs of the Six Nations at Brantford and banished them from the council house, ordering that they be replaced by an "elected" council of twelve, according to the dictates of the Indian Act. The Mounties in that raid also seized the Wampum of the Confederacy, the beaded belts that told the story of the Mohawk people and carried information about their laws and history. The wampum, held to be almost sacred, had been brought to Six Nations a hundred and fifty years before, at the time of the migration after the American War of Independence.

In 1947, when a joint committee of the Canadian Senate and House of Commons met to examine and revise the Indian Act, the Mohawks of Kahnawake delivered a bitterly worded submission which showed their determination and frustration: "We demand the restoration of our primordial rights, the respect and fulfilment of treaty obligations, the recognition as a sovereign nation," they wrote. "We have no desire to be governed in the future by the Indian Act or any other form of government. The Indian Act as it stands today is a detriment to the progress of our people. All the power is vested in the superintendent general of Indian Affairs and the Indian Agent which leave our councillors and traditional chiefs no power to control our own affairs and problems on our reserves, all they can do is offer suggestions in the form of resolutions which often go unanswered. For example out of 485 resolutions passed, the Department of Indian Affairs answered about 40, many unfavourably. The Indian Act is the most bureaucratic and dictatorial system ever imposed on mankind."

More than forty years later the Indian Act, though slightly modified, is still in force. The band council government is the one recognized by the Canadian authorities, but the traditional Mohawk Longhouse government and its Warriors Society continue to exist with sufficient strength that few things happen within the life of Kahnawake without their participation. They brought powerful pressures to bear, for instance, on the school system. The Longhouse people were also strongly behind a move in 1973 to evict a number of non-native families who were renting houses at Kahnawake in order to make room for Indian families who were living off the reserve.

The matter that currently consumes the attention of the people is cigarettes. Cigarettes are a big business in Kahnawake. When you drive through town, and especially on the highway at either end of the community, you see the signs: DISCOUNT CIGS. Some are crudely lettered signs on a piece of plywood outside someone's house while others are flashing, lighted, electric billboards. Some of the shops are trailers, some are not much more than tarpaper shacks. The cigarette trade has been a thriving business for about ten years, and the number of outlets leads you to believe that quite a few people are involved in it, at least in a part-time way. Though no one has exact figures, estimates of the value of the trade run to the hundreds of thousands of dollars; a business worth fighting for.

It started, Earl Cross explains, not as the political statement it has turned into, but as a business venture. "Some young people who didn't want to go off to be ironworkers saw an angle and exploited it," he claims. It works like this: Cigarettes of the major Canadian tobacco companies are manufactured in Montreal and then sold wholesale across the border to dealers in such cities as Buffalo and Rochester. The price at this point (for the sake of argument, because prices fluctuate constantly) is $4.50 a carton. The dealers then re-sell the cigarettes for $7 a carton to Indian reservations throughout upper New York State. Because New York and U.S. law imposes no tax on products sold on Indian reservations, the reservations become, in fact, duty-free zones. Canadian Indians from Kahnawake or Akwesasne or St. Regis take empty semi-transports to the Onondaga and Seneca reservations in New York, load them with cigarettes, for which they pay $10 a carton, and bring them back to Canada. Then they sell them for $18 a carton, which is a considerable discount on the going Quebec retail price. In fact, every time the Canadian government brings in a new budget and raises the tax on cigarettes, the Mohawk business becomes more competitive and more appealing.

However, Indian protests based on the Jay Treaty notwithstanding, the cigarettes when brought back into Canada are considered by Canadian officials to be illegal contraband. They have been sealed for export and then brought back into the country. Those who transport them back are considered to be smugglers. Operating from this position, the government made raids in June 1988 on cigarette outlets in Kahnawake, and in October at Cornwall Island. Both adventures involved arrests: seventeen at Kahnawake, and massive confiscations of cigarettes and money. There are still bench warrants out for some of those charged in Kahnawake, and people live with the fear that the police might knock at the door anytime. The evidence of the raids demonstrated that both sides consider the cigarette trade a high-stakes game: the RCMP raid at Kahnawake resembled a military operation, with heavily armed gunmen and helicopters; on the other hand, the Cornwall Island raid by the RCMP and the New York State and Ontario Provincial Police netted cigarettes and cash, but also guns, automatic weapons, marijuana, and cocaine. Both sides are now locked into a hostile stand-off. Any move, on either side, is automatically a move in a power play. Will the Canadian government assert its authority? Will the Indians thumb their noses at that authority?

I ask Cross what strategy the people want to use in the current situation, and he says they will try to respond politically. "We'd like to negotiate reasonably. On June 1 they came in and raided our community, it was like an invasion. If you want to get real stupid about this, it could turn into Lebanon or northern Ireland, if they want to act so crassly toward our people. We want to deal on a diplomatic level; they insist on treating it criminally."

Earl Cross is disciplined and consistent in his view of the world. His view, and that of the traditionalists, has a strong impact on the Kahnawake people, it creates the identity and self-image from which they operate. "We're not Canadian Indians," Martha Diabo has said, "we're Native North Americans, members of the Iroquois Confederacy." "If you believe in sovereignty," says Earl Cross, "you have to be consistent. You can't say there is no border and then negotiate with the Canadian government to be part of their border patrols."

The bumper sticker on the back of a 1984 Pontiac cruising down the main street of Kahnawake proclaims: "Iroquois Confederacy Has No Border." But not everybody in Kahnawake is an unabashed supporter of this traditionalist view. As I make my way around the community I come upon smouldering pockets of resentment. The Nation office, of course, receives no money from the federal government, that goes to the band office. Its money comes, rather, from a variety of taxes and donations and levies raised within the community, including a tax levied on the cigarettes sold by the cigarette traders. This is described cynically by some as "protection money." There appear to be some deep divisions within the community about the Warriors Society, the Longhouse, the Nation office, and the traditionalist approach. At the edge of town outside an auto repair shop a large sign says: "Mohawk Nation Office and Warriors Society not part of True Confederacy in Kahnawake."

Bob Patton tells me that "more and more people want to get back to learning their culture, and it's important for some of them." Patton, by both job and religion, has made accommodations to the world beyond Kahnawake: he works off the reserve for the Otis Elevator company, installing elevators in buildings in Montreal, and he has been an elder in the United Church at Kahnawake for twenty-five years, ever since he was eighteen. But he says that the pressure from within the community sometimes become almost unbearable. "We're all Mohawks, but sometimes you get the feeling that if you don't belong to the traditionals you're not considered an Indian." Hearing himself make this statement makes him stop and think for a minute, and then he gets angry. "As Mohawks we're proud. If someone says to me I'm not a Mohawk, I say kiss my ass, I'm every bit a Mohawk. There are people, many of them who haven't even lived here long, who've lived in the States, and they show up here with their headbands and their special shirts, and they've got the books with the laws in their hands and I call them 'wannabees.' They're extremists and they don't represent the best of the traditional people, and they have no business to say people like me are not real Mohawks."

Joe Norton is the chief of the band council at Kahnawake. In the struggle between the traditionals and the non-traditionals, this position puts him at one end of the spectrum. But, despite this, he is the first to acknowledge the struggle and how it cuts right down the middle of the community; down the middle of families. "My own sister," he says, "is a traditional, a clan mother." As the Mohawk people of Kahnawake seek strength and direction more and more from their ancient traditions, as they seek to dismiss Canada's or Quebec's laws in favour of their traditional codes, as they abandon Christianity in favour of the Longhouse festivals, as they steer clear of the Indian Act's elections in favour of the hereditary chiefs and the clan mothers, as they look to their own history and the connections with the other Six Nations peoples, even though many of them are on the other side of an international boundary, Joe Norton is caught unhappily, but wittingly, in the middle. "We are going through a very difficult transition," he says. He holds up his right hand with his thumb and forefinger a centimeter apart. "And we are this close to internal conflict." But conflict is nothing new at Kahnawake, he says, and then he sits back as if to enjoy the ride during his moment in a lengthy history. "It's intriguing as hell to watch what's going to happen."

A casual-looking man given to wearing bright sweaters and having his hair stylishly cut, Norton was an ironworker for twelve years and has been a politician since then, chief for eight years. We talk in his corner office in the band council building, a newish frame building in the middle of town with its wood panelling stained dark brown. Wide, electronically operated glass doors whir open to admit visitors, and the vestibule and waiting area hum with the quiet efficiency of a small law office, perhaps in some suburban mall. A couple of well-dressed young clerks are busily processing forms for two band members who want the return of sales tax on newly purchased automobiles. The indirect lighting and silk plants place this office in stark contrast to the atmosphere in the Nation office down the street. If this is a suburban law office, the other – cramped, busy, with garage-sale furniture and clippings tacked up on the walls – is more the university student newspaper office.

Norton is not unsympathetic to the motives of the traditionalists. He appears to understand them and at moments to share them. But he is also in an awkward position. He is the chief. He and his eleven band councillors handle a ten-million-dollar budget from Indian Affairs in Ottawa, and his government has twenty-seven departments to look after garbage, police and fire protection, education, health and welfare, and recreation. To have all that looked upon by a growing number of his fellow citizens not as irrelevant but as a reluctantly accepted colonial evil is disconcerting.

For many years the traditionalists operated more or less underground. Now their growing strength and self-confidence allows them to function openly out of the longhouse itself, or out of the Nation office. Their Warriors patrol the Kahnawake community in greater numbers than the band council's "peace keepers" police force. What the traditionalists lack is the budget money coming from Ottawa and the authority of Canadian law. But their numbers, compounded with the weight of historical and cultural tradition, gives them another authority, one that has become increasingly powerful in Kahnawake and persuades the elected band council people to strive for a workable if sometimes uneasy coexistence. "The mandate of the community," confesses Chief Joe Norton, "is that we move more toward the traditional system."

The week before I visited Kahnawake, the traditionalists made a move in the affairs of Kahnawake life that garnered national attention. One Sunday morning, after a lengthy meeting at the longhouse, the Warriors moved en masse down to the house of a thirty-year-old woman named Evelyn Johnson, knocked on the door, and asked her to leave town. They accused her of supplying cocaine to the young people of Kahnawake. For a number of months, if not years, people had been stymied by the local drug trade. Estimates of the extent of drug use among the young (and not so young) in Kahnawake varies depending on whom you talk to. A survey commissioned by the band itself found that 80 per cent of the fifteen-to-twenty-four age group used drugs and alcohol regularly. People knew roughly what was going on, and who was responsible, yet no one seemed able to do anything. Martha Diabo told me the story of one woman who approached the police concerned about drug use by her son. The police asked her the boy's age, and when she said "seventeen," they told her there was nothing they could do.

Finally the Longhouse gathered the people, and the Warriors acted in the way that they felt was consistent with extreme penalties in traditional Mohawk ways: banishment from the community. Their action was directed against Ms. Johnson, but was also intended as a stern warning to anybody else. Evelyn Johnson, exiled from the reserve, went straight to the news media and, though she admitted she had sold some drugs, complained about lack of due process, abrogation of her rights, harassment, and so on. The news media played it across the country. But in Kahnawake there was solid support for what the Warriors had done, and for the decision of the Longhouse. Even Chief Joe Norton acknowledged that the Longhouse had been able to do what no one else could; act decisively on the problem. "Nobody else could act on that; not the band council, not the local police, not the drug and alcohol program, not the courts, not the provincial justice system. All of us, our hands were tied in the same way." Now, says Norton, the band council is going to respond with a well-publicized edict declaring Kahnawake a "drug-free-zone."

Not always do the factions in the community manage to be in such agreement. As I was leaving Kahnawake, an issue was heating up that had already boiled over in dramatic fashion at the neighbouring Akwesasne reserve: gambling. At Akwesasne the casinos were at issue, at Kahnawake only a bingo hall. But the pro- and anti-gambling groups were marshalling their forces, and the debate about whether a gambling industry was a good thing or a bad thing in the community was simmering busily. And, as at Akwesasne, the factions were debating not only economic merits or social demerits, but were freely peppering the debate with discussions of gambling, as it relates to their rights as Mohawk Indians.

Whether the community's voice remains that of Joe Norton, the band council chief, or that of the traditionalist Longhouse leaders, everybody shares in the consensus that for Kahnawake to flourish, it will somehow have to expand its territorial base. Developments over the last forty years – the seaway, bridges, highways, and the growth of the neighbouring town of Chateauguay – have squeezed the Mohawks to a little postage stamp of their former territory. The feeder lanes running around the edge of Kahnawake and connecting to the Mercier Bridge to Montreal are so scrambled with speeding traffic you might fear for your life when entering the flow. The sound of all this traffic on the surrounding freeways can be heard constantly in the centre of town, and must certainly work away steadily at everyone's peace of mind, the relentless grind of the noise subtly gnawing away at nerve endings and raising anxiety levels.

In the middle of this is Kahnawake's growing population: young families, all wanting homes of their own, all those former ironworkers and C-31 women returning and hoping for houses. There are almost no empty lots in which to squeeze one more house.

One afternoon I stood looking from the family-room window of the new split-level house David Diabo, Gene and Martha's son, has just finished building with his wife Kathy and their two children. Every male Mohawk is entitled to claim an acre of land when he reaches adulthood, and then must build a house on it. To get their houses now, people are taking much less than an acre. David and Kathy's house is in a new suburban tract, one of the last empty spaces left in Kahnawake. When you look out the window you see the roofs of all the other new houses in the tract and realize that there is no more room here. "The situation," I was told, "is getting desperate."

Chief Joe Norton's solution is to send letters, as he did recently, to seven neighbouring municipalities, reminding them that at least part of their land is territory he believes rightfully belongs to the Indians. It is land he refers to as "the Seigneury of Sault St. Louis." Norton argues that the land was first identified as belonging to the Mohawks in the 1600s, and was confirmed as Mohawk land by King Louis XIV of France and by General Gage, who administered Montreal after the British took over in 1763. Historically, the Mohawks lived on parts of the forty thousand acres, moving their settlements and their agriculture from place to place. Though non-Indian settlers moved onto the land, it was still seen as Indian land, and the Jesuit fathers were to collect rent from the non-Indians and keep the money in trust for the Indians. This system functioned for a couple of hundred years, according to Norton, falling into confusion sometime after Confederation in the late 1800s. Now the Mohawks want to see what's what.

The area in question is more than three times the size of the present reserve and would be very useful to the Mohawks. But there are complications: two hundred thousand non-Mohawk people live or work or farm or drive or park or play or go to school on that land. What would happen to them? They are terrified. Will they have to leave? Who will be held accountable for a hundred years of back rent? Must they start paying rent now? Will the governments allow such things to happen to them? From the Mohawk point of view, the land is their rightful territory wrongfully usurped by the whites without their permission or recompense. They are excited by the possibility of collecting the rents, and the unused portions of the lands would be very useful to them. The Seigneury de Sault St. Louis land raises lots of questions; lots of questions to excite the Mohawks and upset the whites.

How the Mohawks will deal with the matter is still being formulated. Chief Norton is careful, cagey. He doesn't want to alienate the local people, and his letters to the seven municipalities were designed to reassure rather than panic them. Nor does he want to threaten or confront the provincial government over the issue. "I'd rather have them see that it's them and the municipalities and us all together against the federal government because the federal government didn't live up to its obligations," he says. At the same time, he doesn't think the Mohawks will go after the federal government through the traditional land claims channels. In that route, he says, you join all the other Indian bands from across the country who have land disputes, you take a number, and you stand in line. The Mohawks feel their case is different; their ownership of the land is firmly established. The only problem is that there has been a hundred-year lapse in the collecting of rents on their behalf. "We're not approaching it on a land-claims basis," explains Norton. "We don't want to fall into the present system of native claims, we don't want to have to stand in line."

Mohawk nationalism and Mohawk commitment to having a community or a territory that is their own fuels their struggle on this and other matters.

One of the important depositories for Mohawk nationalism, culture, identity, and pride are the schools. Over twenty years Kahnawake has made the change from church schools to a unified school committee, which made use of the provincial schools, to finally pulling many of the children out of public provincial schools and establishing local schools. In 1988 the people of Kahnawake took full control of the school system in their community. As a result, the children of Kahnawake, more than on any reserve elsewhere in Canada, are schooled in an indigenous system run and staffed by the local people.

On a grey, breezy Wednesday morning I arrive outside "Karonhianonha," a large-windowed building painted bright-blue and situated on an acre of playground at the southwest edge of the community. This is the Mohawk immersion school and, as I arrive, a school bus drops off a load of six- and eight-year-old children who sprint and scramble up the walk to the front doors. Inside, I meet Dorothy Lazore, a pleasant, cheerful woman in her early forties who is both principal of the school and founder and developer of Mohawk immersion learning. Lazore, a teacher since 1971, was also a Catholic nun for twenty-three years, until she left her order in 1987. She did not grow up at Kahnawake, but on the neighbouring reserve of St. Regis, a place, she says, where the Mohawk language has not been lost to the degree it has at Kahnawake. Three-quarters of the people in Kahnawake, she believes, cannot speak Mohawk. But around her, 210 children, aged five to twelve, jabber away happily.

The immersion program is in its sixth year, and Dorothy Lazore and her teachers have been making up the program, developing the reading materials and the books, making language tapes, working late after school and on weekends and in the summer. It is total language immersion up to grade three by which point the children, Lazore says, are fluent; they can speak, read, write, and understand Mohawk. Then for grades four, five, and six, two hours a day of instruction in English are introduced. Similar to other language school programs, Karonhianonha School is discovering that the learning of one language does not impede the learning of others. Rather, some doors in the brain are flung open and other languages in fact come more easily. The provincial tests done on her immersion students, she announces proudly, "show that even though they get only two hours a day in English, their English is up to par with that of full English students in the other schools. And we are also finding that they learn French more easily than other students. Our French teacher here speaks French, English, Mohawk, and Spanish. She's a good example for the students who complain that they can't learn French on top of the other languages," laughs Lazore.

Both Dorothy Lazore and the community of Kahnawake take the teaching of the Mohawk language very seriously. But why? It is not just the Mohawks, but the Crees of Manitoba, the Kwakiutl of British Columbia, the Maliseet of New Brunswick, the Ojibway of northwestern Ontario and many others who are trying to reach into the recesses of their minds and memories to bring their heritage tongues into the lives and schools of their children. And yet, with the exception of the more northern or remote people, the native language is not something the adults even know or speak. It is not a language that can be used when travelling beyond the confines of the community; when you travel to a foreign country you don't need Mohawk or Cree in order to function. It is rarely, if ever, the natural language of business transaction, even at home. In a region where the predominant language of interaction is French and on a continent where it is English, do you learn Mohawk simply for its own sake? Why is it important to preserve and learn these almost forgotten languages?

The native people who are excited about language have a ready answer. The most important reason seems to be the cultural one. Dorothy Lazore and the Kahnawake people seem to be motivated by a firm belief that language is implicitly and intricately tied to identity, history, and self-worth. "This is the first step," Lazore says, "to bring back our cultural identity and to help the people feel good about themselves." The people, in her opinion, have been lost and language is the key needed to open that first door to rediscover who they are. And if she needs proof to back up these assertions, she can point to the fact that for the first time in twenty-seven years of teaching she sees kids doing well, and enthusiastic about education. The children learn the language easily, and all sorts of other things about heritage and cultural self-image drop almost automatically into place.

In Lazore's opinion all this did not happen a moment too soon, both linguistically and socially. "The parents were aware that we Mohawks were losing our language, that it was going fast," she says. And she cites the social problems that are often interpreted as connected to cultural rootlessness: suicides among native young people in the eighteen-to-twenty-five age range; problems of heavy alcohol and drug use among teenagers thirteen to nineteen. She sees the cultural recovery as a rebuilding, from the bottom back up. "We have nothing left as native people; we need to bounce back. When we get assertive about our beliefs we're not putting anybody else down, we're just saying we need to live by our own beliefs."

The Mohawk immersion program at Karonhianonha has now gone the full distance at that school. The pioneering grade six group will next year leave the school and continue at the junior high school level. Many, if not all of them, will go to the Kahnawake Survival School, which is appropriately considering the introduction of Mohawk immersion into its program.

The Kahnawake Survival School was started in 1978, one of the first of its kind in the country. Its impetus was the Kahnawake community's reaction to Quebec's Bill 101, a language law that swept the Mohawks and all other Quebec residents under its jurisdiction. It insists that, except for certain carefully defined exceptions, all children in Quebec must be educated in French. The Survival School became the Mohawk's carefully defined exception. It exists now as a symbol of the Mohawk's resistance to the French language and Quebec authority. Though French is taught, Mohawk language classes are compulsory, even for the students who have not gone through immersion in the lower grades, and the rest of the school program functions in English. But the impact that the Survival School has had on the people of Kahnewake over ten years has gone far beyond just language. The school is the symbol of the community taking charge of its own education and its own children. The school, as its name declares, is dedicated to the survival of the Mohawk culture, language and much more. The teachers are steadfast supporters of the concept of the Mohawk nationality, the *Seven Generations* is the text for social studies and history.

The Survival School campus is a hundred-acre tract of bush and fields east of the community. The atmosphere is pastoral, despite its being boxed in between a six-lane highway, the seaway channel, and a gigantic smoke-and-dust-spewing scrap-metal processing plant. A dozen buildings housing classrooms, gymnasium, offices, auto repair shop, and cafeteria cluster around the parking lot. In the bush and fields beyond there is room to carry out small-scale agriculture consistent with both traditional farming and the kinds of skills a young person interested in farming now might need. And there is room to practise other aspects of traditional life that the Mohawks consider to be part of their heritage, from ceremonies and sports to the study of nature and the practice of the arts of survival in the forests and waters. But the school is definitely academic as well and struggles, says its principal, Alex McComber, to combine the teaching of what it means to be Mohawk, with an academic credibility that is competitive for the twentieth-century world.

This comprehensive instruction all occurs in the midst of what an outsider might consider to be an unorthodox pedagogical style. The 160 students from grades seven through eleven address the teachers by their first names and seem to have a consistent input into what kind of place the school will be. McComber, a stocky man in his late thirties with short cropped hair and severe rimless glasses, has been with the Survival School for its entire ten years. "Everything about it has to do with who we are," he says as he shows me around. The school is noted around southern Quebec for the prowess of its wrestling teams: "That's a matter of our pride as Kahnawake people." In mid-tour he excuses himself and approaches a lanky young man, a full foot taller than himself, grabs him by the arm, and takes him for a walk down the hall, pressing him for the reasons he is not, at this moment, in class. The problem apparently solved, Mc-

Comber returns to our discussion. "One of my relatives," he says, indicating the boy just talked to. "Another aspect of the school; everybody knows everybody, knows their families, knows what troubles they might be having, knows something of their aspirations."

Less than half of the eligible high school students at Kahnawake go to the Survival School. The rest still leave the reserve to attend provincial high schools in nearby towns. But the Survival School is inching up, annually taking a larger and larger proportion of the available students. On a bright, sunny Thursday morning I get a chance to meet with a group of seven grade eleven students brought together by Harley Delaronde, the social studies teacher.

I want to know what they think; I want to know why they chose this school; I want to know how they think of their future. Also, after journeys that have had me meeting mostly with adult people, I want to meet and hear from some young people.

I certainly hear from them. They are all seventeen, eighteen, nineteen years old. Bright, healthy, attractive, well-dressed, they are the kind of young people who would make any parent or teacher proud and, even at first glance, make anyone despairing for the future of the world relax a little. They are also, perhaps even more than one might expect of high school age students, thoughtful and articulate about why they are attending the Survival School, what they feel will give purpose to their adult lives, and who they are. Harley Delaronde warned me that I would have to pass some tests; the students have had experiences in the past with journalists that angered them, they might be defensive or aggressive. They turn out to be all of these. They are also passionate, full of conviction, angry about the past, and determined to proceed with their lives as Mohawks. Words and language, I learn right off the bat, are important. "We don't call this our 'reserve,' " a girl named Trina corrects me directly when I am making my introductory remarks, "it is our 'territory.' "

The students acknowledge that they pay a price for their attendance at the Survival School. "The kids who go to Howard S. Billings [the provincial high school in nearby Chateauguay]

97

say this is the school for dummies," says Robert Bonspeil, who early on turns into one of the more vocal members of the group. "They say that when we learn Mohawk history and culture and language that we are following the old ways." So the debate about how best to go forward into the twenty-first century is locked, even among these native students and their peers. But if this group feels criticism from some of their peers, they are not intimidated by it. "They are the ones who will be left behind," counters Trina, referring to the Mohawks who are going to the Quebec schools. "We will know who we are."

It only takes a couple of minutes for the conversation to ignite, and no one gives any appearance of reluctance or holding back or being shy. In fact, during our two-hour session together the group is so vocal and willing to talk it becomes difficult for me, the so-called interviewer, to get a word or my questions in edgewise. Peter Montour, a chubby boy wearing a dark blue jacket, cites the value of learning a Mohawk perspective on history. "In the white schools they teach our people lies," he pronounces emphatically. "Our people never lost a war." "It's misinterpretation, maybe, not lies," corrects Robert, at this moment the diplomat. But it does become clear that the Mohawk interpretation of history is not the English interpretation of history. For example, in my school we were taught that the Mohawk Six Nations chief Joseph Brant was a hero. He supported the British during the American Revolutionary War, and subsequently shepherded his people north to a huge land grant in southern Ontario. Both a county and a city were named after him. Brant is seen by these kids, young Mohawks, not as a hero but as a traitor. Why? Because one of the first things he tried to do with the land grant was sell some of it off to white settlers.

If they have any regret it is that they were born too late. Otsitsa Deer, a tall, athletic boy who is on the wrestling team, tells about trips they make as part of their curriculum to help at the junior schools in the community. He talks about how envious he feels when he visits the immersion school and encounters the children who have been speaking Mohawk since kindergarten. He is envious of their language facility, a facility he fears that he, who started later, will never have. "I feel like I'll always talk Mohawk at a grade two level," he says.

When asked what they intend to do after they graduate, all talk seriously about their futures. Robert will go out west to the University of Lethbridge to study business in a special native studies program; Margaret McComber wants to be a marine biologist; Trina Stacey, who says she is almost fluent, wants to perfect her Mohawk language skills, get a teacher's certificate, study political science, and maybe become a lawyer; Otsitsa wants to study agriculture at the University of Michigan; Ben McComber, Peter Montour, and Petal McComber don't have specific plans but say they want to go to English-language community colleges nearby, in Montreal or in Plattsburg, New York. And in the long view, all of them except Margaret, who wants to go to California, say they want to come back to Kahnawake.

These are young people who have not always lived in Kahnawake. Ironworker fathers bounced Ben and Margaret and Peter and Otsitsa through their early years back and forth to New York City and Detroit. Robert grew up in Toronto and the U.S.A. as his father travelled to look for work, and also to escape an alcoholism he feared would overtake him if he stayed on the Indian reserve. Trina moved to Toronto, New York, and Kitchener, Ontario, with a mother who, she says somewhat bitterly, "never knew who she was; an Apple, red on the outside, white on the inside." But now most of them see their futures among the 6,000 people and on the 13,000 acres of Kahnawake. The certainty of coming back and living their lives in this crowded but tidy little community is so strong it startles. Why? Why the pull when most young people in our society seem to be chafing to get off into the world, away from home, sometimes far away from home?

Because this is home, is one reason. "This is our territory," they say. "This, small as it might be, is our nation." Robert will come back, adept in business, not, he says, to make piles of money, but "to give my father something to be proud of." "We'll do whatever we can to help people here," says Trina.

What kind of place will Kahnawake be in ten years if people like Robert, Trina, Peter, Otsitsa, and the others stay and make it their home? What kinds of changes do they want to see? "There will have to be more territory," says one, referring to the forty-thousand-acre Seigneury Sault St. Louis claim. "It's crowded now and the community is growing so we will need more land.' "There will be no band council," says another. "The chief and council are the representatives of the Canadian government and they should be working themselves out of a job. Our government should be our own government, the traditional Longhouse chiefs and the clan mothers should be running this place." "There will be no foreign government," says another. "We are Mohawks, people of Kahnawake; they want us to say we are Canadian Indians or American Indians, but we are not."

These are ethnocentric times among young native people. They are going through the same sorts of identity processes in their own minds that Third World peoples go through just before they overthrow the powers of colonialism and forge their own way. "When I am a mother," says Trina, "when I have kids, I won't have them celebrate Christmas and Easter. We'll have the four festivals of the Mohawks. My mother gets upset when I tell her this, she says 'How can you deprive my grandchildren of Christmas?' I tell her I won't be depriving them of anything, we'll have our festivals." The churches in a few years, says someone else, will be turned into arcades.

There comes a moment when I feel tense sitting there in the roomy office of the school principal, talking to this group of students; I feel both their rising passion, and their anger. The anger is toward Canada and white people. "We don't hate every white person, just the government," someone says, and I try to feel reassured. "It might seem like we're prejudiced against white people," says Trina, "but they killed our grandfathers." "It's the same way the white people would feel," says Peter, "if a bunch of Mohawks had gone to England four hundred years ago and had put all the Englishmen onto little reserves."

In the midst of the conversation I start to worry about my naivete. I know all the stories from the past. But I thought things had changed in recent years, at least among young people. Here we are in the age of television and daily news and pop music and racial mixtures, at least in our large urban centres, that have every colour and culture imaginable. Youth culture, I had come to believe, doesn't even have sex distinctions in the ways of twenty or thirty or fifty years ago. And here we are just across the river from Montreal, one of the most cosmopolitan cities in North America. But these young people are telling stories about making forays into Montreal and getting beaten up, or called "savages," or asked why they don't wear feathers in their hair. I have to try hard to believe it. How do these stories make them feel? I ask them. How do they react?

It makes them angry, they say. They feel paralyzed, frustrated. They don't know what to do. "Sometimes," says Ben Mc-Comber, a slim young man who up to now hasn't said much in our discussion, "when you hear about a cousin who has been walking down the street in Montreal and has got beat up, it makes you angry, but you don't know what to do. Sometimes I just smack my fist into the wall." "We learn to use humour," says Robert. "We crack a joke."

They blame the government, the media, the police for some of the troubles they have with white kids. "Every time we Mohawks do anything, the media is here distorting it, making it look really bad, making us look like a bunch of stupid people and a bunch of radicals." "The government," says Trina, "over the years has done everything they can to make us not like who we are. They can't just let us be and let us become self-sufficient, because then we would be independent. They want us to need them." So the anger builds up and the frustration builds up and the legitimate places to take it out are few. "Three of us are on the wrestling team," says Robert. "Me and Peter and Otsitsa. We wrestle hard for the pride of our culture. But sometimes too I wrestle to get my anger out, so that I can try to hurt a white kid and it will be legal."

A few years ago, before the government sanctioned it for all Indian bands, the Kahnawake people set up the criteria for Mohawk citizenship. They had a debate over the standards and over the levels of racial purity that they would require. Would it be 50 per cent Mohawk blood, or would 25 per cent be acceptable? They settled, with few exceptions, on at least 50 per cent as the rule, and subsequently made it known that anyone marrying a non-Mohawk would face some difficulties. I ask the seven students if they feel they will marry only Mohawks; to a person they assure me that they will.

If you were the Canadian government, I ask in closing, how would you treat native communities? "They should back off. Give us land, give us the unoccupied land so we can become a stronger nation. Then they should back off and leave us alone," they answer.

5   Opinions: Dr. Lloyd Barber
December 15, 1988

Dr. Lloyd Barber has been a member of the Legislative Council
of the Northwest Territories and, between 1969 and 1977, was
the federal government's appointed commissioner on Indian
Land Claims. In that role he led a commission with a nation-
wide mandate. He has developed a sharp overview of the important issues that exist between Indian people and Canada, an
overview that has the important virtue of longevity; Lloyd Barber's experiences go back to the very beginnings of land claims
negotiations.

Barber is a gruff, blunt man with an old-fashioned flat-top
crew cut and an engaging twinkle in his eye. It is difficult to
imagine him having any patience with either bureaucracy or
sentimentality . He knows most of at least the old guard of both
native leaders and politicians by their first names. When I spoke
with him I tried to get him to consider how things had progressed
in the ten years since his involvement in land claims, and also to
reflect on the self-government issue.

We spoke in his office at the University of Regina, where he
has been president since 1976. One of the ventures of the University of Regina of which he is immensely proud is its Indian
Federated College. This is a college within the realm of the
university that is organized and administered by Indian people,
and whose programs are addressed to Indian needs.

Barber: You know, the whole question of education has been at root of the desire for self-determination in a very fundamental way. People who don't have the right to educate themselves really don't have the right to develop in their own image. So I see the manifestation of at least self-determination, if not self-government, in that whole movement for Indian control of Indian education.

Question: Is self-government in fact a useful term at all?

Barber: No I don't think it is; I think it's probably counterproductive. Those people who are legislators, who have the authority or the control over the process, immediately see it as some parallel form of government to the ones that we have evolved, and see it therefore as a threat at worst and a nuisance at best. And some of the rhetoric that people have used over the years reinforces that kind of negative reaction. When I was on the Northwest Territories territorial council a new school was built at Edzo. I kept telling the guys in the Department of Education, the bureaucrats, "Let the Indian people take it over." And they said, "Oh but they don't pay any taxes." And I said, "What the hell has that got to do with it? We're not talking about who pays the piper calls the tune; we're talking about a situation where people won't progress until they call the tune, whether they pay the piper or not! Let them have the bloody school, let them take it over." And they said, "Oh yeah, but, but, but they don't know anything about education." Bullshit they don't know anything about education, they've educated themselves long enough to survive in this country for five thousand years. Just because there's a new form of education – they'll never know anything about it unless you let them take over and fiddle with it.

Finally the school was given to the Rae-Edzo band. And I guess it was the first Indian-controlled school in the country. And yes, it went up and down and there were all sorts of problems, but what the hell, we've never had problems? We didn't have problems with our schools, or with any other forms of our government? Who the hell are we to have a superior attitude towards their ability to create institutions that suit their particular requirements as they see them?

The basic philisophical proposition of the Federated College here at the University of Regina is that Indian people need the necessary skills to compete in this world, but they shouldn't have to cease being Indian in the process of getting those qualifications. The Indians want to offer bicultural, truly bicultural education so they can go either way, and they've succeeded to a greater or lesser extent. And they've had a hell of an influence on modifying programs in, say, business administration, where they now have courses like band administration instead of widget factory administration. Our academic communities had to move over a little bit and recognize the fact that band administration under the Indian Act is a hell of a lot different than municipal administration under the Saskatchewan Urban Municipalities Act. As soon as you start recognizing that, you can evolve forms of institutional change that give them a much greater sense of control over their own lives and their own destiny. That's what it's all about, really.

Question: You spent ten years on the claims commission listening to peoples' problems, their hopes, and the goals that they wanted to achieve. Now another decade has passed since you reported. Have things happened as they ought to have, and as quickly as they ought to have?

Barber: Things probably are not happening as quickly as they should, although if you look at the 1969 White Paper, what changed during the ten-year period after it was, I think, a very fundamental shift in the basic policy direction. The shift was from one of Indian people being wards of the state to the state providing support and services for them to get on with it.

The White Paper was an assimilationist document. If you look at the whole history of Indian relations from Day One it

105

was, "You stay out there until you're ready, and then you come and tell us that you no longer want to be an Indian." The process of putting them out on reserves until they were ready to be assimilated was a process of making them wards of the state.

One time, I remember, I was talking to David Ahenekew [first national chief of the Assembly of First Nations], and I was mad as hell because there was some stupid bloody thing being imposed on these guys, and I said, "David, how can you stand this?" And he said, "Lloyd, you're beginning to understand what it's like to be an Indian." So I keep coming back to this matter of having control over their own lives as opposed to having the will of the majority society imposed in an authoritative way. One of the things that I used to say when people asked me about all this stuff is that the Indians have a capacity for passive resistance that makes Mahatma Gandhi look like an amateur.

My own personal view is that the politicians were too skittish about self-determination or self-government and about putting that in the Constitution. They should have done so and then let it evolve in terms of the various circumstances of various bands. And then they should have managed it. And I don't mean managing in the old-time sense of the Department of Indian Affairs, as a bunch of wards of the state, but managing it in terms of the immediate circumstances. Managing in terms of various kinds of evolutionary, institutional change. Managing in terms of the economics of given bands and the land mass. Self-government in the Northwest Territories is going to be a hell of a lot different from self-government even in the Yukon next door, in terms of numbers and size of the territory and relationship of that population to the total.

I can recall an Indian meeting in Fort Simpson in the Northwest Territories many years back. I walked up and down the street with these guys, Georges Erasmus and others, and I said, "Look, co-opt the government that's there. Don't try to set up a parallel government because you won't get it." And of course since then they've had a majority of representation in the territorial government. So by co-opting the existing form of government they don't get anybody upset; it's not a question of

106

sovereignty outside the traditional forms of government. And unless there's some tilt or schism, in ten years time or fifteen years time they will be self-determined, or sovereign, or whatever you like up there in the Northwest Territories.

But the Tobique band in New Brunswick, I know a bit about that band and have dealt with a number of those people, and it's a pretty healthy band as bands go, good people, a good number of them are well educated and self-sufficient. But can they be different from a municipal government? Can there be a real sovereign enclave within that community, given the history of that part of the world and how long there has been an inter-relationship? I would wonder.

Understand that there's no homogeneity among the Indian people in Canada. I was saying to somebody the other day that if all of the Indians in Canada had been homogeneous: one band, one tribe, and they all lived in a contiguous area the size of southern Alberta, or the size of the Northwest Territories, self-government would take on quite a different flavour. You could make it a province like Quebec, or a principality like Luxembourg; there's all sorts of things you could do. But it's one thing for the Bloods to talk about self-determination, and it's another for Cape Mudge to talk about self-determination. And how the hell any of those things can be reconciled within any given framework is a very vexing question.

But there is no homogeneity among the Indian people in Canada. If they had been one tribe all living in Saskatchewan, we'd have a totally different set of circumstances. Take the Navajo nation in the U.S., living in four states, it's bigger than Rhode Island. They can have a "nation." It's isolated more or less and big enough. They've got some wealth, they can do what they like. The Blood reserve, which is the largest in Canada, isn't big enough to be a Navajo nation in that sense.

In B.C., the history of the differences between the Indian peoples is longer than the history of their commonality. They have commonality in Indianness, but they don't have commonality in terms of the evolution of their lifestyles, their territories or anything else. British Columbia can never have a unified

107

FSI [Federation of Saskatchewan Indians] type of thing. One of the reasons the FSI has been the strongest provincial organization is because essentially Saskatchewan is a Cree province, except for some Dakotas who got shoved in here from the wars in Minnesota. They have to accommodate themselves to the Cree leadership. There isn't the same kind of schism as there is in Alberta between the Crees in the north and the Blackfoot Confederacy in the south. There are some Assiniboines here and a few Saulteaux and some Chipewyans way up north, but the Cree are such a preponderant majority that the others have to follow. There's not so much difference as there is between the Haidas and the Kamloops band. So you get back to this question of what does self-government mean? It means something a hell of a lot different for the Haidas than it does for the Chipewyans at Black Lake, Saskatchewan, or the Lubicon Lake people. People think "an Indian is an Indian is an Indian"; that's like saying "a European is a European is a European." There's about as much commonality between the Micmacs of Nova Scotia and the Haida of the Queen Charlotte Islands as there is between the Rumanians and the Swedes.

Question: What can happen in this country without public perceptions changing dramatically?

Barber: Not a lot. If it hadn't been for the Royal Proclamation and, following on that, Indians having a special place in the British North America Act, the progress that has been made in terms of their place in the country would not have been nearly as great as it has been. There are some basic fundamental legal and constitutional roots for their position: you can't gainsay the Royal Proclamation, you can't gainsay the BNA Act, there they are. They are the only people mentioned in the 1867 BNA Act: Indians and Indian lands. They didn't talk about French people, or English people. Language maybe, but not people.

Now, given the diversity that we were talking about, the fact that they've been a federal responsibility has been a curse in the sense that the federal government has to have policy that applies to everybody equally, right? But the lack of flexibility in that has screwed things up. I've always maintained that it's not the Indian Act that's so bad, it's the administration of the Indian Act that has been hopeless because it hasn't been flexible enough. This is why they need something that says, "Yes, they have the right constitutionally to self-determination." We'll define it as we go along. And it can be something different for the Nishgas than what it is for the Tobique band, or the Whitebear band.

Question: How important in the whole process is this constitutional affirmation of aboriginal rights?

Barber: It is critical symbolically, in the same way it is important for the French to insist that Quebec is not like everybody else. In that sense it's quite critical, and I think if it existed a lot of the heat would go. As long as it doesn't exist, that will be the thing that they beat on rather than getting on with the business. As a practical matter, you can get on with the business without having it; as a practical matter, there are lots of things that are already there if you co-opt them. But the symbolism is very important.

A very good example of that importance is one I ran across when we were looking at the ammunition claim in Treaty Seven. It was probably one of the simplest treaties in Canada, but there wasn't a hell of a lot of progress being made. There was a lot of backing forthing and to-ing and fro-ing and a terrible, terrible bill being presented to the government. They wanted the initial money; they wanted interest; they wanted inflation; and they wanted a payment for deprivation of use. They wanted the whole thing stacked. I forget the numbers now but it was a big, big number, and not reasonable. Until one day the guys from the Department of Indian Affairs came and said, "Okay, we're wrong, we admit we're wrong, now let's really negotiate the number." And the air just went out. Once the department admitted it was wrong and that it owed the Indians, the thing was settled more or less easily.

I've seen many cases where settlements were not reached partly because the existence of the claim was more of a lever than the value of the settlement. Take away a guy's crutch and he loses a prop, he can't beat you with it anymore. So part of the problem of settling some of these claims is exactly that: what are we getting for what we're giving up? Because if we give it up, we can't use it again to get some things that we think we need. I wasn't successful in convincing the legalistic people around Ottawa that it is probably not desirable to say "in exchange for your aboriginal rights" as the treaties all say, because you can come back and say, "You gave up your rights, you have no more right at the trough."

Take Norway House. If there are three thousand people at Norway House you can't say to them in 1999 or 2010, "Oh but you gave up your aboriginal rights. We don't owe you anything any more." You're not going to let them die. So why don't you recognize the fact that what you're dealing with is a social evolution, and leave enough flexibility in the situation. You take the seeds and ploughshares in the treaties and say, "That means economic development." If it had meant that over the years, we wouldn't have the kind of situation we're now dealing with, but it was interpreted to mean a bag of seeds and a shovel and two oxen and a cart. We're finished, right? Right. Now go away and look after yourself.

That same mentality continues to exist. Look at James Bay: "We settled with you, don't come back to us again." If that James Bay thing doesn't succeed there's no point in saying to those guys, "We made a deal with you, now what the hell's the matter with you? Why can't you leave us alone?" "But sir, we're in Canada, we're Canadians, and we're poor. You're taking all that power out of James Bay and you're getting rich on it." Or "We didn't understand there was going to be oil under the Lubicon Lake land." So there's no point in saying it's a final solution; Hitler thought he had a final solution.

The process is important, but you can't solve it. You can't solve human problems. Thank God you can't solve them. Life wouldn't be worth living if they had been solved. Life is a problem. And it's no different for the Indian people. People go around saying "We've got to have a solution to the Indian problem." But every goddamned solution hasn't solved anything. The problem is, people are looking for a solution instead of a process. That's what putting it in the Constitution would be. And you come back to your point about self-government. It's not self-government, it's "You bastards, let us in your Constitution. We were here first. You talk about TWO nations. Piss on you." You think about it in those terms and it is incredibly simple. And thoroughly understandable.

Question: What would be the worst thing the government could do?

Barber: Return to its pure assimilationist policies. Not recognize that these people are a distinct people, a distinct people with both moral rights and legal rights going back to the Royal Proclamation and through the BNA Act. And they are not going to be assimilated.

6   Cape Mudge, British Columbia

Jimmy Sewid was a well-known man, a famous elder among the Kwakiutl Indian people who live up and down the coast of British Columbia, from Campbell River to Port Hardy. He was a leader of his people, one of the important elders, who had taken on as one of the last jobs of his life a lengthy fight to secure the return of the Kwakiutl people's ceremonial regalia.

The regalia had been missing for sixty-five years, ever since the government had outlawed the potlatch and had scooped up the masks and adornments. It was for the Indians' own good, they said. And then they had sold the individual pieces to museums in Ottawa and all over the world: in Germany, the United States, England. The museums were delighted to receive the booty, and for the next two generations they held, like prisoners, the fierce masks, the sheets of ceremonial copper, the elaborately painted screens from inside the longhouses. All was kept behind glass cases in galleries and museums so anthropology students and the general public could "ooh" and "aah" and say how quaint but frightening they were. And wasn't it true that the West Coast Indians were known to be slave-keepers and cannibals?

Jimmy Sewid and a group of others like him had come in their later years to view the 1921 and 1922 confiscation of their ancestors' ritual regalia as a supreme indignity. Traditionally proud and independent people, over the years they had ceased to be intimidated by or deferential to even the federal government. So they started to put voice to their belief that the artifacts

112

belonged not in the big national and foreign museums, but at home, in the small museums of their own Indian villages. For years, Jimmy Sewid and the others worked, pressured, negotiated, lobbied, and pushed to get the government, the diplomats, and the heads of the large museums to agree with them, and agree to return the Kwakiutl heritage. And at his death at age seventy-five, much of the regalia was back where it belonged, safe on the shelves of small local museums like the one at Cape Mudge.

For this, and for his many other accomplishments, Jimmy Sewid was known as an important man, and when he died, many people came to his funeral.

It is a hot day in early spring. I travel across to Campbell River, where the funeral will be held, on the ferry with Dan and Alberta Billy, Kwakiutl people from the Cape Mudge band on Quadra Island. The Billys are related to Jimmy Sewid; one of Dan's sisters is married to his son. But almost all Kwakiutl people have some family tie to almost everyone else; there are only eight thousand of them to begin with. The family ties are cherished and nourished in conversation and lore these days almost as assiduously as they were in the pre-European contact heyday of West Coast Indian culture. Then, every marriage, every birth, every death, every name, every clan and family connection, was known by everybody and woven with ritual significance.

The big BC Ferries Corporation boat carries us across a channel that is as busy as a highway with gleaming white cruise ships heading north from Vancouver to Alaska, little silver runabouts from a tourist lodge, tugs loaded with oil drums, and other tugs laboriously pulling booms of logs toward the pulp mill at the north end of the city of Campbell River. Overhead, flurries of gulls swoop and scream. In Campbell River, spring is bursting; school children can hardly suppress the joy of being out of doors.

After the funeral, hundreds of people gathered for a feast in the big hall next to the Campbell River community centre and hockey arena. The room is enormous, one of those wide, all-purpose halls with a well-equipped kitchen, and lots of parking on the gravel lot out front. But so many people are there, jammed into the hot room, it is still almost not big enough. As the feast runs to its end, the elderly women gather their blankets and, as elderly women at Kwakiutl funerals for hundreds, or thousands, of years before them have done, they start a dance and a chant.

When I first make my way to Cape Mudge, I fly north from Vancouver to Campbell River on a little Air BC Dash 7. We are fifty-five minutes in the air. Campbell River is a bustling new town of twenty thousand people on the inner coast of Vancouver Island. It is, except for some fishing and the fast-growing tourist business, essentially a one-industry town. Its huge pulp mill continuously spews white smoke into the leaden sky. To get to Cape Mudge from Campbell River, I must take the ferry to another island, Quadra, a twenty-minute ride away.

The people on the ferry to Quathiaski Cove, Quadra Island, say that Campbell River is ugly, Quadra is beautiful. What they mean is that Quadra is unspoiled; unspoiled by the pulp mill, unspoiled by the litter and random development that in our society is too often taken to mean that the economy is going well. Quadra, by contrast, is Indian and, to a degree, reminiscent of those 1960s utopian places the hippies loved. On the ferry I meet a woman named Wineva, a petite Californian dressed in a loose cotton dress and dangly jewellery. She has lived on Quadra, where she teaches kindergarten at the island's only school, for fourteen years. She is married to a Japanese man, who works as an administrator for the Indian band in neighbouring Campbell River. When we get off the boat he is waiting to meet her in a brand new, smoke-blue Mercedes.

A girl on the ferry, a young white woman towing two children, friendly but bland, says she came to British Columbia with her parents from Sudbury, Ontario. She asks about my visit to Quadra, and when I tell her, she says she hears "the Indian men are all raping the Indian women." "Where?" I ask. "In B.C.," she guesses. She heard it on the news.

On Quadra Island I wait in the parking lot in the rain for a few minutes, and then Alberta Billy arrives to meet me. I don't know the Billys well and I am presuming on their hospitality, which they are most generous in offering. Alberta and I drive in her new Oldsmobile down the two kilometres of road to the village, and pull into the driveway beside their house.

Alberta and her husband, Dan, are in their early fifties and have three grown daughters. Alberta is an active participant in the United Church, at home in her community, and right up to its national level where she sits on a council that looks after the affairs of churches in native Indian communities. In 1986 the United Church wrote an agonized apology to native people in Canada and issued it publicly. In it, it declared that it did not apologize for teaching the Christian gospel to Indian people, but it realized, in retrospect, that it often confused western European culture and values with the teaching of that gospel. For that, it was sorry. Alberta Billy was one of the people active behind the scenes to persuade the church to make the apology. Now she watches anxiously to see how it will be received, and what will happen next. Indian people, for their part, acknowledged the apology, but have not formally accepted it.

Alberta Billy is a strong, pleasant woman with dark hair framing her face in a halo of curls. Dan is a small man, an inch or so shorter than Alberta. He is compact but strong, with slicked back black hair and an abundance of quiet dignity. You might tend on first impression to say he is aloof, but that would be misinterpreting his shyness. When he is moved to show or explain something, it is done with an effervescent burst of enthusiasm. Alberta and Dan have been married for twenty-seven years. Their three daughters have all moved out, though all live nearby. Two are married and the Billys have three grandchildren in whom they take an obvious delight.

The Billys are fishermen, as are most of the people of Cape Mudge. It is hard to tell at this stage if Dan and Alberta's prosperity is greater than that of other people in the community. The entire community is tidy and pleasant, built in a half-moon

115

crescent facing the water on flat ground below a steep hillside. The hillside is dense with fir and maple trees; the community is spotted with flowering trees, lilac bushes, and bushes bursting with yellow flowers. Twenty six well-built and well-maintained houses stand in a row facing the waters of Discovery Passage, which looks across to Campbell River. Enough other houses are stacked up behind, to make a community of about sixty dwellings. In the middle of the community is the new museum with three totem poles, "welcoming poles," in front of it. Beside it are a soccer field, tennis courts, a children's playground, and an old elementary school now used as a nursery school. Almost in front of the museum, facing the road and the water, is the graveyard, a fenced-off area with about two hundred gravestones. Most of the markers are small crosses or simple concrete slabs, with plastic flowers and silk wreath decorations. The legible names say things like; "Skookum Jack, 1918" and "Major Dick, 1914" or "Baby Dick, 1908, age three months."

In the other direction from the museum, is a short street with the church, the fire hall, and the old band office. At the extreme end of the community is the new band office, a sprawling building constructed early in 1988, and in front of that, a substantial community wharf and dock where the people tie up their fishing boats. To complete the well-equipped feel of the place, there is also a modest, new dry dock where the people can pull their boats in for repairs.

The general prosperity of the community is evident. Alberta explains, with no small pride, that "the Kwakiutl are Salmon People." Fishing is obviously a big operation. On the living room wall are three pictures: a painting, a colour photograph, and a pen and ink drawing of the *Susan Laverne*, the Billy's fourteen-year-old boat. The pictures show the boat in the three phases of its work: herring fishing, which is done in March, far up the coast and out on the open sea; trawling for salmon; and seining, which is done in July and August when the boat pulls a huge 220-fathom net that catches more salmon. Sockeye, they explain, is their main livelihood. The name of the boat, *Susan Laverne*, is that of their youngest daughter.

The investment in the boat, Dan explains, is about $800,000, and its refit this spring alone is running to almost $100,000. To be an efficient fisherman, he says, requires a boat with all the latest gadgets: radar, radio, depth-sounding equipment, and efficient winches and hydraulic systems to pull in as many as six thousand salmon at a haul. The intensity of the fishing business becomes clear when you understand that it is all done in a mere fourteen days of the year. This is because fishing is not only a big operation, it is also a highly regulated one. Licensing is controlled stringently by the federal government's Fisheries and Oceans Department. The department, through its licences, divies up the locations and the times for every commercial fisherman's activities. The herring fishing in March, which is physically the hardest of all his work, according to Dan, must be done in only one or two days. The boats travel a great distance; it takes the Billy's forty hours to get the *Susanne Laverne* from Cape Mudge to Prince Rupert and the herring grounds. Then, in March weather that is frequently inclement and on seas that are treacherous, the captains jockey for position and fish as though there were no tomorrow. Likewise with other species. Dan says he used to have a halibut licence but if you don't use it for one year, you lose it. He surmises that there are now probably only two native halibut fishermen left on the entire coast. He also feels the percentage of native fishermen in general has gone down. It used to be 18 per cent, and now is perhaps only 5 per cent of the total.

The fishermen of Cape Mudge are all small enterpreneurs, independents. The Billys' fifty-five-foot boat requires a crew of five, relatives and close friends, for those exhausting days of fishing. The other families of the village all crew their own boats. The catch is sold through one company, B.C. Packers, which is owned by Weston Foods. Then it is either canned or frozen, and marketed, much of it going to Europe or Japan. A combination

117

of good catch and good price is what the fishermen need to be successful.

The Billys express a predictable irritation with the rules and the workings of the fisheries officials. Part is the natural irritation entrepreneurs feel for bureaucrats; part is also the resentment Indians feel for the white man's government. Alberta says that in the original agreements between the Indians and the government, "the old people trusted the government too much."

Fishing is a lifestyle of hard work and industriousness, but no amount of hard work alone can guarantee its future. There is fear that the future of all commercial fishing is in jeopardy. Fish stocks are depleted, and the reason, in Dan Billy's now decidedly heated opinion, is not because of the commercial take, but because of sport fishing, and, worse, environmental damage. Mining and lumbering activities have destroyed river mouths. "Trees cut at the mouths of rivers ruin fishing, mine tailings ruin fishing," he says, becoming visibly angry. "We could be the richest country in the world if we would learn to work together and understand how everything we do affects everything else. But instead, everybody is out only for the immediate dollar. If people would just think," he pleads.

The real fears these days of people like Dan and Alberta Billy concern the possibility that the provincial government, instead of the federal government, will take control of fishing regulations. The Indian people seem universally mistrustful of the provincial government. If they don't like the federal government, they like the provincial government even less, and fear that it would never respect or consider the Indians' best interests. "If our fisheries ever get into the hands of the provincial government, that would kill us," says Alberta.

Another issue is the competition between the commercial fishermen and tourism and sport fishing. Tourism is now king in British Columbia, and the fishermen fear the ramifications. If the government has to choose between tourist dollars and fishing dollars, the Indians fear tourist dollars will win.

A recent innovation on the British Columbia coast, which the commercial fishermen find threatening, is fish farming. Introduced only a few years ago by Norwegians, it is nonetheless enthusiastically supported by the provincial government. Fenced-off compounds of domesticated fish in coves up and down the coast may soon account for half of British Columbia's marketable fish. This makes the Billys angry. They claim to worry about diseases introduced into the natural stocks, and argue that the farm fish is of inferior quality. It is mushy, not as tasty, and has no protein value, according to Alberta. Consumers are being poorly served. Alberta laments that even some Indian bands are getting into fish farming. She dismisses them for seeking only the fast economic return. "I don't know what the advantages of fish farming are, except for people who want to make a quick buck by abusing our natural resources," she says.

Fishing, still, has been good to the Billy family. They live in a rambling, twenty-year-old, cedar-panelled ranch-style home. A Ford half-ton truck and the 1989 Oldsmobile Regency Brougham sit in the carport. Each winter there are regular trips to Hawaii. On Sunday afternoon the Blue Jays-Chicago White Sox game is on the television, and the picture window across from the living-room fireplace, and across from walls lined with local art and prints and carvings faces past their deck, to a spectacular view of the waters of Discovery Passage. Among the pictures on the wall is an enlarged photograph, taken in 1972, of Pierre and Margaret Trudeau with Louise Howell, Alberta's grandmother.

Discovery Passage, outside their window, can be as busy as the English Channel: boats loaded with pulp from the Queen Charlottes, a fishing boat going after halibut, smaller pleasure crafts fishing for salmon. In summer, when the tourists come, the exhaust and noise from the boats that line the shore just outside their house, Alberta says, chokes them. But now all is peaceful. Gulls scavenge the shoreline; pairs of ducks, old squaw and harlequins, bob in the water; eagles circle over the forest in back of the house. Not twenty feet from shore a lone sea-lion, looking at first glance like a Labrador dog, swims leisurely yet purposefully.

On Sunday evening we walk over to the Quadra Island United Church, a white-frame building with a blue roof and a steeple built in 1931. The stained-glass window in the front of the church was donated by Alberta's mother. In blue, grey, green, and white it shows a seining boat caught in a storm.

Extensive missionary activity occurred among the Indians of the B.C. coast a century and a half ago, and between 1860 and 1910, 90 per cent of the Indian population was converted to Christianity. In 1893 the chief at Cape Mudge, Billy Assu, wanted a school, so he bargained with the churches and held out for the denomination that would offer him the best deal. It was the Methodists who came through with the school, and so it is that Cape Mudge went Methodist and today is United.

The signboard at the church says the minister is the Reverend Dan Bogert-O'Brien. Inside, the church has been modernized and is bright and comfortable. It is large enough for eighty people. Behind the altar is a brilliant circular carving on yellow cedar of a male and female salmon pursuing one another. It was carved in 1984 for the church by Jim Hart, a student of the famous Haida carver Bill Reid. At this Sunday evening service in spring, the altar is decorated with a sprig of blue-flowered camas. Camas bulbs, I've been told, were used by the Kwakiutl in times past for food; somewhat like potatoes, they are a source of starch.

Dan Bogert-O'Brien, a gangly man in his mid-thirties with intense blue eyes, a shock of red hair, and a red beard, takes his place at the front of the church. The theme of the service is "words": how imprecise words can be, and the theological significance of "the word becoming flesh." "Word" is an appropriate topic. Earlier, before dinner, Dan had initiated a brief conversation about the loss among people his age of the Kwakiutl language. Dan was one of those whose hands were strapped at residential school when he spoke Kwakiutl, and he says he now has a mental block about his language.

The importance of language is also an appropriate topic given the ethnic mix of the congregation. The Quadra Island United Church was built in 1931 by a group of devout Cape Mudge people. The people who come to the church now, though, are island people, and mostly white. There are three or four Indian elders, including eighty-three-year-old hereditary chief Harry Assu and the mothers of both Dan and Alberta. But the rest of the group is an eclectic mix of the people you might expect to find these days settled in out-of-the-way, upper Pacific coast islands; left-over hippies, retired people with gardening interests, people with esoteric tastes. A gentle-looking man named Ray with a shaved grey head, is a teacher who has just published a book on the Taoist perspective on relationships. His wife, who is the organist, favours us with an intense solo on the cello, something from Vivaldi. A shy man in heavy wool pants and yellow slicker has arrived from town on his bicycle, his bald head and bearded face shining from the exertion. Two retired couples from town and a few other women fill out the congregation.

The Indian people of the British Columbia coast have lives and histories, land, cultures, and economies unlike those of any other people, anywhere else. The coasts, north from Vancouver, are a territory of steep mountains, deep water, a repeating pattern of fiords and misty inlets, of rain, cedar trees, and dense undergrowth. The landscape is overpowering, tempting superlatives, weighted with visions of the mysterious. The Indians, before the arrival of the Europeans, lived off a natural abundance. They situated their camps and villages in sheltered coves close to salmon spawning grounds rich beyond imagination. The waters also yielded cod, halibut, herring, shellfish, and the tasty, oily oolichan. The oil is used as a condiment to freshen up almost anything the Kwakiutl eat. If fish were not enough, there were sea mammals and, in the rain forests, an abundance of fruits and berries.

The climate made subsistence a relatively easy matter. The people, intelligent and imaginative, used the resulting leisure to develop rich and complex political and cultural systems built on complicated schema of rank, lineage, mythology, and ritual.

The northwest British Columbia coast has certainly changed in the two hundred years since European contact, especially for the people of the Indian nations: the Nishga, the Nootka, the Bella Bella, the Bella Coola, the Salish, the Kwakiutl, the Tsimshian, the Haida. But the sense of power and mystery possessed by the land of rain-shrouded slopes and deep tidal channels persists, mindless of all the scratches of human change.

There are 197 Indian bands in British Columbia. Many of them are small, with only a couple of hundred people and a few acres of land. There are six hundred people on the Cape Mudge band list. Cape Mudge has a large land base for a coastal band, though certainly not large by, say, prairie standards. It has 11,400 acres on Quadra Island, which includes the village, and a forest reserve. There are two other properties, of 254 acres and 287 acres, on other spots on the island. The band has turned one of these into a public campsite, and gains some revenue from that. As well, the band owns another 240 acres on Vancouver Island at a place called Quinsam, and some of the band members live there. Of the six hundred people who are members of the Cape Mudge band, slightly more than half actually live on the reserve. The three Billy daughters, for instance, all live off-reserve – two on non-reserve land, and one, with her husband, on the Campbell River Reserve. The provisions of Bill C-31 are bringing Indian women back to reserves in British Columbia, too. Ruth Billy, who lost her status by marrying a non-Indian man, says she would now like to return to the village at Cape Mudge and get a house in an area already identified as a new sub-division.

The band has managed its forest reserve for the past twelve years. They manage it assiduously; no clear cutting is done, but they thin out 600,000 board feet each year, which brings in about $70,000. The forest is healthy and a pride to everyone. But it is not the land the Kwakiutl people are most interested in; it is the ocean, coastal rights and water rights, for they are fishermen. Cape Mudge has a band government made up of six councillors and a chief councillor, all of whom serve voluntarily. For sixteen of the last twenty years, Dan Billy has been a councillor, and every week or so must donate at least half a day to a council meeting or some official business. The band also has eight employees, including band manager Don Assu and Daryl Wakelyn, a white man who acts as economic development coordinator.

A friendly, open-faced man in his middle-thirties, Daryl Wakelyn worked for Indian Affairs from 1980 to 1987 out of the Campbell River office, where he was in charge of band government and alloting money for the housing program. He takes some time and is able patiently to explain to me the ins and outs of Indian administration in British Columbia.

Wakelyn left the employ of the federal government because of "devolution," a term that refers to the government's transferring responsibilities and programs to the hands of Indian bands or tribal councils. At the Campbell River office the staff of civil servants was cut from twenty-seven to six. Devolution also meant the divesting of some responsibilities. The traditional responsibilities of the Department of Indian Affairs were education, social development (welfare), lands reserves and trusts (administration of Indian trust reserves), economic development, housing (a capital program), and band government. The skeletal Indian Affairs staff that remains still holds, explains Wakelyn, "incredible authority over program funding and lands and trusts. These are also called their residual responsibilities." But in the main, the federal employees are responsible now for handing money over to the bands and tribal councils who spend it themselves. This has meant a tattering of the morale of the once all-powerful department. It also means that the real action now seems to be at the band and tribal council level. The process has done funny things for the people who work in the "Indian business." Ironically, people like Daryl Wakelyn are still doing their jobs, but they have shifted over and now have the Indian band councils instead of the minister of Indian Affairs as their bosses.

Whether this is "self-government" is an entirely different matter. The money for administration and programs is handed over but is strictly controlled by regulations. The Cape Mudge Band is currently squabbling with the government over education moneys. Don Assu and Jimmy Wilson, who is the band's community planner, explain that there are 110 students from Cape Mudge who leave the reserve every morning to attend public schools – the elementary school on Quadra Island or the high school in Campbell River. The federal government pays $3,500 for each Indian student, giving the money, under something called a "Master Tuition Agreement," directly to the provincial school boards. This amounts to almost $400,000 for Cape Mudge students.

Wilson and Assu are quarreling with the government about the quality of education the children receive. Wilson claims the education the provincial schools provide is inadequate, and doesn't equip the Indian children "for anything except working on the reserve." The band council feels the provincial school boards are making a profit from the agreement at the expense of their children. But because it is a matter directly between the federal government who provides the money and the provincial government who runs education, the band has no say in it. The band feels that if the money were given to them they could provide their own education, or they could at least negotiate a better deal and better services from the local school board. These kinds of squabbles seem to go on continually.

Despite devolution, the federal government remains the major and in many cases the only source of money for Indian bands. There is a provision in the Indian Act for bands to raise some of their own revenues through taxation, as municipalities do. Few bands do this; most manage to subsist on the Indian Affairs allotment. The allotment to the Cape Mudge band is approximately $300,000 a year, which gets augmented in their budgets by money they obtain for a host of programs from other federal and provincial government departments, lending agencies, and so on. The band gets some small income from such things as garbage collection fees that are levied on its citizens. A cream-coloured garbage truck with the label "white trash" painted on its hood lumbers each morning through Cape Mudge Village.

Daryl Wakelyn observes that the manner in which bands receive money is "not that much different" from the manner in which most municipalities function. Even if they raise revenues through taxation, municipalities (and provinces) depend to some degree on equalization payments from higher levels of government. What makes the Indian bands different and vulnerable to criticism is that they contribute very little in any obvious way to the larger government revenue pie. Status Indians pay no sales tax, no income tax on moneys earned on a reserve, no land tax or property tax. This is resented sometimes by non-Indians. "It is difficult sometimes," says Alberta Billy, "to explain to the stores that we don't have to pay sales tax. They resent it." But the Indian response, consistently, is that giving up their land should be the only contribution required of them; a one-time-only, major contribution to the Canadian purse. "Look at what we've already paid," says Alberta Billy.

The federal government's Alternate Funding Arrangement (AFA), the same arrangement that is being pursued by Norway House, is available to bands in British Columbia. Some are considering it. Daryl Wakelyn describes it as the latest attempt both to simplify things in the Indian funding business and to shift more of the initiative to the Indian bands themselves. He mentions a band on the west coast that has just signed an agreement to receive $55 million over five years. The money will have to finance and maintain all of the band's programs and services for the five-year period: new housing, welfare payments, education, health services, garbage pick-up, recreation, band administration, and so on. But in Wakelyn's eyes, and in those of some British Columbia bands, an AFA is not an unmixed blessing. They fear that the increased autonomy in the setting of their own priorities is in part illusory. The government still has stringent guidelines and the Indians perceive (with basis, says Wakelyn) that they are being backed into a corner. Once they sign such an agreement, they can't return to their old system. Furthermore, the government holds the unilateral right to reduce the budgets, if necessary, but gives no corresponding guarantee that they will be increased. For the Indian bands, signing into an AFA is a gamble; a good one if government funding and budgets on the old basis continue to decrease in the future, a bad one if they don't. It's a high risk, says Wakelyn, to tie into a base budget so unequivocally: "The bands are right to be mistrustful."

Wakelyn's job with the Cape Mudge band is to coordinate a venture they are undertaking in an attempt to cash in on the current tourist boom in the Campbell River-Quadra Island region. "The tourism industry in Campbell River is growing in leaps and bounds," says Wakelyn. Cape Mudge intends to get a slice of it by opening a tourist resort. The band has identified a site where they plan to build a twenty-five-unit lodge and five cottages. The site is on a lovely piece of ground directly above a narrowing in Discovery Passage, where the water is fast and the king salmon lie in wait. Eagles circle high above the surrounding cedars. It is the best fishing spot in the area.

The project will cost $2.5 million, none of which will come from Indian Affairs. An additional three- to five-million dollars will build a marina at the south end of the village that will accommodate 40 commercial boats owned by band members and 150 pleasure craft. Profits from the undertaking will go back to the band, which has incorporated for this purpose as Cape Mudge Development Ltd. As well, the fifty to one hundred projected new jobs running the resort will take up all the slack in the community's labour pool.

It sounds good on paper. Daryl Wakelyn says that the band has planned the enterprise carefully, going through all the appropriate stages of land-use studies, engineering studies, cost-benefit studies, and a business plan developed by a consulting firm that specializes in tourism ventures. Only three people in the village oppose the idea, two of them are Alberta and her nineteen-year-old daughter, Susie. Susie argues that the site picked for the lodge is sacred ground and should be left alone. It is a spiritual place where she goes sometimes to play her drum. The band counters that they will use the project to educate people about Kwakiutl culture. The museum in the village will be an important component, as only a quarter of the tourists would come for fishing. The others would come for conferences, or for holidays during which they could learn about Indian culture. The band believes that a huge market for such a vacation spot exists. Daryl Wakelyn has been told by one tourist agent that he could deliver two busloads of European tourists daily to such a lodge.

I drive around the island with Wakelyn in the sunshine of a warm afternoon. We stop at various points that are reserve land. We pass an area with twenty or so campsites occupied by fire pits, picnic tables, and a smattering of recreational vehicles from Idaho and Oregon. The scenery is breathtaking; harlequin ducks bob in the shallows, the tide is out. In the near distance is a spit of land populated by tall cedars, now a provincial park. Wakelyn says the Kwakiutl people believe the spit was once Cape Mudge land, but they were cheated out of it by some private individuals and the provincial government. Future land negotiations will try to get it back.

Wakelyn was an accountant before he got into the Indian business. His career choice was made with the best of motives: he wanted to give and to help. He does not always meet with the same spirit in other whites who work for the Indians. He recalls a couple of stories about the callousness with which his fellow whites, including some from his former department, treated Indians. He names bands that were moved wholesale from remote areas to reserves on the edges of urban areas, and then had their old houses burned so they wouldn't be tempted to return to their old site. He is appalled by some of these incidents, and is all the more appalled by the fact that they took place so recently. "Some of these things happened in our lifetime," he exclaims, "while we were students at university."

Less than seventy years ago the government and the missionaries cut down the totem poles, carted off the regalia and masks to museums, and banned the potlatch. It is not much longer ago that white men used their guns to fire on Indians for sport ("to see them jump" according to the account of one such sportsman brought to discipline), and less long ago that Indian children in residential schools had their fingers strapped for speaking their languages.

The problems facing Indians today have the same root as the problems faced throughout the history of their confrontation with the white man. Indians are still victims of callous government regulations and decisions concerning the natural environment and industry, recalcitrance in aboriginal claims settlements, and unscrupulous operators who are only too ready to go in and make a quick buck whenever Indians have money to spend. "Sometimes you think that not much has changed. Indian leadership is becoming more cagey and sophisticated, but there are still an amazing crew of consultants, some of whom are slimy low-lifes," accuses Wakelyn, "prepared to give bad advice for good fees to unsuspecting bands." When economic development schemes go wrong, he says, it is usually a good idea gone bad.

While some Indian Affairs people are just bureaucrats filling chairs, says Wakelyn, others are sincere and believe in what they are doing. There is some paternalism but also genuine care. There is also frustration. The Indian business is one in which a new broad theory promising to solve everything comes along about every eight years. A bandwagon forms as everybody, the bureaucrats, the politicians, the academics, the media, all jump on, believing a great answer has finally come to light. Then when it doesn't work out as it should, or as quickly as it should, disillusionment sets in and everyone waits for the next bright idea to emerge. Wakelyn lists the panaceas of his short career, since 1970: education and assimilation, economic development, band management, and self-government. Four panaceas in less than twenty years. Each in its turn was a bandwagon movement that didn't work, wasn't allowed to work, or didn't have enough time to work. He looks back to the past, when children were sent to residential schools and the potlatches were banned, all by officials and politicians and a public who believed that what they were doing was wise and right. He is conscious that he is now an official and the thought makes him pause. "What if we look back in twenty years and our strategies look just as bad in retrospect?"

Alberta Billy has a licence plate on her Oldsmobile that reads NATIVE. She is intensely proud and pleased to have the licence plate, the only one of its kind in British Columbia. She and her family have never doubted who they are, and have never been shy to proclaim it. When she and Dan go to Hawaii on winter holidays, they look up Hawaiian natives and compare cultural notes.

At dinner at the Billy house, Alberta's mother, Ruby Wilson, a handsome woman in her seventies, tells how as a child she was sent out to residential school in Chilliwack. She was twelve years old. The school was run by the Methodists, later the United Church, and she stayed until she was seventeen. Residential school ran for ten months of the year and in the summer the children were allowed to go home to the communities scattered up and down to coast to be with their families.

It was not an easy life for a twelve-year-old, and it had moments that are still poignant, when remembered. If Ruby Wilson was good when she was at the residential school, she would be invited out to dinner on Sundays at the homes of white families who lived near the school. She remembers that once she started high school, the local buses would not pick up the Indian children to transport them the extra distance to the high school. "So the government bought us all bicycles."

Contrary to the stereotype, however, she did not find it a negative experience. "If I hadn't gone there, I wouldn't have got an education," she says quite matter of factly. "I wouldn't have learned to play the piano either." The only really bad thing, according to Mrs. Wilson, was that they were not allowed to speak native languages. Ruby Wilson's only real regret is that she didn't go back for one last year, graduate, and go on to become a nurse. She had the aptitude; one year, she says, she had the highest mark in all British Columbia in a St. John's Ambulance first-aid course. "I'm not bragging," she says now, almost sixty years later. "It's true."

Harry Assu is eighty-three years old, but he could pass for sixty. His hair is still jet-black, shiny, and slicked-back. His skin is smooth and his eyes look soft and friendly and alert behind his heavy-framed glasses. He dresses well and might pass for a retired country doctor or a gentlemanly small town businessman in the real estate or general insurance field. The only clues to his age are a stiff leg and a hearing-aid in his right ear.

Harry Assu is aristocracy in the Kwakiutl and Cape Mudge world. He is a wealthy man; he was very successful as both a fisherman and businessman, and he is a hereditary chief from a bloodline that goes back hundreds of years. His father was Chief Billy Assu, a man of considerable fame and reputation among West Coast Indian people. Billy Assu was a chief of the Cape Mudge people, a wise man, everyone will tell you, who governed for sixty years until his death in 1964. There is now a large totem pole in his honour inside the entrance to the Cape Mudge museum.

Within the last fifty years the hereditary chiefs have essentially been replaced for purposes of band government and administration by elected chiefs and councils. But that notwithstanding, the tradition and culture of the coastal Indian peoples continue to hold the hereditary line in high esteem. In the powerful legacy of Kwakiutl culture their place remains intact, the bloodline remains strong. Like the ideal of aristocrats in the best sense in all cultures, they have a moral authority that is never in question and cannot be denied.

Sometimes the hereditary chief and the elected chief turn out to be the same person. That, however, was not the case for Harry Assu. He gave up his role in active governing, he says, shortly after he assumed it on his father's death. He preferred to go herring fishing and couldn't reconcile governing with staying away from the community for the extended periods of time his fishing demanded. His life has thus been that of the fisherman, not the chief, and he lives, perhaps, somewhat in the shadow of his famous father. He has, however, a bit of fame in his own right. In 1958 the government of Canada put the picture of a seine boat on the back of its five-dollar bills. The picture was of Harry Assu's boat.

Harry Assu is an excellent fisherman. He knows everything there is to know about fishing the west coast and still faultlessly advises the fishermen among his twenty-three grandchildren which tidal and weather signs to follow in order to achieve a good catch. Harry Assu lives now, in retirement, in a modern and comfortably furnished house facing the water, the first house past the new band office. He is asked regularly by visiting journalists and television crews to take them on tours of the village. He has been on television, he says, three times in the last year, and the morning we meet he is awaiting the arrival of a woman from a radio station in Vancouver who is flying in to interview him. He has been to Japan, Alaska, Hong Kong, Hawaii (nine times); he owns a nearly new Oldsmobile and he is a Shriner. "It's a good club to belong to," he says. Though he declined to be a political leader, his offspring have shown more interest. His son Don is the band manager and has been for thirty years. A grandson in Vancouver is a lawyer.

Chief Billy Assu was instrumental in having Methodist missionaries come to Cape Mudge and build the local school. The school however, was not of great benefit to his son, Harry. "The teacher," says Harry, referring to the missionary, "was awful. If we spoke at all we were strapped. Every year when we went back to school we started out again with ABC, which was what we had learned the year before. I hardly gained anything in four years, so

131

I quit and went to work." When his own children reached school age, he sent them out of the community, south to private schools.

Harry Assu never lived in a longhouse but he remembers the existence of the large cedar buildings with their fire pit in the middle and their apartments in the four corners where various branches of the extended family lived. He was born in 1905, and in his childhood memory the longhouses stood vacant and rotting while the people replaced them with "modern" single-family houses down along the shore. One of his father's greatest achievements, he says, was bringing water and electricity to those modern houses in 1923.

The memory of the longhouses is a mixed one. Harry Assu seems to have welcomed modernity, but recalls the past being destroyed with a cruel brutality. The law banning the potlatch was passed in 1884, but it was not until 1922 that the government witch-hunt actually got around to Cape Mudge to confiscate ceremonial objects. Harry Assu remembers when they came in the spring of 1922. It was, he recalls, "a real sad day. I was right down on the beach. They had a scow. I don't know how much they took, five hundred masks anyway. The Indian agent was here, a man by the name of William Halliday. The Indian agent and the missionary, they were working together. They towed the scow to Campbell River and loaded everything on the CPR boat. Lots of it went to museums, some of it was sold to Germany. 'If you keep it back, they'll put you in jail,' that's what they told the people. There were two nice big totem poles, they took them down to the beach and burned them." A letter from Halliday to Duncan Campbell Scott, the superintendent of Indian Affairs (and also the famous poet) dated 10 April 1922, describes three hundred cubic feet of confiscated potlatch paraphernalia stored in his woodshed prior to display in the Anglican hall in nearby Alert Bay. The letter also recommends sale of the materials to U.S. museums saying "many of the American museums would simply jump at the chance of getting it."

The next spring, in 1923, Billy Assu directed the band to level what was left of the longhouses, and an era passed.

Harry Assu credits his father with two important decisions that affected the economy of Cape Mudge. In 1917 he borrowed $5,000 to buy a steam donkey. With its aid, twenty-seven men spent the winter logging and cutting a million board-feet of lumber. Billy Assu got his men to agree to only half wages, $1.50 a day, and with the money they saved, he paid back the loan in the first year. The next year, carrying no debt, he was able to pay the men $9.00 a day for their work. "That's how the village became prosperous," says Harry Assu.

A second story: Until 1921 the Indians had been permitted only to troll and to use gill nets when fishing. In that year Chief Billy Assu, at the behest of the owner of the cannery, went to a public meeting and persuaded the local MP to get the rules changed so that the Indians could use seine nets for their fishing. Indians and war veterans, the new rules said, could now use seine nets. Production was thereby vastly increased.

One evening when we were tying up the boat, Dan Billy got angry. It was a sudden, inexplicable burst of anger, a flash from out of nowhere on a fresh spring evening at sunset. Dan had steered the fifty-five-foot *Susan Laverne* back from the dry dock at Quathiaski Cove. He had slowed the engines and was trying to squeeze into a spot at the band's dock in front of a boat that was owned by a white man from down the coast. The boat had been out halibut fishing and had incurred damage to its hull when it struck a rock. "The guy must'a been asleep at the wheel," muttered Dan. The boat had been towed in to Cape Mudge to get repairs. But the situation simply served to irritate Dan. It reminded him of one of his pet peeves: that few Indians have halibut licences. And from that exploded the anger.

Beyond us in the gathering dusk a sixteen-foot aluminum outboard with the logo of April Point resort drifted by, a young couple in rain gear desultorily trolling for salmon. Earlier in the day Dan had settled the bill for repairs to his boat. It had been in for over a week and the mechanics and shipwrights had been working on it for $40 an hour. "They don't want us to have nothin'," Dan exploded, suddenly, as if opening the steam valve on his anger. For a moment everything was silent until he decided to talk more. "It's anti-Indian," he said, grasping for any argument he could muster. "I don't know how they want us to make a living, what do they want us to do?"

The explosion was a little out of character and might have been sparked from the repair bill he'd just paid, or the sight of the white man's boat licensed to fish halibut when he couldn't, or the sight of the tourists who seem to be taking over all the fishing. In fact, Dan does well fishing. In two days of herring fishing in March, Dan's boat netted thirty-eight tonnes at $2,500 a tonne. And this in what he considers to be a bad herring year. In the summer he will fish for salmon catching maybe six thousand fish a day at $6 a fish. But he has just spent a hundred thousand dollars on his boat, and finds himself limited stringently to fourteen days of fishing this year, and around him he sees sport fishermen at the end of their shift at the mill in Campbell River or up from Vancouver or up from the United States catching what they please for the price of a $10 licence. "The government says 'conservation first.' They don't have to tell us about conservation, we conserved for thousands of years. They're not for us, we should tell them where to go. We could have our own government; we governed ourselves for thousands of years."

"You can't know anything about these people unless you understand what fishing means to them," Joy Inglis tells me. "They are fishermen and their whole identity is tied up in that." Joy Inglis is a white woman, an anthropologist who got her master's degree twenty-five years ago with a thesis on the people of Cape Mudge. In 1973, she and her husband, Bob, moved to Quadra Island to live out their retirement. They bought some land on the opposite side of the south coast from the Cape Mudge reserve.

Joy is a pleasant, serene-looking woman with straw-grey hair and pale-blue eyes. Her current project is to work with Harry Assu to put together the history of his family and to get it published as a book. She talks about the pleasantness of the island and the industriousness of the people. "I can honestly say that in all the years I've been here that I haven't witnessed a single drunk Indian," she says conjuring up the time-worn stereotype. "Not in this community. Way back in 1891 Chief Billy Assu was determined to keep liquor away from his people and, perhaps with that in mind, forged a fortuitous alliance with the Methodist missionaries, who were themselves death on drink." Cape Mudge has since then been officially dry. Inglis recounts times when a person who arrived at a public function in the community a "little bit tight" would be met at the door and unofficially hustled off to someone's house, away from the public event. When the new museum was opened in 1979, officials from Victoria suggested a wine and cheese party for a celebration. This threw band manager Don Assu, grandson of Chief Billy, into a dilemma. "He had to consider for a long time before saying, yes, he guessed it would be okay."

Joy Inglis is modest about her work, though she doubtless knows a great deal about the Kwakiutl people and about this community. And the people in the community speak very well of her. She is not the only official anthropologist in Cape Mudge, however. One afternoon at the museum I am introduced to Marie Mauze, a petite, serious-looking young French woman who first visited the community in 1980, and since then has been returning regularly to write her two volume PhD thesis, *People of Fire in the House*, for the Laboratoire d'anthropologie sociale in Paris. Another anthropologist, Erich Kasten, a young German from Berlin, is working farther up the coast. The area has been a rich vein for students of that discipline since Franz Boas, the pre-eminent specialist in the culture and languages of North American Indians, first set foot on Vancouver Island in the late nineteenth century.

The anthropologists are assisted by the tenacity and enthusiasm the Kwakiutl people themselves display for their history. At the Kwakiutl Museum in Cape Mudge, a young woman named Debbie Wilson spends three hours showing me through the artifacts and regalia gathered by the museum since 1979. She proves extremely knowledgeable and unrelentingly enthusiastic, showing me the collection of masks used in various phases of the potlatch, discussing the theatrics involved, and explaining how Kwakiutl dances differed from those of, say, the Salish people. She also carefully takes me through an explanation of the return of the masks and artifacts. For Debbie Wilson, the experience of watching the traditional objects of her people slowly come back home has been overwhelming. So far 135 pieces have come back from the Royal Ontario Museum in Toronto, and more have come from the Museum of Civilization in Ottawa, the Museum of the American Indians in New York, from Philadelphia, from West Germany.

The artifacts were attached to the ceremonies of the potlatch. Put very simply, the potlatch was both a ritual expressing the complexities of one's status in the Indian world, and a complicated bit of theatre. The objection of the whites, notably the missionaries, came on both counts. Held in the wintertime, potlatches provided an occasion for the people's ritual ceremonies and dances. They were also a means to redistribute wealth through the competitive giving away of goods, to choose leaders from among the aristocratic cadres, to acknowledge deaths, births, marriages, and the giving of names. Peter Macnair, in his essay "From Kwakiutl to Kwakwa ka' wakw," in *Native Peoples: The Canadian Experience*, says "the Potlatch was society." Margaret Seguin, a professor of anthropology at the University of Western Ontario, describes the coastal communities as "village worlds" where the chiefs "conducted themselves with the formality and concern for protocol now associated with international diplomacy." Jimmy Sewid, who among his other accomplishments also wrote his autobiography, *Guests Never Leave Hungry*, describes the potlatch as an obligatory exercise any time family honour needed to be restored, even, he says, to make reparation for your child getting into a fight with his chums.

Historically there existed within the potlatch an elaborate system of reciprocity obligations centred mainly on the holding of feasts and the giving of gifts. A man or a family cemented a reputation for wealth and power by being generous with that wealth, giving gifts extravagantly to all guests. There are stories of potlatches where a chief would give away a thousand blankets, hundreds of bags of flour, cooking utensils, boats, untold quantities of money and material goods. At one level this was a ritualized means of redistributing wealth; at another it was simply a display of power and a variation on our ethic of conspicuous consumption. There are accounts of a chief destroying valuable items, tokens of wealth, simply to show that he had more than he needed. This offended missionaries and government officials who felt they ought to be teaching the value of frugality, to the Indians.

In the ceremonies that accompanied the feast, rituals were elaborate *coups de theatre*. Sewid's autobiography describes the initiation rituals of young boys into the secret societies, notably into the hamatsa or cannibal society. "At the beginning of winter as whistles were heard in the woods near the village, the novice would be abducted or disappear voluntarily into the woods. The first to disappear was a boy to be initiated into the hamatsa society. He was believed to be at the home of the Cannibal Spirit. During the day he would be met by other hamatsas and taught the dances of that society. At night the entire village gathered in one of the large houses, and a master of ceremonies would direct the performances of singing, dancing, supernatural feats, and other dramatic productions. The Kwakiutl were unsurpassed among North American Indians in their theatrical skill. Huge masks with movable parts were danced around the fire. Trap doors in the floor enabled dancers mysteriously to disappear. Lifelike heads carved of wood and carried on top of a dancer's costume were skilfully cut from the body. Then a powerful shaman would revive the decapitated person to the amazement of the audience. The most important secret was the simulated nature of these dramas which the uninitiated believed to be supernaturally produced."

The theatre was so good that some white observers were taken in. When the hamatsa appeared to bite members of the audience and to draw blood, the early missionaries panicked, believing they were witnessing some strange ritual of cannibalism. And so these sophisticated, ritualistic, celebratory societies that knew how to make clothing out of cedar bark, store perishable foods under ground, build canoes and huge wooden houses, encountered the so-called "civilized" European world.

Debbie Wilson completes the tour of the museum by showing me information on the cedar tree, the great provider, the "tree of life." The tree was offered god-like reverence, for it provided almost everything they needed. The cedar contains a natural water-resistant preservative, and every part of the tree was used by the Indians: The inner bark provided soft, water-resistant clothing, mats, twine, and baskets. Roots and small branches were also woven into ropes and into baskets. Planks were split off standing, live trees using yew wood wedges and stone mauls or hammers. The aromatic wood provided houses, canoes, storage and cooking boxes. Dan Billy explained that the cedar, as well, has a natural insect-repellent and that a cedar growing in the midst of a forest of fir trees will help keep the insects and diseases from attacking the other trees.

There are about eight thousand people now in the Kwakiutl nation. Those who have not moved on to Vancouver, or Victoria, or to other places in North America live in a dozen or so villages stretched along the British Columbia coast from Cape Mudge in the south, to Bella Bella and Bella Coola in the north, a distance of some four hundred (air) kilometres. The exact number of villages is imprecise because some of them have been abandoned, their houses and totem poles decaying in solitude in the coves of small steep-sloped islands. Peter Macnair in his overview of the Kwakiutl people reckoned twenty groups settled in winter village sites that date back eight thousand years. Margaret Seguin wrote of those village societies that "to enter the territory of another village (or even another lineage segment) was to enter a foreign land. The inhabitants of each domain figured as reciprocal, symbolic 'others,' providing an important component of a view of the universe as a place of many worlds."

Nowadays the Kwakiutl people, in their entirety, are represented by the Kwakiutl District Council, a political body that represents twelve bands. The Kwakiutl people share a common language (though few of them now can or do speak it), and they share a blood relationship. They reaffirm their connections through periodic, and regular, grand get-togethers.

Since the government ban on the potlatch was repealed in 1950, the tradition has been renewed. The modern potlatches, however, are more gentle and are used mainly for renewing family acquaintances. The competition formerly expressed in gift-giving is now more likely to centre around fierce competitions on the soccer pitch between teams of young men representing each village.

In the spring of 1988 I had the good fortune to be invited to such a gathering at Kingcome Inlet, an isolated village some two hundred and fifty to three hundred kilometres north of Cape Mudge.

At four in the morning, everybody in the Billy house is up for the trip to Kingcome Inlet. We will be travelling on the *Susan Laverne*. Dan figures that a five o'clock start will make the best use of the tides on what is bound to be at least a twelve- to thirteen-hour trip. When your boat travels at nine knots, it is better to have a five-knot tide in your favour than against you. Up until the last minute, no one is certain who will be going: Dan and Alberta; their daughter, Susie; Tom, Susie's boyfriend who also works with Dan fishing; a niece named Michelle, a pretty young girl who arrives wearing white leather cowboy boots with silver spangles, a red sweater, and striped black and white trousers, the dress of every high school girl in North America; and Anthony, almost three years old, the eldest of the three Billy grandchildren and the apple of his grandparents' eye.

At five o'clock daylight is breaking and a fine rain drizzles down on the grey waters of the channel. The mountains around us disappear, like myths, into the ghostly vapours that whisper over them so that you truly cannot tell if any of them have tops. If the mountains seem endless vertically, their ranges also seem endless horizontally. The sheer-sided peaks and islands hung with thick dark green carpets of spruce and hemlock and cedar go on forever, to Alaska. At least it certainly seems like forever when you are making slow journey past them. Dan takes his coffee to the flying bridge to steer the boat's passage; the teenagers disappear to the bunks in the bow to the fore of the engine room; and Alberta busies herself cleaning the galley and the bathroom to her satisfaction rather than the satisfaction of the men who have been working on the boat down at the boatyards in Quathiaski Cove these last two weeks.

Within an hour, the rain falters and the sky breaks, although it remains overcast. The *Susan Laverne* chugs northward past mountainsides green with cedar but also, with depressing regularity, showing the striking shave of recent clear-cut logging. Periodically the green of the mountainside will change in hue as a new-growth forest in various stages takes over from a cut. From time to time we meet a tug pulling barges of timber from some northern cut to some southern mill. Frequently we pass sport boats from Campbell River or some outlying resort bobbing by the shore, their occupants trying to coax spring salmon to their hooks.

Dan knows the coastline at this juncture like the back of his hand and points out places where he has fished in the past. The sounder, a black television screen to the left of the wheel, shows that we are passing over waters that go to a hundred, a hundred and sixty, two hundred fathoms in depth. Little yellow masses pass across the screen; Dan says that they are herring and judges them as to their yield: a hundred tonnes, two hundred tonnes. We regularly spy bald eagles circling out over the water and back to their trees; grebes, which Dan calls "hell divers," bob along the surface looking for herring below; a couple of porpoises play off starboard at one point; and two raccoons are spied scurrying along the rocky edge of an island, a half-metre above the water level. We hail a boat of prawn fishermen and purchase sixty dollars worth of their catch to take with us and, a little after noon, we pull into a cove and put ashore to dig for a pail of cockles. But mostly we keep journeying on toward Kingcome Inlet.

Alberta's father was born at Kingcome Inlet, but she herself has never visited there. She is visibly excited. "I feel like I am going home," she says. She tells Anthony more than once that he will meet many of his relatives when he arrives. This is mid-week; the events at Kingcome village will have been going on for three days already when we arrive. The potlatch has been called to celebrate the fiftieth anniversary of the building of the Anglican church and the raising of the main totem pole. Some of the older people, I have been told, sense the irony and are a little at odds about whether to have a potlatch to celebrate the church that took such an active role in the suppression of that very ceremony. But the people of Kingcome are devoted to their church; 98 per cent of Kwakiutl people are baptized Christians, and the potlatch is their traditional way of gathering and celebrating. History and competing cultures have somehow made peace. Two weddings will be celebrated during the gathering, as well, and then the week will turn into a sports festival with an ongoing soccer tournament, feasting, and dances.

Kingcome village is about as isolated as you can get: three dozen houses, a half-dozen totem poles, a band office, a band store, a trim white house that serves as medical dispensary, and the school: two square buildings set side by side connected with a plywood covered walkway. In front of the public buildings is a broad playing field with soccer goal posts at either end, a tiny children's playground with swings and slides at one side and a gigantic spruce tree at the other. At the end of the village is the Anglican church, dressed in a fresh coat of white paint and with a pink metal roof that makes you think for a second that the whole thing might be made out of gingerbread and icing. The village is on a small, flat, alluvial plain with mountains closely surrounding it; so close, and so enfolding, that it could be mistaken for Switzerland. The only motorized vehicles I see are an aging white tractor, which hauls the garbage wagon, and a shiny new ride-around lawn-mower, which is used to trim the soccer pitch. And of course there are the boats; runabouts that line the river shore like cars in a parking lot.

We have to moor the *Susan Laverne* about five miles below the village at the head of Kingcome Inlet and come up the river, treacherously shallow with deadheads at every turn, in Dan's flat-bottom herring punt with the outboard motor. Everybody else has had to do the same and there are, at the end of the river, seventeen big fishing seiners of various shapes and sizes with names like *The Pacific Dawn* and *Discovery Bay S.* all moored shoulder to shoulder. Many fly red-and-white Native Brotherhood of B.C. flags from their masts. On the way to the village we pass a tiny logging camp, a small herd of about eight black Aberdeen Angus cattle grazing on an alluvial island, and a broken-down fishing camp. The owner of the camp is seen later, a red-faced white man in a shabby, oversized coat wandering alone at the edge of the potlatch festivities looking forlorn and a bit lost. I am told that he is the son of William Halliday, the Indian agent who, seventy years ago, engineered the confiscation of the Kwakiutl ceremonial regalia and potlatch equipment.

When we finally pull in at the river shore, Alberta has tears in her eyes and Susie and Michelle say, "Gee, I wish we could live here. I wish Cape Mudge was as isolated and as quiet as this."

The soccer teams competing on the grassy pitch have names like "the Breakers," "Cormorants," "Warriors," "Wolves," and come from villages called Gilford Island and Alert Bay. The soccer tournament is serious business: referees from the British Columbia Soccer Federation, tall blond men with British accents, have been flown in all the way from Victoria. The pitch is a bit bumpy, but green, manicured by the little ride-around lawn-mower. The crowd lines up in lawn chairs along one side; dogs and small children occasionally wander onto the ends where play is not in progress. The children are hastily hustled off, the dogs are left on their own. In the back of the pitch the Anglican church and the totem pole sparkle, presiding proudly and with serenity.

It is a good brand of soccer by any measure, the teams are tough and fiercely competitive. They play a round robin, which will see ten games before a championship match on Sunday. Dan tells me that there has been soccer among these people for a long time. He doesn't know how the game got here, but Erich Kasten suggests to me that it might have come through the residential schools. Dan played all over the coast when he was young and holds a record for the fastest goal: thirty seconds from the start of the game, in the Upper Island Soccer League. He is still an avid fan and goes to Vancouver whenever he can to watch professional matches. Even two-year-old Anthony can tell you that Diego Maradona is the greatest soccer player in the world. Dan points out a halfback on the yellow-shirted Breakers team and explains that he could have gone pro. Susie was invited to try out for the Canadian women's national team, but was prevented by an injured knee. Dan clearly measures a man by two gauges: skill as a fisherman and prowess as a soccer player. Repeatedly he mentions men he has known: "He was an awfully good fisherman," or, "He was a real good soccer player."

A good sense of humour and joviality is regularly in evidence. The serious soccer is interrupted at one point when an "old-timer's game" is announced. A group of out-of-shape middle-aged men go on the field amid lots of laughter and clowning around. They put on a good show with much humour, playing the parts of men who are no longer "real" soccer players. But when the young men take to the field again to resume the tournament, the enterprise is once more totally earnest.

The gathering itself is the important thing. Dan is all smiles; "I've met relatives I didn't know about," he says. Alberta busily takes Anthony around from house to house and through the great hall to show him off. I get the impression that if a family tree were drawn on a great board, all fifteen hundred or so people who have visited the community this week would be on it, and its interconnections would make it look like an urban street map. The gathering is important in other ways, too; the young girls have clearly taken a fancy to boys from other communities. Michelle Billy and Leslie Wilson are bubbling over with sly and shy talk about a certain boy from the Sliammon soccer team, and how they hope to go to a tournament in June in Alert Bay in order to run into him again.

During the week everybody eats in the community hall, which has been arranged with twenty long tables. The old people are always invited to be seated first. They are called "elders" and are deferred to universally. When a voice on the public address system announces that the table is set for the elders, all the young and middle-aged people are suddenly on their feet, assisting grandmothers and grandfathers and elderly aunts, taking them by the elbow and gently steering them up the steps of the community hall. The old people continue an uninterrupted visit with one another, graciously enjoying this homage from the young.

When the elders have finished eating, everybody else lines up in the community hall, paper plates in hand. Much of the food is "southern" – roasts of beef and turkey, potato salad – though for one lunch I did have a fine fish chowder with pieces of halibut, vegetables, and clams.

The kitchen is a constant hive of work, run mainly by the women. Women from Kingcome and women who grew up in Kingcome and moved away but are back for the potlatch do the work of this celebratory week. A weary-looking woman of about forty tells me this is her community, though she has lived for years now in Vancouver where she is a teacher. She came back for the celebrations and to see her parents and family but has spent most of her time in this kitchen, working until both her hands and her eyes are red. She explains that the food bill for the week will run to about $20,000.

Around the edge of the gathering the anthropologists wander. Marie Mauze complains that "unless you are doing contemporary," the field work is hard to do; the reliable past is truly gone. She talks about how some anthropologists are experimenting with new methods. Since virtually every primitive society has now experienced some contact and outside influence, anthropologists will have to alter their methods and start to reconstruct the past in the form of story. I imagine it might be like creating historical novels. Erich Kasten, the young German anthropologist, is a tall, pleasant, dignified young man with a trim goatee and a bush of greying hair. He has been coming to Kingcome Inlet for two years. He came to Canada initially to see first-hand the subjects of the lectures he was giving in Berlin and was appalled, he says, to discover the inaccuracies he and others were perpetuating. So he moved to Canada and now has a house on Saltspring Island. He hopes eventually to immigrate. He isn't writing a thesis, but is investigating the life of the Kingcome community, documenting much of it photographically. He was up earlier in the spring for the oolichan fishing; the catching of masses of smelt-like fish as they head up the river to spawn, and the making of the thick oil that is used extensively in Kwakiutl cooking. He will return later in the year for other events. He organized a visit by twenty Kingcome carvers and dancers to Berlin in 1989, and hopes that an exchange will develop from that. He has had to be careful, he says. In a small community there are many rivalries and if you are seen too soon to be close to one family, a rival family will have nothing to do with you. "To get a true picture you have to walk a fine and careful line." When I ask how he is received, he says that there are always some who wonder why he is there, but he feels most people see him as an ally in documenting their culture and history, and making it understood.

Billy Wilson is a Cape Mudge boy who is now a lawyer in Comox. One of his clients is the Kingcome band. He is a sturdy fellow in his early thirties with smooth skin and an even gaze. At the lunch table in the Kingcome community hall he sits, wearing a dark blue University of British Columbia sweatshirt, with Dan Billy. "He's quite radical," Dan told me, "but I'm starting to agree with him." At the lunch table Billy Wilson is talking politics. "We've got to leave the past behind," he says, "and we've got to stop fighting among ourselves." Dan says that Billy Wilson wants to urge the people to proceed quickly with their land claims.

Early in the morning, Alberta, Dan, two women from Cape Mudge, Lily Billy, and a woman named Harriet, all of whom are riding back down the coast with us, are having coffee in the galley of the *Susan Laverne*. Also present is Ernie Scow from Campbell River, who is on his way home from Kingcome in his own boat, and with him is Albert, a cousin of Alberta's from Gilford Island. They are talking politics with an edge of sharp anger. All day yesterday Dan had wanted to fish in the bay at the mouth of Kingcome Inlet but was prevented by the presence of an RCMP boat moored on a log boom just down from where the Indians' fishing boats were tied up. The presence of the law irked him, he kept looking over at the police boat wondering if it would move out. It stayed all night. This morning Dan and Ernie Scow and the women are talking about the Vietnamese who have moved in lower down on Vancouver Island, about how they believe the thorough and scouring clam-digging styles of the Vietnamese, the newly-arrived population on the Pacific coast of Canada, are ruining the clam beaches.

"They go up the beach side by side, shoulder to shoulder, and they dig everything," says Ernie Scow. "When they're done there's nothing left and the clam bed is ruined forever. When we dig clams we don't take the little ones, we don't even take all the big ones, so the supply doesn't get wiped out." Feelings apparently have run so high recently that on a couple of occasions Vietnamese fishermen and native fishermen confronted one another with guns. To Dan it is another example of how the Indians are getting the shaft. "The provincial government allows them to do it," he says. "They police us but they don't police them. I'm getting tired of it. We gotta take these waters back, we gotta police them ourselves. They're our waters. I didn't used to feel like this," he continues. "I used to believe we should share what we had. But I don't believe that any more. We've been abused too much. Now I want them to go after land claims and fishing claims and our aboriginal rights because these lands are ours."

That night, we dock at the wharf at Gilford Island. Gilford is a pretty spot with only about a dozen houses. An old man, accompanied by a shaggy yellow dog, opens up the longhouse for our benefit, so we can see it. The longhouse is over a hundred years old but has been restored, its totem poles and *sisuitl* mural have been touched up, and the hall is now used for gatherings and potlatches. It is silent and chilly inside but there is a powerful sense of spiritual presence.

Alberta steers Anthony through the correct way of entering the longhouse when you go in for a ceremony. And then, for a long time, the little group of us just sit on the row of hard benches, no one saying a word. The visit serves as a reminder of the efforts the Kwakiutl people are making to recover a sense of the past that was stripped from them. Alberta uses the opportunity to tell a little story about the day, a few years ago, when the first shipment of masks and regalia arrived back at the museum at Cape Mudge. For two nights the museum's alarms inexplicably went off in the fire station at Campbell River. They figured it was a short circuit but nobody could discern the cause or the location of the short. "We couldn't say anything to them," says Alberta in retrospect, "but I know what caused it. The spirits of our ancestors were dancing for joy."

Later, on the way home, we stop to fish and a successful catch seems to calm Dan down. It helps him forget his irritation at the RCMP boat, his anger at the Vietnamese, his frustrations with the government. After some trying he jigs two rock cod, two ling cod, and a fifty pound halibut that gives him quite a fight. The whole day looks brighter. Porpoises play off the starboard bow, we see more than a dozen eagles, and the girls, from the stern, see a killer whale leap twice from the water.

7   All Is Politics; All Is Words

The Conference Centre in Ottawa is an old railway station, an imposing grey structure built in the classical style. Situated on the Rideau Canal, it is just across the street from the even more imposing, turreted Château Laurier hotel, and close enough to the Parliament Buildings that the walk over can't even qualify as exercise. For decades dignitaries and members of Parliament arrived for their sojourns in the capital at this railway station. When the times changed, and such people ceased to arrive in Ottawa by train, coming instead by airplane, the old station underwent a conversion and became a centre for meetings. The huge central lobby with its high, vaulted ceilings was turned into a kind of amphitheatre where the prime minister, premiers, and other political leaders could sit facing one another at an expansive circle of tables and, from that position, make their speeches and conduct their negotiations.

This is an interesting manner in which to exercise public policy making. The whole set-up is engineered to treat public policy making as theatre, and to turn public policy making into theatre. Everything that happens in the old railway station conference centre is an event staged for an audience, albeit one that is reached primarily through the vehicle of the media. And the very physical design of things not only accommodates that fact, but ensures it. Everything operates in circles. Beyond the circle of the main actors themselves, at centre stage, is the larger circle of

148

the main actors' advisers. The people sitting in this circle shepherd fat briefcases, sometimes two per person; they have intense, worried looks on their faces, jot things down on pads of paper, consult pocket calculators, and listen carefully through their simultaneous translation earphones. Behind them is the circle of the media, primarily television, the electronic media. There are lights, cameras on dollies, cameras on tripods, cameras handheld by technicians who wear blue jeans and tennis shoes and step gingerly over kilometres of cable. And in the midst of the cameras, resembling Hollywood stars, are anchor persons and reporters with make-up help perpetually powdering and buffing their shiny or sweaty brows.

In tiers of rising theatre seats behind the stage is the audience circle. The house audience is infinitely less important than the television audience but, like a studio audience, it is necessary for background noise. As well, since these are government productions, a gesture in the direction of old-fashioned democracy dictates that there always be a house audience, just as there will always be tours of the Parliament Buildings and a gallery in the House of Commons whatever may be the pressures of security and efficiency.

Behind the studio audience, beyond the great hall itself, is the rest of the Conference Centre, like a theatre backstage. It is a vast infrastructure of offices and smaller meeting rooms used primarily by the media. Most are equipped with desks, telephones, computers, and all manner of technical back-up. But it is the main room, the central amphitheatre, in which we are most interested, for it is there that the public drama takes place. That is the room we see on television.

What happens in this room, and has happened for more than twenty years, are the momentous meetings of our democracy. (Who could forget that it was at one of these that a youthful Pierre Elliot Trudeau, then justice minister, first looked good on national television?) Federal-provincial conferences, they were first called; meetings of First Ministers they are called now. They

149

are meetings that play out in a delicate teeter-totter of pre-written script and wild-card spontaneity the formulation of what we as a nation profess to agree to.

What is agreed to either makes policy or confirms policy. But because of the highly public nature of the meetings (they not only make the news, they often preempt television programing, at least on the CBC, and become like on-going mini series), just to make the agenda is a monumental achievement. For three days in the early spring of 1987, Canada's aboriginal peoples, or Indians, were the agenda.

In 1982 the repatriated Constitution of Canada did two things with regard to aboriginal people. It affirmed aboriginal rights in the broad sense and opened the door for land claims, and it specified a period of time and a series of meetings through which the aboriginal people could approach the government leaders, the prime minister and the provincial premiers, to negotiate whatever further desires they had. March 1987 was the time of the final meeting and the last opportunity for the aboriginal leaders to present their case. The aboriginal leaders thus felt there was some urgency, and they had decided on something they all wanted. They wanted self-government for First Nations, as they were by then calling themselves, and they wanted that right to be written as an amendment to the Constitution of Canada.

History shows that they did not get what they wanted. When all votes were tallied, three western premiers: Grant Devine of Saskatchewan, Don Getty of Alberta, and Bill Vander Zalm of British Columbia had not agreed. (Quebec at that time had not signed the constitution and could only be an observer at the meetings.) The argument went back and forth for three days, and what ultimately could not be resolved was the question of whether to include the idea of native self-government in the Constitution in principle, and work out its details and defini-tions later, or whether the definitions should be worked out first and written into the Constitution after the terms had been fully discussed and agreed on. The nay votes decried the lack of definition: if it could not be defined, they would not go along with it.

Politics being process, it is nonetheless worthwhile to consider that event in the spring of 1987, mainly because it still represents the apex of the self-government discussion. At the circular centre tables sat Prime Minister Brian Mulroney, then well into his first term of running the country, and his minister of Indian Affairs, William McKnight, a no-nonsense Saskatchewan Conservative fast gaining a reputation among the Indians for his tight-fisted-ness. The provincial premiers were Brian Peckford of Newfoundland, Joe Ghiz of Prince Edward Island, John Buchanan of Nova Scotia, Richard Hatfield of New Brunswick, David Peterson of Ontario, Howard Pawley of Manitoba, Grant Devine from Saskatchewan, Don Getty from Alberta, and Bill Vander Zalm from British Columbia. On the side of the aboriginal leaders, the main spokesmen were Georges Erasmus, national chief of the Assembly of First Nations, the organization that had grown out of the old National Indian Brotherhood and represented most, though not all, of the status Indian people in Canada; Louis "Smokey" Bruyere from the Native Council of Canada, representing non-status Indian people; Zebedee Nungak and John Amagoalik of the Inuit Committee on National Issues; and Jim Sinclair, from Saskatchewan, representing the Métis National Council.

It was a male-dominated group; should women wonder whether any of their number were involved in the discussions, they should know that the only woman I saw seated at the inner table was federal cabinet minister Barbara McDougall. There were no women arguing on the aboriginal side. Women are abysmally under-represented in native politics. Only fifty-five chiefs of almost six hundred bands in Canada in 1989 were women. But there was youth on the aboriginal side, a far cry from the old days when elderly chiefs carried the Indian message to Ottawa, and the young deferred to their wisdom. It is an acknowledgement, no doubt, of the youth of the native population, 55 per cent of which is under the age of twenty-five. Nungak, Amagoalik, and Erasmus, all in their late-thirties, early-forties, are younger than the prime minister and all the premiers.

Two things need to be highlighted: One of them is self-government, since that is ostensibly what the meetings were all about.
The other is the increasing adeptness of native people as politicians. Should we ever be in search of a new diplomatic class, a
species schooled in but also naturally skilled at public process
and negotiation, a group like the Chinese mandarins of dynasties
past, we might consider recruiting from among the Indians. The
performance of the First Ministers was often unimpressive. They
would bluster on, occasionally betraying an astonishing lack of
understanding of the issues. Bill Vander Zalm delivered a "some
of my best friends are Indians" speech until he was drowned out
by the boos of the crowd, and, although everyone knew he would
vote against the proposals, he went on at length describing what a
good job native soldiers from Canada had done fighting to
liberate his homeland of Holland in the Second World War.

By contrast, the speeches of the native leaders: Amagoalik,
Sinclair, and Erasmus, were passionate, clear, leavened with
humour, and to the point. What's more, the Indians both at this
national level and on the reserves I visited show an extraordinary
patience with the tedium and boredom and endless meetings of
politics. And they have an extraordinary appetite for watching it.
There were, at the Ottawa meeting, journalists accredited to fifty
separate native news organizations, from small radio stations on
Baffin Island, to bi-weekly newspapers in British Columbia. The
tunnels and corridors and back rooms of the Conference Centre
were crawling with native newsmongers all hanging on every
word, every implication, every speculation that the negotiations
brought forth.

My visits to reserve communities brought home to me the
importance of politics. In most native communities, politics is
bread and butter; all good and all ill come from it, it is the only
game in town. There is virtually nothing that happens in the life
and the economy of an Indian reserve that is not governed by
politics. For Indians, preoccupation with politics is as natural as
a gambler's preoccupation with basketball scores and the race

results. Public money figures hugely in almost every project, and in almost everyone's salary. Many Indian reserves are like Ottawa: virtually everyone is on the public payroll. The difference is that the payroll for an Indian reserve is very much leaner.

But try to imagine a situation where almost all subsistence comes from public money, either as social assistance, or as the salaries of those who are on the community payroll. They are on the payroll either directly, as bureaucrats or employees of the band, or indirectly as employees of one or another community project initiated and supported by public money. Add to that a plethora of government rules, right down to rules about who may or may not be defined as a member of the community. If you can imagine this, then you can appreciate the life-and-death power, in such a world, of politics.

A native politician's job is to pry funds out of the federal, and to a lesser extent the provincial, government and distribute those funds locally. A successful politician pries lots of funds, distributes them in a way that is seen to be equitable, and so keeps most of the people happy most of the time. The skill needed to practise this art is extraordinarily high.

I made this observation to a civil servant in the Indian business in Manitoba, and he agreed. Indian political leaders are highly sophisticated, he said. A chief, even from a remote corner of the bush, will have been to Ottawa countless times and will likely have experience in high-level negotiations exceeding that of a provincial cabinet minister. Moreover, my friend went on, an Indian leader, even at a local level, understands that every act is essentially political. "He will be superbly conscious of public relations both at home and in the larger context. They know how to use the media, they know how to get attention, they know how to play on weaknesses and guilt."

There is an underlying principle, tacitly agreed to by both sides, that informs the relations between Indian politicians and both the government and the general public in Canada. The basic tenet of this understanding is that the government and the

153

Canadian public owe. They owe a debt to the Indians for two reasons: First, because Indians are suffering from well-demonstrated social and economic inequities and this, after all, is Canada where the job of the government is to right wrongs and ensure equality. Second, for historic reasons: the European immigrants took the country from the Indians and must pay. An analogy being used more and more by native leaders is that of the landlord and tenant: Indians own the country, non-Indians must pay rent. The whole country could be Kahnawake's Seigneury of Sault St. Louis. More than one leader used this image in rationales about the nature of their relationship with the rest of Canada. A good native politician understands both of these principles very well, understands their power, and plays them skilfully for all they are worth. And most native leaders are good politicians. They are, apparently, not always good administrators; the television reports and news articles are full of horror stories about administrative ineptitude, budgets gone awry, moneys gone astray, boondoggles of one sort or another. But while their administrative skills may be from time to time disputed, their political ability never is.

I mentioned to my friend my observation that native politicians also seem to have a good understanding of nepotism and patronage. "Yes," he responded, "but they don't call it that, they call it self-government."

One of the most perplexing issues in the whole Indian discussion is the question of words. Words, and their meaning, and their adequacy to describe, emerge constantly, so much so that you can feel at times that were certain semantic problems solved, all else would surely fall readily into place. Difficulties in the interpretation of treaties and statements of aboriginal rights often boil down to interpretations of words. Does a "medicine chest" imply total health care? Does a "bag of seeds and a plough" imply economic development in its broadest sense, and in perpetuity? Does "as long as the sun shines and the rivers flow" mean, literally, forever? Does the "Great White Mother" mean

Queen Victoria, or all subsequent governments? And so on and so on.

Because the English language, the French language, and many native languages are all involved, the matter of translation also becomes important: the accuracy of translation and the conveying of imagery from one language into another. Indian people remark frequently that their forefathers didn't understand what they were agreeing to when they signed treaties. Either they didn't understand exact wordings, or they didn't understand the breadth of the implications behind the words that they thought they were agreeing to. The argument most often used here appeals to our common sense: "They couldn't have understood what they were giving up because no one in his right mind would so easily sign away total territories and rights and livelihoods." That may be so. It may also be that the Indians didn't share or perhaps even understand the European idea of ownership of land, and consequently couldn't see that they were giving up access to it.

The upshot, though, is that agreements were made, in words. And as the fight over what is implied in the various treaties or in the broader notion of aboriginal rights goes on among the Indian leaders and the Canadian politicians and the lawyers for both of them, it is these words that are being struggled over, pulled back and forth like the knotted handkerchief at the centre of the tug-of-war rope. And you know that without agreement on the meaning and the implications of the words, nothing will ever be resolved.

If you add to this an almost full-blown industry around the creation of new words, the Indian discussion becomes a semantic minefield in which agreement in terminology is often totally elusive, and it is impossible to be universally up-to-date with current terminology. As I travelled across the country from one community to another, I could never be sure which words were going to be in usage and which words were going to be passé. A word in common usage in one place might as easily give offence when used somewhere else. Indian bands are now commonly,

155

but not universally, referred to as "First Nations." In Kahn-awake I was chastized for using the term "reserve" when the Mohawks wanted their land to be known as "territory." In Norway House the term "self-government" is avoided, even though self-government is a very general and current catchword used by both Indian and government leaders across the country. In Norway House everything that is implied elsewhere by "self-government" is expressed by the term "local control." Self-government, I was told there, is a negative term that upsets the local non-status community, which fears that the Indian band is about to take over everything at its expense.

And so it goes. The term "Indian" itself can by no means be taken for granted. There is, among those who fancy themselves in the know, a cachet to being the first to adopt a new and more sensitive designation. It is similar to being in the United States where only the most uninformed, for example, would be caught using the term "Negro" these days instead of "Black." But even Black may be on the way out it would seem, as those really in the know prefer to use "Afro-American."

The same is the case in the semantic footrace here. In Canada the term "Eskimo" went out long ago, replaced by "Inuit." The term "Indian" has been a little more difficult to get rid of, mostly because so many Indian people still seem to be content to use the word themselves. The term "native people" had currency for a time, sometimes in upper case, "Native People." "Aboriginal people" also gets used. Judge Murray Sinclair, who gained prominence as one of the commissioners of Manitoba's year-long Aboriginal Justice Inquiry burst out at one point with an aside to the media about the inappropriateness of the term Indian. Its use, he said, perpetuated an historical inaccuracy: Columbus had not happened upon the Far East and had not encountered the Indians he had expected. Sinclair is quite right, but rejecting the term "Indian" does not solve the problem. Communication requires language that is agreed upon and understood. If no one agrees on the terminology, how can communication take place?

If communication can't take place, how can understanding ever be reached? How can anything ever be settled or achieved?

It might be helpful, rather than trying to identify the group with one name, to bring into greater use the names of the individual tribes (or First Nations; here we are again with a semantic problem). We could try to speak less with a blanket term and more with the specific names of the dividual peoples: the Cree or the Mohawks or the Maliseet or the Hurons or the Ojibway or the Blackfoot or the Kwakiutl. This route would both serve to be more specific, and it would also serve to underline something that seems to be too often glossed over by non-Indian people; the fact that Indian (or native or aboriginal) peoples are very, very different, one from another. They are different in ethnicity, in language and tradition, in governmental and religious and cultural practices. That an Indian is an Indian is an Indian is no more the case than is the case that a European is a European is a European. There are probably more differences separating the Haida of the Queen Charlotte Islands from the Micmac of Nova Scotia and the Navajo of the American southwest than there are separating a Turk from a Lithuanian from a Scotsman in Europe. Pan-Indian, which expresses the idea that North American Indians are similar to one another and have the same interests, is a recent and rather shaky notion that by all evidence has more going against it than for it. But the fallacy in the non-Indian mind that all Indians are alike persists, even, discouragingly, at the higher levels of government.

There are lots of theories but not a great deal of clear definition and agreement over what self-government means. This is what frustrated some of the Canadian politicians at the First Ministers' meeting and allowed them their out; if it couldn't be defined, they didn't have to go along with it. Some observers point out that the country being as large and as diverse as it is, the concept can never be defined in any universal way, nor should it. Lloyd Barber feels that the aboriginal leaders in Ottawa were really seeking a symbolic nod. "Acknowledge us," he believes they were saying. "Acknowledge in a broad way that we have rights and skills and can look after ourselves."

It must be acknowledged that thinking on Indian government has moved a tremendous distance in the last twenty years. In 1968, just as his government was preparing to bring forth its famous White Paper on the assimilation of Indian people into the mainstream of Canada, Prime Minister Pierre Trudeau said: "If we think about restoring aboriginal rights to the Indians, well, what about the French who were defeated at the Plains of Abraham? What about the Acadians who were deported? What about the Japanese Canadians who were so badly treated at the end of or during the last war? What can we do to redeem the past? I can only say as President Kennedy said when he was asked about what he would do to compensate for injustices that the Negroes had received in American society: We will be just in our time. This is all we can do, we will be just today."

In 1973, a short five years later, after intense political pressure and lobbying by Indian groups and their leaders, Trudeau had a change of heart. He told an assembly of native groups: "Well, it looks like you've got more rights than I thought."

But if it is self-government that Indian groups want, then what does that mean? Can anyone define it in ways that can be understood? People try. In 1988, in a special edition on Indians and self-government, writers in the *Winnipeg Free Press* tried to speculate on what self-government might look like. To do so they produced the following scenario: The buyer of a new pickup truck from a First Nation auto dealership would pay sales tax to the band, not the provincial government. The policeman issuing speeding tickets would wear band or tribal council uniforms. Revenue from the tickets would go to an Indian justice system; or motorists could fight tickets in an Indian court, before Indian magistrates. It would be a First Nations chief at the news conference announcing that Inco Ltd had opened a new mine in the North. Grade six history lessons would teach reserve children why a chief had selected a certain piece of territory for their reserve.

Within twenty years, the *Free Press* wrote, "Indian leaders expect their bands to withdraw from federal jurisdiction and the Indian Act and be constitutionally recognized as a First Nation, with a government elected by its members, responsible only to its members, collecting taxes and royalties from resource projects within their boundaries, and competing with the provinces for transfer payments from Ottawa. Provinces would give up control of resource development – mining, forestry, hydro – within First Nations, which could opt for development or collect royalties from firms operating within their boundaries. First Nations would be compensated for existing projects that have developed on their land."

Maybe the future will look like this, maybe it won't. Maybe it will look like this in some places but not others. The above is an ideal that may, through negotiation, legislation, and constitutional amendment, be worked out. Likely there will be some compromise, and different versions will be worked out in different ways in different places across the country. What Canada will look like and what Indian Country will look like in twenty or thirty or fifty years is still a matter of broad speculation. Some people are ready and willing to dream, but the dreams they come up with are different often from the next person's dream. The *Winnipeg Free Press* in an editorial observed; "even after a decade of debate, rarely are any of the power brokers talking about the same thing."

But if the experience of, say, Norway House is an example, things change in small but positive ways all the time. And the changes, by and large, seem to be accepted positively by the people. The shift in budget administration over the past decade has been significant. For instance, according to the Department of Indian Affairs, $1.7 billion is the cost (1987 figures) of annual Indian programs in education, economic development, and social development across the nation. However, only $394 million of that is administered by the department. A further $219 million is administered by the provincial governments, while $1.1 billion, or 64 per cent, is administered by the various bands themselves. As recently as 1982, Indian bands administered only 55 per cent of the money. The government's "devolution" is gradually taking more jobs and more responsibilities away from government bureaucrats and placing them in Indian reserves.

To succeed in some of their wishes, Indian First Nations are going to have to deal with provinces and provincial governments, which is something they traditionally have not liked to do. The mistrust between aboriginal leaders and the provinces is historic and differs little from one end of the country to the other. However, it is land and control over natural resources that First Nations want, provincial jurisdictions are automatically involved. Non-reserve Crown lands in Canada belong to provinces, as does control over natural resources. The federal government cannot give either away without provincial agreement.

Some observers point out that aboriginal leaders would do well to understand their potential power in the provinces, and the impact they can make even without constitutional changes. They have clout already and they should make use of it. There is some understanding of this in the Northwest Territories, where Inuit, Indian, Métis, and non-status people make up 60 per cent of the population. This fact is reflected in the make-up of the governmental assembly; there are fourteen native and only ten non-native elected legislators. So there, and in the northern reaches of many of the provinces, aboriginal people seem to be already in a position to carry their issues into prominent places in the public agenda.

8   Opinions: Keith Penner
October 20, 1988

In 1982 the Parliament of Canada struck a special committee and charged it with studying the issue of Indian self-government. For the next twelve months the all-party committee criss-crossed the country listening to representations from dozens of individuals and groups. In October 1983 it tabled a two-hundred-page report in the House of Commons.

Six months later the government changed and nothing in the way of legislation really ever emerged from the recommendations in the report of the Special Committee on Indian Self-government. But the fact remains that the hearings took place. Ideas were raised and recorded; issues were thought through, committed to record, and distilled into recommendations. The report is still referred to when people talk about Indian issues in Canada. Its impact has been substantial, and might be said to be an important turning-point in the thinking of a lot of people in Canada on issues of Indian people and government. The chairman of the special committee was Keith Penner, a Liberal member of Parliament from Cochrane-Superior in northern Ontario.

I met Keith Penner on a day when the news was full of the stories of the Lubicon Cree in northern Alberta. The Lubicons, in an act of exasperation, had built barricades across oil exploration roads. There they had set themselves up, keeping warm beside bonfires while they waited for the police to come to remove their barricades and while they waited for politicians in

Edmonton and Ottawa to respond to their demands for land for a reserve.

What would happen to the Lubicons was close to Penner's thoughts on this day. The television set in his parliamentary office flickered images of Chief Bernard Ominayak walking away from an Edmonton courthouse and toward the CBC cameras. In a level voice he stated that the Lubicon Cree would no longer see themselves as subject to Canadian laws.

At the time of this interview, a federal election campaign was in full swing. (Penner, after twenty years in politics, wasn't running.) And though Georges Erasmus, chief of the Assembly of First Nations, had vigorously proposed that the federal political leaders include a debate on aboriginal issues in their agenda, nothing had come of the suggestion; neither the politicians, the media, nor the public had shown any enthusiasm.

So where are we now, I wanted to find out from Keith Penner.

Question: As the self government negotiations continue, do you think, based on your background in the subject, that Indians know specifically what they want?

Penner: There are variations across the country. The special committee made it very clear that we're not dealing with a homogeneous community. When you move from the Sechelt people, to Indian people on Vancouver Island, into the North, the Mohawks in Quebec, the Six Nations around Brantford – you're dealing with different peoples. So that difference had to be acknowledged in any kind of public policy formulation. And that's an obstacle for the federal government, which, being a national government, likes to have a single, clearly defined, totally applicable policy. That's what they prefer. And if parts of the country can't accept this overall policy, they can use the opting-out provision [of the Constitution]. So it's an extremely difficult task for the federal government to move toward a policy formulation, and for that reason I think you have to go back to the issue of constitutional recognition.

Once you have constitutional recognition, then negotiations as to what the people want can be worked out differently for different people. Some First Nations are very ambitious. They're talking not only about control of education and health care, but they want to negotiate certain responsibilities in the field of the administration of justice, economic development, resource development. There's a great deal of variation across the country. For anybody who understands the aboriginal communities across the country this poses no problem. But for policy makers in Ottawa it's enormously difficult to comprehend all of these negotiations going on, adapting to different demands and needs across the country.

Question: Did you find that the delegations who came before you were very definite about what they wanted in their own locality?

Penner: Some were very definite and presented briefs in which they actually described in extensive detail how their governments would function, how representatives would be chosen, what responsibilities they would have, how their officials, their bureaucracy would function. The Federation of Saskatchewan Indians gave us enormous amounts of documentation dealing with education and a justice system and economic development and so on. We found many others, however, who said all of this is really interesting but academic until we have the right to self-government recognized first. That has to be the first building block. A lot of the negotiations that are going on now to accommodate what is wanted are terribly unfair because the two sides at the table are in such a state of imbalance; the federal negotiators have got all of the high cards, they've got all of the legalisms, and the aboriginal people really have to play from very low cards.

Question: Did you ever, during the process or before or since, imagine how you would have handled it had you been in charge in 1888 or 1688? We're dealing now with three and in some

163

places four hundred years of accumulated history. What mistakes were made?

Penner: There were several possibilities facing the colonial power in dealing with aboriginal people. They could have gone for conquest; they could have decided that these were simply a savage people and they were going to eliminate them. But they didn't. They chose instead to recognize. Colonial policy actually did establish the *modus operandi* for dealing with aboriginal people. They recognized first of all that there was a great deal of variation. In the Royal Proclamation of 1763 they talked about the many tribes and nations. They actually used the word nation, so when First Nations today use that term, people of Canada ought not be offended, because that came from a very early colonial concept. They knew that people were, in many cases, extremely well organized, that they had a cultural identity, that they had language, that they interacted with other tribes and nations. So, therefore, the decision was made not to conquer these people; these people have certain rights. What rights did they have? The rights that they had were aboriginal rights.

I think most Canadian people see this as just some other kind of right. They see that there are all sorts of rights around and we're always talking about rights – human rights, women's rights, rights of sexual preference, and so on. But I would contend that when you talk about aboriginal rights you're talking about something that's totally and completely different, which was recognized by the better thinkers in the colonial period: there is a right that is inherent, that comes with being there first.

I keep looking for examples that will justify this. Here's one. If you ever line up for a ticket at a motion picture theatre, if you want to go to a popular movie and you get there first, you have a place in line. There's a right for being there first. Somebody can't come along and push you out unless they're bigger and stronger than you and knock you to the ground, in which case you can use the criminal laws to get redress. Somebody could come along and say, "Look I really want to take my girlfriend here, will you accept eighty dollars," but there is a right for being there first. In land, if a person in Canada occupies a piece of land for a long enough period of time unchallenged, he has a certain right that can be upheld in law. If you have used an access for a long period of time, let's say to get to a water supply, and then it's later discovered that you're cutting across somebody's property, there are legal precedents that say that the right of access cannot be denied to you. There is a right in being there first.

Now there's been an enormous job to leap from that understanding to the concept of title. That's a huge leap. Prime Minister Trudeau, who was a brilliant constitutional lawyer in his own right, had great difficulty making that leap until the Nishga case or the Calder case in the Supreme Court. Here we had six out of seven Supreme Court Justices who said they could understand the title that aboriginal people had, that they had title in terms of the English understanding of law. Now where the Supreme Court split was over the question of whether that title could be asserted today, or whether it had been extinguished. Three of them, one group of three led by Justice Judson, said that it had been extinguished. But the other group, led by Justice Emmett Hall, said that title could be asserted today. It was that that changed Mr. Trudeau's mind and opened the door for land-claim negotiations and for a comprehensive claims policy in Canada. But this direction was really established by the Royal Proclamation.

I don't want to make too much of the Royal Proclamation. I mean it's not the New Testament, it's a colonial document, and it has to be seen as that. It doesn't do many favours for aboriginal people. But it did at least recognize these rights, and it pointed in the direction of how you solve those rights when they are challenged. What you do is negotiate, on a government-to-government basis, agreements or treaties or arrangements that are fair and satisfying, so that the newcomers and those who were here first can interact, coexist, and share.

Question: So a reasonable course was charted by the Royal Proclamation, and the problems have really been our deviation from that?

Penner: Yes. By the time John A. Macdonald and George-Étienne Cartier and Tupper and the others began to talk about confederating, they wanted to get out of the colonial basket, and in their desire to do that they simply forgot. All of this political action was going on, but there was a group of people on the fringes who didn't get involved, and as events moved toward Confederation they were simply overlooked. So our first consti-tution, the BNA Act of 1867, almost entirely overlooked them. Section 91 defined the federal authority, section 92 defined the provincial authority, and then, like throwing an extra turnip into the stew, they tossed in Indians and lands reserved for Indians, without any great thought.

Later the new government of Canada was reminded by the court that the section didn't mean anything at all until they legislated it. So they brought out the most terrible piece of legislation to be found anywhere in the free world: the Indian Act. And the Indian Act did everything that the Royal Proclama-tion had said not to do. It imposed the will of a new colonial power, namely Canada, on the aboriginal people and it said "This is the way that you shall govern yourselves. You shall govern yourselves as bands and you will elect your councillors in this way." And it laid down in minute detail how they were to conduct themselves, what rights they had and what rights they did not have. They were obviously looked upon not as Canadian citizens, because these people had no right to vote. If they wanted that right to vote, or if they wanted to go to a saloon or a bar to drink, they had to rid themselves of their "Indianness"; they had to cease being Indians and they had to become enfranchised.

Obviously the government at that time did recognize that they were a separate and a distinct people. That's the only good thing that can be said about the Indian Act. But they said, "This situation can't last, it can't last because you can't have a separate

166

and distinct people. So what we'll do is we'll have various kinds of enticements and gradually we'll draw them in." This was the beginning of assimilation.

The most clear-cut case of trying to assimilate was the Liberal government's White Paper of 1969. It fell on hard soil and eventually died, but we still see it from time to time. And many Canadian people say, "Well, you know the only answer to the so-called 'Indian problem,' " – and I put that in quotation marks – "the only answer is that they've got to become like us, they've got to become familiar with the Protestant work ethic, they've got to realize that we do certain things in our society and they're expected to follow suit."

Question: What do you say to people who say, "Listen, history is history but this is today and we can't have hyphenated Canadians. There are people from all over the world here and we can't have special groups"?

Penner: What I say to them is "face reality." We can philosophize, or we can dream all we want. "There should not be hyphenated Canadians and nobody should have special rights. We're all Canadians together and we should all be governed by the Constitution. We should all be governed by human rights codes, the Charter of Rights and Freedoms," and so on. Well that's a very fine theory and maybe if we were writing a new version of Plato's *Republic* we might say this is the way we would like to have it. But the fact is that we have to face reality in Canada. And to some extent we have faced reality. Who would bring back the theory of Lord Durham about French Canadians and say the only way Canada can be strong is if we assimilate French Canada into an anglophone North American society? It's idiotic. The French in Quebec and the French outside Quebec have struggled hard to maintain their distinctiveness and their identity and their rights, and they have succeeded. Why? Because they've had strong political leaders and they've got leverage.

That's what the aboriginal people of Canada want. They want their distinctiveness, their separateness, their cultural identity retained, and the majority of them want to do it within the context of our Canadian Confederation. The only way they can do that is to have their rights recognized and to be allowed, through agreements, to pursue those areas that are essential to their culture and are essential to their meaningful existence.

Question: So, in your view, there is a moral imperative about political power.

Penner: It's much more than a moral imperative, it's a geo-political imperative. I'm always worried that people think "Here is just another bleeding-heart liberal concerned about these poor Indian people," and I have to say that initially, way back in my own development on this thinking, that's probably where I was. But it goes much further than that. These people exist here, they have certain rights to be here – political, economic rights. What's happened is that a dominant society, with force, has pushed them to the fringes.

In most areas, when it comes to developing policy on matters that Canadian people are concerned about, we do pretty well. For instance in the social areas, with elderly people, with children. It takes the government a while – you have to keep hitting them over the head – but after a while it gets through to the thickheads in the government that you have to do something. They suddenly realize now that you have to do something about the environment, for example. But with aboriginal rights, it never gets through. We have an election campaign going on now and nobody is talking, none of the political parties is saying this is an important issue for Canada, we're not going to be a healthy nation, a whole nation until we solve it. There is almost complete silence. The newspapers and other news media respond a little bit if there's a confrontation, with the Lubicon for example. But otherwise nobody is talking about the way to go.

168

The sad thing is that we know where to go, the public policy is there, the agenda. You could put it in neon lights, it's perfectly clear. The public policy has been developed. Indian Affairs couldn't do it. I was told by a deputy minister of Indian Affairs when we set out to do our report, "You are wasting your time my friend. I've been working at it for three years and it's like tilling hard ground, you'll not break any ground." And he was right, because they can't do it over there in the glass towers of Hull where Indian Affairs is located. They can't do it because they're bound by parameters.

Now I want to be clear that the Special Committee on Indian Self-government didn't develop public policy. I would be so proud to say that we had if we actually had, but we didn't develop one small iota of public policy. What we did was recognize that we were in total ignorance and darkness, and we went out and said, "Shed light, let there be light, because the public policy exists." There are chiefs and elders and scores and hundreds of Indian people in this country who know what the answer is, and they know where the beginning point is, and they know how to get from the beginning point to a satisfactory conclusion. The route is as clear as following the Macdonald-Cartier Highway from Montreal to Toronto. So what our report did was simply take that information, that knowledge, and put it into the kind of language that they use in government.

We looked at a lot of options and we said every single option should be pursued and, you know, it has happened. For example we said, "Let's try the legislative route." Now the legislative route has been a total and complete disaster. It's not very fruitful. The answer doesn't lie in looking to Parliament to legislate self-government; there are too many obstacles, too many problems along the way.

First, the government would like to have a single bill. That's the way they work over here. They like to have one thing and get it over with. So even though the special committee report said that we should look at the legislative route, we can clearly see now that it will never be the answer. It might be necessary to use it in certain cases in order to meet requirements of law, requirements of the system, but it must not be seen as an answer.

We also said in the report that you could go the bilateral route, and the government and Indian Affairs has grabbed hold of this and they've gone into this bilateral approach, or community-based self-government. Which means that the department sits down and negotiates self-government terms with those bands or First Nations that they judge capable of going into these kinds of negotiations. But I tell you, that is another route that leads nowhere. There's too much suspicion on the part of the aboriginal people. They've been fooled and hoodwinked and tricked so many times, and they're so fearful, that they keep going back and back again. So these negotiations become protracted and almost endless.

The other factor is that all the power is on one side; you can't have meaningful negotiations unless the two sides are in some kind of balance. The federal negotiators think that they're handing something over – money or certain powers. But then in the back of their minds they're concerned about the Financial Administration Act; they're concerned about the auditor general; they're concerned about how they're protecting their minister. And so it doesn't work. The only good thing that can be said about it is that they're sitting down and talking, and that's always valuable, I mean there are probably more bureaucrats today who are doing more talking with Indian people and that in itself is valuable. But it's not the answer.

I'm absolutely convinced that the answer has to be within the Constitution; you have to recognize, or you have to define, aboriginal rights in the Constitution. The right to self-government has to be in the Constitution. We've got to a point now where senior politicians talk about this – the premiers, the prime minister, and the first ministers – they actually talk about Indian self-government, aboriginal self-government. But they're terribly frightened of it, which is curious, because you're dealing with only a small number of people. It's hard to understand what their fear is.

The fear is expressed as, "All right, we will recognize this right when we know exactly and precisely and in minute detail what's involved." That's what we call a contingent right: "We will recognize self-government contingent upon these agreements." Aboriginal leaders have rejected that, and quite rightly. Because how can you have a right that is first clearly defined and fenced in? Surely a right has to be open! And there might be a conflict; aboriginal rights could conflict with what we call third-party interests. Well, we know how to deal with that kind of thing; you deal with it through negotiations, you try to sit down and work it out. If necessary you can deal with it through the courts. There are all sorts of ways of settling disputes. If we're good at anything, it's settling disputes. That's why we've been a nation for a long period of time; if we couldn't settle our disputes neighbour to neighbour or government to government, we couldn't be a country. So aboriginal people say we can settle these things easily, but to settle them they need their rights recognized. So that right has to be inherent.

What is it that the political leaders fear about an inherent right? There are two things they fear. One has been voiced by the federal government; the other has been voiced by the provinces, particularly Ontario. An inherent right, says the Minister of Justice, means that you're granting through the Constitution a sovereignty to aboriginal people. Now what happens when a sovereign nation like Canada has within it a group of people who have sovereign rights? "It's incomprehensible," says the Minister of Justice. "You can't do that." The other argument, which has been voiced by Ontario, is the fear of litigation. If you have an inherent right, they can take this inherent right and wave it under the nose of a judge, and who knows what the outcome will be. It could be anything. As [Ontario Attorney General Ian] Scott said, we're not going to let seven senior citizens over there in the Supreme Court decide on matters like that. That belongs to politicians to decide. What I want to say to both the Minister of Justice and the Attorney General of Ontario is that they're both wrong on those two counts.

Question: Does the enshrining of the inherent right in the Constitution remedy the problem of the imbalance in powers?

Penner: Exactly. It would go a long way. I'm not saying that that in and by itself it would give you complete balance. It certainly would not give aboriginal people some kind of upper hand, which is what the premiers are afraid of. They wouldn't be able to start kicking the premiers around, kicking the resource companies around, kicking third parties around, asserting their power. I don't think it would do any of that, but what it would do would be to provide for meaningful negotiations. They would have what I call the constitutional imperative to negotiate, and they would be able to negotiate from strength. They would have strength and they could use the courts. Ian Scott is concerned about that, but the courts have a very mixed history of what they do for native people. There have been victories here and there, and there have been some really silly decisions. But sovereign, inherent right is what gives aboriginal people standing or status at the bargaining table. It also gives them standing and status in court. And what would flow from that would, in my view, be justice.

I guess the real question for Canadian people is, "Should that be feared?" I have to throw the question back to them. What are you afraid of? Are you afraid Indian communities will no longer be little poverty-stricken ghettos? That these people will have schools and hospitals and houses and businesses that are as good as we have in towns and villages in this country? Are you afraid of that? Are you afraid that there will be fewer native people, Indian people, in our jails? Are you afraid that they will take steps to protect their fishing grounds and maybe ask for some role with conservation enforcement agencies? What would they be afraid of in Kenora, Ontario, for example. Would they be afraid that they won't have the beaten Indian person, dejected and depressed, having no status and no wealth and using the meagre dollars they have to try and forget their desperate plight and be inebriated on the street? Is that what you want? Or do you want a person to walk proud and be an economic force in your community?

It's amazing, when there is economic power, how quickly people change their minds. I know when the Cree of northern Quebec had economic power and said that they were no longer going to be subservient and taken advantage of by airlines that brought their supplies in, and they said, "We'll develop our own airline," how quickly one of the other airlines said, "Well, we'll go into a joint venture with you and help you develop an airline. We'll show you how to do it. You can use our expertise and, later, when you've got it, you can go on your own." That's the kind of thing that happens when you have recognition and agreements and self-government. What we're doing is taking a serious illness in our society – the illness being the poverty and the rejection and the pushing aside of a significant number of people, a proud people who have a culture that's been retained through all of this history – and we're going to give these people an opportunity to participate in society, not on our terms 100 per cent, not on their terms 100 per cent, but through a combination of agreements.

Question: You prescribe the constitutional route as by far the most important and the best of all routes?

Penner: I think it's the only one.

Question: How optimistic are you that politicians will agree? Will they come around? What will it take?

Penner: It's inevitable. It will happen. It absolutely will happen. And the key to it happening is public pressure. We need pressure from more people, and we're getting a growing number now.

What they required in the time of the French Revolution to get rid of the *ancienne régime* was *les philosophes*. We need people who write. We need the academics, we need the writers, we need the lawyers, we need the politicians. There are very few politicians in this field because it doesn't get many votes. In Parliament, aboriginal affairs are just about at the bottom of the Order Paper. Most of the time they're not even on the Order Paper, they usually have fallen off somewhere. The native leaders can't do it by themselves; although they're respected by their own people, they're sometimes considered suspect by the rest of society. So there needs to be tremendous support in Canadian society. And this support really has to go well beyond the bleeding-heart liberals or the moral support, the caring concern. I don't want to bash that because it's a very good beginning point. If you have a church group or a school group or students at a university, begin there and say "You know we should care about Indian people in Canada . . ." You can begin there but you can't stop there. If this could be understood by more Canadians, then they would say to the politicians "For goodness' sake solve it!" I've seen so many problems that you never would believe could be solved in Canada; all of a sudden, one day, it becomes a ripe piece of fruit and it falls off the tree.

Question: Do you sense frustation on the part of the aboriginal people at the failure to achieve sovereignty, and do you get a sense of where that frustration might go?

Penner: The frustration is growing daily and is turning to anger. The aboriginal people are enormously patient. To see this all you have to do is watch Chief Ominayak [of the Lubicon Crees] in action. He is not a wild revolutionary; he is a highly intelligent man with enormous patience, and he's done everything according to the book. And after forty years of failure by his people to get their land base, now they're trying something else. Frustration is growing and growing and growing daily. Why is it growing? It's growing because the agenda that I talked about is growing. In reality it's more developed than a lot of other public issues. You can go talk to John Amagoalik, or Georges Erasmus, or Smokey Bruyere, or a hundred other outstanding leaders in this country, and they can tell you all about that agenda and that policy. But where are we in implementation? We are way back here; we've made hardly any progress at all.

9   Tobique, New Brunswick

In 1987 a group of women of the Tobique Indian band in New Brunswick published a book. It took them three years to put it together, but with the help and the tape recorder of a doctoral student from Manitoba named Janet Silman, who had spent time on the reserve doing research for her own thesis, they finally got their stories down on paper. When it came time to give their book a title, the women did not hesitate. *Enough Is Enough* they called it, leaving no mistake about the depths of feeling that had provoked them.

Enough Is Enough is an anecdotal book; the presence of the tape recorder is strongly evident. It is oral history and oral protest. The women, about a dozen of them, talk about their recollections of childhood and what their lives and their community used to be like. There are some funny stories and some warm ones, but there are some brutal anecdotes, too. Tales of poverty and hard work, of leaving home and wandering across the country and the continent in search of work; tales of feckless men, dependent children, drinking binges, getting beaten up, all delivered in flat, matter-of-fact monotone as if that is what life is all about. Finally, the book chronicles the tough struggles made by these women to overcome the disastrous events of their lives.

Mostly unsophisticated, and with only a rudimentary education, these women describe themselves as victims and they are tough in the way that victims can be, tough enough to keep taking it all. But they are tough also in a way that victims often don't get to be. For some reason, in the struggles of the fifteen

176

years prior to writing their book, the group of Indian women learned, as not all victims can, how to be defiant. They fought battles and won small victories, and each victory gave them courage for the next battle. They knew who they were, and gradually they learned who and what they were fighting against, even when what they were fighting was their own insecurities.

A federal government study cited in the introduction to the book describes Indian women as ranking among the most severely disadvantaged in Canadian society. "They are worse off economically than both Indian men and other Canadian women," the study decided, "and although they live longer than Indian men, their life expectancy does not approach that of Canadian women generally." The women of Tobique, however, don't lash out only at the inequalities of Canadian society, the Canadian economic system, and the rules and regulations that govern and control Indians. With considerable risk, they lash out also at the structures of their own community and the sad and sorry ways in which people in their own backyard have battled and damaged one another.

Tobique is famous as one of the communities from which came the leadership for the fight to have Bill C-31 enacted. One of the critical moments preceding the enactment of that legislation was a month-long march on Ottawa by Indian women in the summer of 1979. The march on Ottawa, inspired by the Poor People's March on Washington D.C. in the United States, gathered native women from all across Canada along its route. It was organized by the women of Tobique. Forty women and children from Tobique trudged through the July heat up the highway from Montreal to Ottawa. They hoped their effort might make a point with the Minister of Indian Affairs, and maybe there would be some attention from the media. As their demonstration gained momentum they realized they would succeed beyond their wildest dreams. Before they left Ottawa they had even achieved a meeting with the prime minister, Joe Clark.

Another victory in the battle for C-31 was a 1981 condemnation of Canada by the United Nations Human Rights Committee. When the United Nations chastised Canada for breaching the International Covenant on Civil and Political Rights, to which Canada had been a signatory, it was in response to the representation of a Tobique woman. A small, deceptively shy woman named Sandra Lovelace, backed by the other women and by the New Brunswick Human Rights Commission, had lodged a complaint at the international body about the loss of her Indian status. And the U.N., in response, slammed Canada.

Sandra Lovelace's story represents those of many women of Tobique. Like many New Brunswick Indian people, upon reaching adulthood she left home and crossed the nearby border into Maine to look for work. She worked for a while in a potato factory in Maine and then wandered further into the U.S.A., living for a while in Pennsylvania, and then moving to California, where she married a non-Canadian, non-Indian man. After some time the marriage broke up and Lovelace and her son, Christian, returned to Canada, New Brunswick, and Tobique, hoping to rebuild a life for themselves.

Upon her return to what she believed was "home," she discovered that she no longer officially belonged. According to the Indian Act she had voluntarily given up her status by "marrying out" and no longer had a claim to any of the rights and privileges Indian status carried: the right to live on the reserve, the right to be provided with housing, the right to be provided with health care and with education for her child. She was astounded. "We are Indians," she says. "It never occurred to us that we could lose our Indianness. And this community is our home."

She soon found that she was not alone. Many other women at Tobique, women she had grown up with, women who were related to her, were in the same boat. All had tried to live in the world beyond the reserve, all had watched their options run out, all had returned home seeking refuge, all were uniformly astonished to learn home was no longer officially home. All felt they had no choice but to stay anyway and fight for something they believed was their right.

Locally, the matter was complicated by a chief and band council in the mid 1970s who believed in adhering to the letter of the law. Tobique, like almost all Indian reserves, was a community where there was never enough to go around: never enough houses, never enough jobs, never enough welfare money, never enough land. So if somebody was not officially an Indian, that was one less house you had to provide in the midst of a shortage. The band took this line, and treated the women and children like usurpers. The women, who felt their options close in around them, did whatever they could.

When she couldn't get a house from the band, Lovelace lived in a tent that she pitched by the band office. Other women were in even worse shape. With no legal leg to stand on, they frequently found themselves at the mercy of the men. A woman who no longer had status would strike a liaison with an Indian man, and she and her children would move into his house. If the relationship got rocky, though, the man could, and did, pitch the woman out of the house, and she would literally have nowhere to go. When Juanita Perley was thrown out of her home by an alcoholic "husband" in the fall of 1976, she and her ten children and a grandchild moved straight into the band office and refused to budge.

What embittered the women even more was their observation that, while they and their children were without any Indian rights, white women who had married Indian men at Tobique were in a position to enjoy all the privileges they had lost. This realization stuck like a bone in their throats. In 1977, in an act of defiance that surprised even themselves, the Tobique women occupied the band office building and refused to leave until the chief paid some attention to their grievances. In 1979 came the march to Ottawa, in 1981 the U.N. decision on the Lovelace representation, and in 1985 the passage of the federal Bill C-31, which returned Indian status to the countless hundreds of Indian women and their children who had lost it by "marrying out." The political awareness fostered by these events and their sense of victory was the impetus for the women of Tobique to publish, in 1987, the story of their battles.

On an early November morning in New Brunswick wet snow covers the ground thinly. Mists drift like magic down from the wooded hills of the St. John River valley. The river itself is still and black and glistens like a mirror. I have driven into a town called Andover, a village of 1,800 people, having passed through country that is strangely, hauntingly beautiful in the melancholy way country that is worn out and hasn't got much of an economy left can be. The leaves are gone from the forests – woods, as people in New Brunswick call them – that cloak the steep hills that climb up from the valleys. On this the first day of snow, stiff winds have blown the leaves from the lawns of clapboard neo-colonial houses, and churches, and stores that are as sturdy as the New Brunswickers and New Englanders who live inside them. I have come from Maine and have passed the hilly fields from whose tired red earth the brown potatoes once more have been mined.

From Andover I cross a lengthy span of iron bridge, its girders painted green. The railroad bridge beside it was taken out by the thundering ice of the flooding St. John River two springs ago, leaving only the concrete pilings. On the Perth side of the bridge I turn sharply and follow the narrow pavement that hugs the other shore. I can see Tobique below me, on the other side of the dam and bridge at Tobique Narrows: the church, red-roofed and white-steepled, the clutch of frame houses, wood-smoke sifting from chimneys. It is a pleasant-looking village, built on the point of land where the Tobique and the St. John rivers join in the fullness of their force to flow on south past Fredericton to St. John, the Bay of Fundy, and the sea.

The people of Tobique are Maliseet Indians. The Maliseet first encountered Europeans about four hundred years ago, even earlier if they lived near the coast. European fishing expeditions touched in at regular places along the Maritime coast for years prior to any actual European settlement. Contact with the Indians was frequent, if sporadic. By 1605 Samuel de Champlain was trading with the neighbouring Micmacs from the French post at Port Royal in Nova Scotia. The Maliseet people signed their first treaty of friendship with the British Crown in 1725. The people of Tobique took possession of the land that is now their reserve in 1801. Theirs is the second largest of fourteen reserves in New Brunswick, a band of 1,307 people (857 living on the reserve) on 6,731 acres of land. They also claim a further twelve thousand acres, including two thousand acres immediately downstream, upon which is built much of the town of Perth. That claim is frequently a source of friction between the Maliseet and the white townspeople of Perth, New Brunswick.

At Tobique two adolescent children move in the company of a brown and black dog up the middle of the street toward the Mah Sos school. Or maybe they are going to the arcade, or the Eagle's Nest restaurant. They pass the white clapboard Ste. Anne's Roman Catholic church, which looks in splendid dignity out toward the river that has been at its front door for a hundred years. A Franciscan brother, dressed in a belted brown robe, like Friar Tuck, watches the children from the upstairs balcony of the big, white-framed, red-roofed house where he lives with three other priests. The house rambles back through a series of connected sheds and summer kitchens and garages and old stables, to the slope of its back lawn. The lawn runs down to the cemetary, where the more recent graves, shiny granite stones topping them, are lying right up against the white wall of the band office. A yellow "Maliseet of Tobique" crest with an arching salmon, entwined green fiddleheads, and paired eagle feathers, is tacked onto the wall of the band office that faces the graveyard.

The band office is in a relatively new two-storey building that resembles a tourist lodge or a golf club or a large suburban restaurant. Its newness and its imposing nature, however, are appropriate to the role band government plays in Tobique. The band office is the nerve centre, the centre of everything, the ganglia out of which the jangle of all energy and activity proceeds.

Seven people are in the tiny reception area joking and filling styrofoam cups with coffee as fast as Elaina Daigle, the office receptionist, can get it made. There is a sign that reads "Coffee 50 cents," but everybody ignores it. Not everyone in the room works in the band office. Three of the men are in construction boots, heavy jackets, and baseball caps, ready to go on to other jobs. But a stop at the band office for coffee, a few jokes, and a chance to hear the current gossip, is a morning ritual. There are election jokes this morning, none of them complimentary to Prime Minister Brian Mulroney. There is also commentary about the local Liberal candidate who came by the previous day hoping to put up some of his signs on the reserve, but refused to make any promises, about anything, when pressed. A young man wearing a San Francisco Giants baseball cap periodically breaks into the conversation as he tries to get commitments for donations of food for a community lunch which will follow the Remembrance Day ceremony at the end of the week.

I am met in the reception area by a woman named Karen Perley. She escorts me through a maze of offices, introducing me to a different person with a different title at each door. Eventually we reach her small office where she works as an assistant on Tobique's self-government project. An attractive, engaging woman, neatly but casually dressed, Perley is, I judge, in her late thirties. She has four children: the eldest is twenty-one and lives in Fredericton with her own children, while the youngest is only three. Karen Perley's husband, Carl, is a former RCMP officer who is now living in semi-retirement on the reserve. Her brother-in-law, David, is the chief.

I am surprised at first by the eagerness of the Tobique people to meet me. I made my approach to them in much the same way I did with the other communities, though I had more apprehensions because Tobique was new territory to me. I had read *Enough Is Enough*, and on the basis of that I had written a couple of letters: one to the women, one to the chief. I then received phone calls from several of the women enquiring as to when I would be there and assuring me of their desire to meet with me, yet another writer. Still, the welcome surprises me. It comes like a gift that you are not expecting. People often ask how I feel when I approach strangers and a strange community, and I say, invariably, "self-conscious and apprehensive." And then they ask how I am received and I say, "with hospitality, patience, and kindness." On this Monday morning, the friendliness of the welcome continues. Before I know it, I am heading back outdoors to Perley's car for a quick tour of the reserve.

Karen Perley takes me on a tour around all the curving, snaking junctions of the reserve. We go up and down roads, through bush, across bridges, over hills, into laneways, around corners, until I am totally confused as to where exactly we are. We pass houses built in rugged clearings in the bush, and the grounds by the river where the people have, for the past three summers, defied the provincial game wardens by netting salmon. Along the river we see, skimming effortlessly above the tops of the trees, one of the five eagles Karen says now reside here. We drive around a corner and inspect the sprawling alcohol and drug rehabilitation centre, just built and looking like a first-class resort. But it functions for the time being, explains Karen, with only two clients because "there was funding to build it but no funding for programing."

Housing, Karen tells me, is in short supply. That was the story in 1977-79 when the women held the protests that led to their book, and the situation became even more critical in the past two years after the return of two hundred women and children to the band rolls as a result of the C-31 legislation. All available buildings have people living in them. We pass old houses, new houses, a gas station that has been transformed with tidy yellow curtains in its windows into someone's living quarters. While the rest of the population of North America ages and declines, the native population grows and gets younger. "We're fucking like rabbits," one fellow in the band office will say to me later. Twenty-nine per cent of the Tobique band members are under the age of fifteen.

On our way back to the village Karen Perley explains that part of the economy of the reserve are the small businesses that people run out of their homes: a dozen small stores, restaurants, variety outlets, craft shops, ice cream parlours, video stores. It is worth remembering that Tobique is not only an Indian reserve, it is in the Maritimes. But unemployment at Tobique, Chief

David Perley will tell me later, is 80 to 85 per cent as opposed to the New Brunswick average of 30 per cent. The chief has approached all the provincial government employers in the area: hospitals, the Ministry of Education, the Department of Highways, and the Rotary Club in Perth-Andover, to try to push more of his people into the employment market. The response over and over has been: "Unemployment is high for everybody, everybody needs jobs." "So they give what jobs there are," he says, "to their own people first." The Tobique people are left with what they can get on the reserve, working for the band, or in the traditional seasonal work of the area: fiddleheading in the spring, blueberry raking in summer, potato and apple harvesting in the fall, and cutting hardwood in the winter. Otherwise they are required to travel, as they always have, to find work. They go to Fredericton or St. John or Moncton or other parts of New Brunswick. Or they go across the line, to the factories and construction sites of Maine, Massachusetts, and Connecticut.

Often, on an Indian reserve, the chief is the most difficult person to see. He is too busy. Though Indian bands have elected councils as well as chiefs, and though they have civil service bureaucracies of varying sizes like any government, unlike other governments, save perhaps a charismatic dictatorship, everything leads to and stops at one person: the chief. No matter how much a chief may wish to delegate or how well organized he has been in constructing appropriate channels for everything to flow through, nobody feels really satisfied on any matter until they have dealt with him. This is the case whether it is a citizen with the smallest complaint about a malfunctioning sewage system or late welfare cheque, or whether it is a meeting in Ottawa at the Department of Indian Affairs. The chief has to deal with it personally. Chiefs, as a result, are in constant motion, pulled in every direction, their time and energy constantly in demand. They are consistently over-booked. Politics, you soon realize, is the real industry on all Indian reserves, and the self-generating momentum of politics and administration on even the tiniest, most insignificant reserve turns the position of chief into a more than full-time job. The demand for personal, hands-on attention on every matter, and the calls for meetings and conferences and confabs at every level of region and nation are so insistent that the chief can find himself travelling with a schedule that would rival that of the head of a European state.

For this reason, I am in a state of total surprise when I get to meet Chief David Perley on my first day at Tobique. It is past noon and I have just finished a lunch of thick homemade vegetable and beef soup at the Eagle's Nest restaurant, when Perley, Tobique's chief since 1983, walks in and says he has an hour on his hands; do I want to talk?

Perley is a slight man with clear eyes behind the sort of plastic-framed glasses an accountant might wear. He has quick movements, a pent-up energy, and is almost fidgety. His greying hair is cut modishly short. He is articulate, and could pass as someone from a civil service or academic background. It turns out he has both. He has a degree in sociology from Carleton University, and in 1979 and 1980 he worked as a policy analyst for the Department of Indian Affairs in Ottawa. Part of his job was to be one of two Indian members of a national social assistance review committee. What he heard during his tenure there disturbed him: "Senior management people were essentially saying through the review that it was cheaper to keep us on welfare." And even though talks were moving in the direction of self-government, the focus of the department seemed to Perley "still to be how do we [government] maintain some control of what Indian communities do. That was disappointing for me. I didn't want to be identified with any initiative that controlled Indian people."

Perley left the security of the civil service, and with it what he felt was a mistaken notion that you can help your people through the system. He decided to go back to school, did his MA in sociology at the University of New Brunswick, and started a PhD on the subject of race relations and education. He got halfway through that when his own community, Tobique, prevailed on him to become involved in local politics. For a number of years

Tobique had been the fiefdom of a rather autocratic chief accused (depending on who you talk to) of lining his own pockets and paying his friends. Perley took a look and decided to get involved. He was elected chief in 1983 and again in 1985 and 1987. He heads a twelve-person band council.

In the Eagle's Nest restaurant, little children zoom in and out among the tables, playing tag. The chief's sister, Faith, who owns the restaurant, stands behind the counter with a proprietary air, her arms folded. "The Price Is Right" is on TV, video games whir and beep in the background. David Perley sits under a broad white banner tacked to the wall "Wolastokwik Negoot-Gook, Maliseet Nation at Tobique," and absently stirs his coffee. Above the cash register is one of his old re-election posters. He talks about the hectic job of being chief, the incessant demands, the constant travel. The next morning he will leave for Fredericton to attend a three-day national conference on child welfare. The Department of Indian Affairs has recently consolidated its operations, closing its Fredericton office and placing all operations for the thirty-one Atlantic-area reserves in an office in Amherst, Nova Scotia. For Perley this now means a six-hour drive to get to the meetings he has to attend for every little negotiation with the department. Frequently he flies to Ottawa to plead his case to the national ministry. "You have a choice," he says with a wry smile. "You can stay here and keep in touch with the people, or you can travel all the time to get funds."

Perley and his council administer an $8.5 million annual budget. His current frustration with the government is over the building of houses and the provision of services – education, health, social welfare – to two hundred new band members either reinstated because of Bill C-31, or newly in Tobique because of the return of band members from non-reserve locations. Tobique, he says, had the highest number of women and children applying to return under Bill C-31, 363 people by 1988, many of their applications are still to be processed. The band council got funding to build thirty-one new homes, but the funding was for materials only, not labour. What ensued was the kind of bureaucratic runaround with which only Indians would have any patience. Other conventional financing sources, like banks, wouldn't lend the band money to pay for labour when they found out it was for C-31 housing. "That's a special federal government undertaking," they told them. The band went back to the federal bureaucrats who told them to build fewer houses than budgeted and use the money saved to pay for labour. They did that for two years in a row and as a result ended up with ten fewer houses than they had forecast needing, and that they in fact needed. Reimbursement for those houses was promised for October 31, 1988. That date came and went, but there was no cheque. On my tour of the reserve, I passed eight poured concrete foundations for new houses whose construction was halted in mid-stride when the special Indian Affairs grant ran out.

Life in the administration of an Indian band seems to be one long constant litany of squabbles and frustrations: irresistible forces meeting immovable objects. The Indian bands want and need; the government decides and gives. The bands want more; the government gives less. The interchange, the push and pull goes on daily and the uncertainty, the inability to forecast or plan or take anything for granted, becomes a fact of life. Because the added population put pressures on all facets of Tobique's budget, they ended the 1987 year with a deficit of $700,000 or about 7 per cent of their budget. This made the government unhappy, and it responded by withholding cash-flow moneys from the band until they could come up with a financial management plan. "The people controlling the purse strings hold all the power," Perley says bitterly. "They can delay cash flows, they can refuse to transfer funds. Once the bureaucratic system is in place the bureaucrats maintain that system. The minister from time to time makes nice statements about the Indian nations running their own affairs, but when you get right down to it there is all kinds of bureaucratic resistance. The government should support the First Nations in fighting the bureaucrats."

Perley continues with his complaints about the games bureaucrats like to play, and his distaste for civil servants is palpable. "The New Brunswick chiefs all rejected the current master contribution arrangement, the government's contract for money for the current year. It gave us no room to move and forced us to return to the government for every item. But it was the end of March, the end of the fiscal year. Everybody was strapped for money. The government guys said, "Fine, we'll continue talking about it until the end of April." Some of the smaller bands were so strapped for funds they couldn't wait that long. They signed the agreement against their better judgement. We're fighting a very powerful organization and we're in a very weak position in the negotiating process; a weak position because they control the funds."

Perley's solution is for Indian bands to become economically self-sufficient. "If we were more independent in terms of our own finances," he says, "we could tell them to go to hell."

The problem is they are not economically independent. They are, in fact, so dependent that 85 per cent of the band is unemployed and social assistance is the biggest item in their $8.5 million budget. Also, in a frustrating Catch 22, virtually the only source of investment financing for an Indian band is, you guessed it, the federal government. Banks seem loath to lend to Indian bands, and Indian bands on their own are not considered to be corporate entities with borrowing powers. The two most commonly used sources of economic development money from the federal government are the economic development budget of the Department of Indian Affairs, and a program under the Department of Regional Economic Expansion called the Native Economic Development Program. This program had $345 million, but its mandate was for only three years, which ended in the spring of 1989. The economic development initiative through Indian Affairs is a paltry $1.4 million, just 2 per cent of its spending in the Atlantic region. This places economic development at the bottom of the department's list of priorities, after social development, education, and housing.

Perley's dream is to initiate community or band-owned enterprises through a community development corporation. Tourist
facilities, a store and recreational complex, a bingo parlour are
discussed. But the two most original notions are an aquaculture
business that would hatch and raise 200,000 salmon fry for sale
to stock New Brunswick rivers, and a hydroponic gardening
enterprise that would deliver ten thousand kilograms of fresh
vegetables a week to the grocery market of western New
Brunswick. Each of these enterprises would create employment
and, in the dream, create profits that that would spawn future
enterprises and pay for band services that would help make the
band independent. "I guess it's the socialist model," says Perley.

At Tobique, two people in the band office are in charge of
further development of these economic strategies. One is a husky
thirty-year-old named David Paul. In another society he might
be a candidate in the management stream of the Bank of Commerce, just awarded his first branch. But then he would be
discouraged from wearing his hair tied back in a long, glossy
pony-tail. The other economic man is an ex-hippy, ex-radical
who travelled all over the country in his self-admitted drinking,
dope-smoking, demonstration-attending days. Gerald Bear is
the band's finance officer. With his long shaggy hair and
moustache, he looks a bit like an Indian Frank Zappa. Now,
however, instead of placard waving, he sits surrounded by his
IBM computer equipment on which he is trying to develop a
database and a financial records system that he would like to sell
to other comparably-sized Indian bands to aid them in handling
their financial recording and transactions. "Integrated Band
Administrative Support System," he calls his program.

On the day I see him, David Paul is interested in a scheme that
has been tried in some Third World locations, most recently in
Bangladesh and Latin America. It is called a "micro enterprises
loan program," and what it has been in the Third World situations is a bank loan guaranteed by a charitable foundation. The
loan is made jointly to a number of small entrepreneurs who in
turn take responsibility for one another keeping payments up

and on time. If one defaults, the others have to make up for it, so there is considerable peer pressure exercised. The scheme, explains Paul, was introduced in Canada through the Toronto-Dominion Bank to Indian reserves in southern Ontario and has worked for a number of years with no instances of default. The Maliseet of Tobique are in the process of negotiating with he Toronto-Dominion Bank in Fredericton for a $15,000 loan. The band would guarantee the loan and redistribute or re-lend the money to twelve small enterprises on the reserve: an auto mechanic, a furniture builder, a lawn-care service, gift shops, and crafts makers. It's a small but first-step remedy, believes Paul, for the frustrations of depending on government economic development money.

Gerald Bear offers to explain the status of the aquaculture and the hydroponic gardening projects, and does so with the ritual preamble about the frustrations of working with government. "As far as the government is concerned," he complains, "the price tag doesn't come along with the increased responsibility. We have the administrative capacity to undertake some business ventures but not the resources." He then launches into the tale of their adventures in getting their aquaculture project to the state it's in now.

The Maliseet have fished the rivers of New Brunswick for thousands of years. But recently, a combination of polluted waters and the heavy demands of sport fishing have taken their toll on the salmon. As a symbolic protest, the Indians set up a fishing camp each summer on the Tobique River just north of the village and, using nets, catch salmon which they then distribute to band members. However, netting salmon is against provincial game laws and the Maliseet have been watched warily from the other side of the river by provincial wardens. Although shots were fired during one highly publicized outburst, no arrests have been made. It is rather like two fighting cocks ruffling their feathers, or a Mexican stand-off, each side aware of staking territory.

Having made their point about what they believe to be their fishing rights, the Maliseet investigated how they might replenish rather than take from the dwindling salmon stocks. They came up with the aquaculture idea. The initial investment would be $2.5 million, says Bear, and seven jobs would be created. But down the line tourism, and even a salmon cannery, might result from the project.

To get the $2.5 million they had to approach the Department of Indian Affairs. Indian Affairs commissioned a feasibility study "which told them," says Bear, "all that we had told them in the first place. Lawyers and consultants," he complains, "are the only ones who make any money around here." The band then formed a company and applied for their funding (financing is always called "funding" in the Indian business), which required them to answer 150 questions on a government form. Eight months passed. The minister of Indian Affairs approved the project but then another three months passed before the signed agreement arrived at the band office.

The band then called tenders for the equipment and buildings to set up their salmon hatching operation but, explains Bear, "the tenders were way out of whack with the consultant's predictions. So we missed two deadlines and the project had to be delayed a year and had to be rescheduled to open in the spring of 1989 instead of 1988."

And so it goes. Everything is somehow damned. It isn't even Burns's "best laid schemes o' mice and men," it is more a cloud of dull throbbing continual impossibility. It's hard to maintain enthusiasm even for the good schemes when they are continually opposed and thwarted. The chief says that the government feels it is cheaper to keep people on welfare than to fool around with economic development. It is also a lot easier.

The schemes that work best are, ironically, those that grow from the roots of the people's desperate hopelessness. The real economic gold mine at Tobique, as on many other Indian reserves across the country, is bingo. People spend the little money they have whiling away the time with the vague hope of hitting a lucky jackpot. At Tobique, bingo is played almost every night of the week, with people coming from as far away as Grand Falls, New Brunswick, and Presque Isle in Maine. Various organizations sponsor these bingos, including the band itself, which last year made $210,000 from the games. The money was turned around to support six full-time and fifteen part-time jobs, and to finance a number of community recreation projects. But the fuel that feeds it is hopelessness.

"On Friday you get paid," explains Gerald Bear. "You go to the liquor store or you try to find some drugs. The kids pick up their welfare, buy a few joints, and listen to music. The women head off to bingo." When a health study was done of the Tobique band, it was calculated that 84 per cent of health problems in the community were related to the over-use of drugs or alcohol, and 45 per cent had some connection to inadequate housing. "Because of paternalism and the conditioning of a hundred years," Bear continues, "it's hard to persuade people here to be independent."

"Welfare has ruined many a good man," says Victor Bear. I have gone for a drive on a bright, sunny morning with Victor Bear in his new red GMC Wrangler half-ton truck. We drive off the reserve and west out of Perth-Andover, then cross the U.S. border at the customs stop at Aroostook, where Victor seems to know and have an opinion about everybody in both offices, American and Canadian. Passing through the hilly Maine countryside, he shows me where the air force bases used to be, and fields where he picked potatoes as a child and where his twelve-year-old son Victor Jr. now picks in the summers.

Back at Tobique we pull up to the three-year-old blue frame bungalow he shares with his wife, Mary, who is the community health worker. He describes his house as one of the few privately owned homes on the reserve. It is up the hill from the village, surrounded by forest, and near to the homes of his brother and his mother.

192

Victor is highly sceptical of self-government and the band's economic ventures. "They haven't been trained to use the power or to make the money last," he says. "It'll be like giving a bag of candy to some kids and saying, 'Make this candy last a year.' What will happen when they run out of money after nine months?" At one point we talk about how Indian stores don't seem to work, and Victor says: "Indians won't buy from Indians. They won't do business with Indians." This is one of the reasons for his scepticism about band-owned enterprises. "You watch," he says, "as soon as those businesses turn a profit, will it go back to the community? No. Each board member will then start taking a fee every time he sits down to a meeting. It'll be the same old story."

There is, in Victor Bear, a streak of independence that makes him feel this way. It makes him live off, away from the village, surrounded by his family. At one point, it made him pull his children from the reserve school and send them down to Perth to the public school. When he was fourteen, Victor Bear left home and headed south. He worked the potato fields for a summer and fall, and then ended up Lowell, Massachusetts, working in a dry-cleaning plant. He made $42 a week. With that, he rented a room with a hotplate for $12, spent $10 on food and incidentals, and saved $20. He later worked in a mattress factory, took a carpentry course, and eventually became a journeyman carpenter. He worked on construction projects, building houses on and off Indian reservations all over New England.

When he was twenty-one he returned to Tobique. He was always industrious; he ran a contracting business and drove a school bus. At forty-four, though, he has been diagnosed as having angina, and now he waits to be scheduled in a Halifax hospital for coronary by-pass surgery. He spends a lot of time waiting around his house, cooking meals, or going for long drives in his truck. He doesn't look well. He tires quickly and his face is pallid. Even with the heart problem, though, when his doctor insisted he had to drop heavy work he bought two lawn-mowers: a riding mower and a push model, and he and his twelve-year-old son set out to get lawn-cutting contracts both on the reserve and in the town of Perth. When the lawn-cutting season ended, he repaired to his work-room behind the house and kept himself busy, as much as his strength and stamina would allow, making potato baskets, a traditional Maliseet handicraft made from strips of ash and now sold as souvenirs to tourists. When he is hard at it, he says, he can make a hundred baskets a week; they sell for ten dollars apiece in souvenir and craft shops as far afield as Bangor, Maine. And all the while, as he awaits his heart surgery, he fantasizes about the next business his family might get into.

"The problem with welfare," Victor complains, "is that with a job on the reserve you're really no better off than if you're on welfare. It's interchangeable. If your brother or cousin is the chief, then you get a job. When a new gang comes in you are out of a job, so you go on welfare. It changes back and forth. But it's all public money, one way or the other." This brings him to politics. On a reserve, every job is a political appointment and paid out of the public purse. Political connections land the jobs, patronage is the rule. Graft is an ever-present threat. Welfare, another form of public largess, helps you survive when you can't get the job. It's a sour pool and no one is ever happy. The system is rife with inefficiency and corruption, but what does it matter? What goes around, comes around.

Victor complains about the stupidities he encountered as a house construction contractor. He claims he could build foundations for half what the band pays outside (white) contractors. His methods would be more labour-intensive, he argues, so more money would stay in the community and be spread around among local labourers. His comments are a criticism of inefficiency and short sightedness and greed and politics deciding everything, even at the expense of efficiency, fairness, and economy. However, if Victor has been badly treated by the political system, he also knows how to make it work to his advantage. When he found out about his health problems he offered to quit his bus-driving job, but first he held up the band for half a year's salary.

The decorative sign that greets you at the entrance to Tobique tells you that the reserve was formed in 1801. When I want to really start looking for the history of the community, though, I am directed to a back corner of the basement of the band office, to a cubby-hole office occupied by Wayne Nicholas. I've been advised that Nicholas knows everything there is to know about the subject. If he doesn't have the information in his head, it must be somewhere in the twelve-inch-deep jumble of papers, documents, reports, books, and studies that clutter his desk. He greets me, and lights a Player's Plain, adding to the haze of blue smoke that seems permanently installed in his office. He asks me to sit down.

Wayne Nicholas seems well-suited for his role; he looks like the kind of fellow who might spend all his time in this cluttered room, surrounded by his smoke and his documents. He has a small body and a long face topped by an enormous mop of greying hair. He is oddly gentle, soft-spoken. But when he gets on his favourite topic, land claims, his speech becomes insistent, almost tough. In 1801, he says, the people of Tobique possessed land on both sides of the river that covered twenty thousand acres, roughly three times the size of the present reserve. When Europeans arrived in the upper reaches of New Brunswick, squatters settled on the Indian land on the east side of the river across from the present reserve. There ensued a sporadic series of disputes over trespass that led to attempts by the colonial government, in 1844 and again in 1854, to dispose of the land in favour, Nicholas says, of the settlers. In 1867, with the British North America Act, the federal government inherited the matter and in 1892 achieved what they believed to be the surrender of the Tobique land. Some land was then sold to the squatters, some became Crown land, and some – two thousand acres to the south – became the site or the town of Perth.

Everyone was happy except, of course, the Maliseet. For them, the land loss was a grievance that smouldered over generations. In 1972, when such matters were coming back to attention all across North America, the Tobique people looked into their grievance, found what they believed to be a hitch in the legal process of the 1892 surrender, and resurrected it as a claim. They demanded the return of a portion of land and $98 million. Ten years later, in 1982, the minister of Indian Affairs "validated" the claim, meaning that the government agreed that the issue deserved investigation. This led the Maliseet to believe they would be compensated in some way for the injuries of history. In 1985 Wayne Nicholas came on the band office staff and took over the negotiations.

The story is like a broken record. Land is taken; people are moved around; a new society is built. A new legal system is incorporated; then the new legal system is appealed to, and yellowed, weathered, ancient parchments are hauled out in an attempt to prove or disprove the question of wrongs perpetuated by and to ancestors. The media waits in the wings with cameras whirring. The government wants it to seem that justice has at least been nodded to. Lawyers and negotiators are hired by all sides and the paper starts to move back and forth.

Nicholas takes me earnestly through the procedures of the Tobique band's thus far futile quest. The band engaged a lawyer from Fredericton. They spent $800,000 on lawyers' fees, consultant's fees, land appraisers, geologists, trips to Ottawa, and expenses, and collected six boxes of papers supporting their claim. In Ottawa, the Department of Indian Affairs brought over a negotiator from the Department of Justice and assigned him to the task. The Indians have a cagey understanding of how the process works and of everyone's roles. Nicholas describes the government negotiator's job as "trying to get a settlement that avoided giving away the store."

The Tobique representatives had thirty-three meetings with the Ottawa representatives between 1985 and 1988. The government "funded the claim" on a yearly basis, which is to say, they paid the expenses to keep the process going. The Tobique Maliseet revised their claim downwards from $98 million, a figure even Wayne Nicholas acknowledges as "outrageous," to $15 million, and told the government they would negotiate separately for the territory on which was located the village of Perth. The government, however, felt otherwise. After examining the evidence from their standpoint, they decided there was a "technical breach" that got them off the hook. They announced that there was "no claim" and, supported by the signatures of the minister of Indian Affairs at the time, William McKnight, and the minister of state for Indian Affairs, Bernard Valcourt (who by coincidence happened to be the MP representing Perth Andover and Tobique) they curtailed negotiations in March of 1988.

The decision was a blow, but the Maliseet did not lose heart. It may be said that they expected something like that to happen and were mentally prepared for it. In fact, it is as if the move-counter-move is a game that both sides understand and fully expect to play. Though the Maliseet feel wronged in history and would like to increase their land-holdings and cash equity for the benefit of their community and their people, there is also an unmistakable sense that the game is worth playing for its own sake. I know this is not how any of us have been taught to look at things: one seeks to solve problems, to look for just solutions, to be efficient and deal with matters economically. But the game of Indian land negotiations rarely seems to work like that. If it never solves anything, an enormous economy and people's whole careers can still be built around its being played. This is not to accuse anyone on either side of any particular cynicism, but just to acknowledge a profound sense that, in many cases, a state of negotiation is how things may well always be. The final goals move into a sort of abstraction, the government pays the expenses, and the moves and countermoves go on and on.

Immediately upon the government's curtailing of negotiations, Wayne Nicholas had three possible countermoves at the ready. He endeavoured to explain them to me and I had the feeling that the negotiators on the government side would be disappointed should he not hit them fairly quickly with one of them. They could spend, he says, an additional $250,000 and take the matter to court. They could wait for a political change; at the time we spoke a federal election was three weeks away, and Nicholas could hope that a Liberal government might be elected, and be better disposed to settling with the Maliseet, or at least starting the negotiations all over again. Or they could "exercise jurisdiction over the land in title." What does that mean? Nicholas smiles. The Maliseet can occupy the land, he says. Interrupt logging operations on it, blockade roads, erect a building, carry out demonstrations and protests, cause problems. "It would become very contentious locally," he promises.

Such tactics would not be new to the Maliseet. In 1982 their confrontation with provincial game wardens over fishing rights in the Tobique River escalated to the point of gunfire. In 1987 a number of Maliseet occupied disputed land at a place where a white person was busy building a house. They set up a road block around which the poor fellow had to try to move his materials. They are good at using the media at such events. "How does the government respond to such acts?" I ask. "They call us immediately," explains Nicholas, "and ask for a meeting."

A day later I encounter Wayne Nicholas hurrying through the hallway of the band office. He is buoyant and excited. "I've just discovered something new," he says, "a litigation fund the federal government has that we didn't know about. It could pay for our court challenge." He rushes into an office to call the chief who is in Fredericton. He hopes the two of them can fly to Montreal to meet with well-known lawyer James O'Reilly, who has represented the James Bay Cree and the Lubicon Cree, to see if he will take their fight to court.

Tobique claims to be the first reserve in New Brunswick to look seriously and comprehensively at self-government. But their idea of self-government is not, Chief David Perley told me, self-government as the federal government might see it. "The government likes to perpetuate the municipal model and try to explain to the First Nations, thereby reassuring both themselves and the Canadian public that in the end it will be like having three hundred more municipalities, three hundred more town councils with dog by-laws and water, sewage, and fire department responsibilities." That is not the way the Indians see it, and David Perley is one of those whose persistence and developing vision is helping to formulate it otherwise.

Whether the vision of people like him will ultimately prevail, of course, yet remains to be seen. But he is adamant and insistent in presenting it. He, like a growing number of Indian leaders, is very careful that the choice of his words themselves move the speaker and the hearer into another realm of concepts. He uses the term "Indian band" rarely, usually it is the term "First Nation" as if, should you hear the terminology often enough, it will stick. A concept larger than a "village-sized group of people on welfare" will settle into the collective consciousness; the image will be rather that of proud nations, with statesmen leading them and with political and cultural traditions intact, ready to pitch for themselves in the world. "Local control in the eyes of the Department of Indian Affairs," says Perley, "means they give us the funds and they control the guidelines. Control for us means we develop policy, control legislation, and implement the programs. We would like to be a third level of government, not a municipality."

This system, Perley acknowledges, is contrary to the government's agenda in a number of ways, but it would be the best of all possible worlds for the Indians. The Canadian taxpayer, for instance, would still pay the bill. "I don't believe in taxation," says Perley, meaning he doesn't believe in taxing Indian people to pay for their own affairs. The money they get and hope to get in the future he prefers to think of as "one of the benefits that emerged from the relationship between the First Nations and the federal government, and it should continue." Neither does Perley want to have anything to do with the government of the province of New Brunswick. Like most other native leaders, he says, "I don't approve of the transfer of First Nations to provincial jurisdiction. I do approve of shared services, schools, hospitals, but the services should respond to our needs."

Perley explains the Indians' antipathy to provincial authorities in several ways. Part has to do with history, part with self-
image, and part just simply with the preference for dealing with a
certain type of bureaucracy, a certain type of bureaucrat, and a
certain type of politician. "The historical relationship," says
Perley, "is between the First Nations and the federal government. The BNA Act supported this. It's bad enough to have to
deal with one government, let alone two. In the lower levels of
government there seems to be more resistance, more, dare I say
it, racism. The provincial governments tend to be anti-aborigi-
nal rights, they want us to become municipalities, which is
something we will never do."

In terms of their self-image, Indian people use the language
more and more of their societies being peers with the societies of
the United States and Canada. An Indian reserve, therefore,
should be seen as akin to Luxembourg in the European community; tiny but every bit an equal to the other jurisdictions. The
Indians like to remind people that their ancestors signed treaties
with national governments. "We didn't," explains David Perley,
"sign treaties with provincial governments. We signed treaties
with a nation that decided to become a nation within our nation.
They have the power because they have more people and more
wealth. Now they say, 'My God, we have to go from reserve to
reserve to reserve,' well, who made the reserves?"

This line of thinking is what makes the constitutional entrenchment of aboriginal rights so important to Indian people. A
place in the Constitution would acknowledge the place that they
see for themselves in the North American community. When
they talk about aboriginal rights they are not talking about
human rights or Charter rights. They are talking about the rights
of nationals. They are descendants of people who once had a
homeland. Now with the meagre exception of patches of ground
that are the reserves, they feel they are deprived of homelands
much as the Palestinians, for example, feel deprived of homelands. Though a Maple Leaf flag flaps away here and there, in

front of someone's house or beside a store, Maliseet after Maliseet told me they do not think of themselves as Canadians. "We are North American citizens," one man at Tobique told me. The creation of the nation states of the United States and Canada is irrelevant to them. The constitutional entrenchment of aboriginal rights would be a further acknowledgement of that, a latter-day treaty, if you like.

But Perley, for one, doesn't believe the provinces of Canada will allow that entrenchment to happen, at least not in a form that would be satisfactory to the First Nations. Since the Indians are not likely to succeed in that venue, Perley believes they may end up having to go through other routes. He mentions "the court of public opinion," or appeals to international bodies such as the United Nations or the World Court. Indian people, he emphasizes, "do not want to be subordinate to the federal government."

Chief Perley's man in charge of developing the self-government proposal is a jovial sixty-five-year-old grandfatherly man named Ray Trembley. A Second World War veteran, former chief, and twenty-year employee of the Department of Indian Affairs, Trembley understands both sides. He jokes that after his retirement from the department in 1983 people told him his attitude changed. "I told them that my attitude hadn't changed, it's just that now I was free to let it out."

Trembley took on the enormous task of formulating a self-government strategy for Tobique with all the zest of a retired man given a challenge he enjoys. "The term self-government was used and nobody knew what it meant, and they don't yet. Everybody has a different view on it." He doesn't exclude the federal government from this confusion. "The people the government hired to work with us didn't know what the hell they were doing. Guidelines hadn't been written yet when we all started, so we go along; everybody's learning something."

The government, too, was enjoying the process almost as if it had a new toy. It announced in 1987 that $4 million a year would be available until 1990, so everyone better set to work. Some forty bands in Canada, including Tobique, entered the development stage of self-government.

At Tobique, Trembley asked Karen Perley, the chief's sister-in-law, to work with him, and they set out on two strategies: to discover models of government that would be appropriate for a band like Tobique, and to carry the people through the education process that would help them both understand what was going on and have some input. A delegation from Tobique paid a visit to the Navajo Indians of Arizona and New Mexico. "They have their own justice system and everything," explained Trembley. "They were a big help to us." They also visited the Sechelt people of southern British Columbia, who had just been granted a local governing system through a special act of Parliament.

Trembley and Karen Perley organized six workshops at Tobique with local people and, over the course of two years, wrote three proposals, which they submitted to the federal government. Their submissions stated that they wanted to develop a constitution for themselves and sought authority over citizenship in their band; land, water, and air; forestry; minerals, oil and gas; migratory birds and wildlife; fisheries and conservation; the environment; economic development; education; social development; health and welfare; marriages; cultural development; communications; justice; law enforcement; taxation; and financial resources. They stated that they wanted control of these matters on their land and for their people, and the right to develop policy and pass legislation in these areas.

The proposals then began to move back and forth. The legal people in the government responded with a discussion paper. The Tobique people didn't like what the discussion paper said and responded with their own discussion paper. Response at the community workshops was mixed, says Trembley. "The first community workshop got a good turnout, but like everything else, you've got two sides." Local politics were never far from the scene, and those opposed to the present administration on the reserve tended likewise to oppose the self-government notion. At the same time there was a sense of fatalism. "Indian people," explains Trembley, "know that when the government has some kind of program, it's going to happen eventually. They say it doesn't matter if we like it or not, it's going to happen so let's get prepared for it."

Ray Trembley, however, is determined that things go ahead, if only to prove that they can. People, in his view, must do something for themselves as he did when he joined Alcoholics Anonymous in 1958 and quit drinking. "All those years," he says, "we're sitting here feeling sorry for ourselves but not doing anything. A lot of things that happened to us Indian people is our own damn fault because we let it happen. The easy way out is to blame somebody else." Trembley seems determined that that won't happen this time.

Sandra Lovelace is an Indian again. She is also a carpenter, which is not a bad thing to be in a community that claims a chronic housing shortage. The woman whose story got Canada reprimanded by the United Nations is now in her late thirties. She drives back and forth every day across the border to the University of Maine, Presque Isle, where she continues to take courses toward her papers as a carpenter. The rest of the time she lives in Tobique with her son, who has also been given status as a treaty Indian, and with her mother, Cora Hofmann, who like many others came back to Tobique after years in the northeastern United States.

There was a grand celebration and dinner dance at Tobique in 1985 in celebration of the passage of Bill C-31. But though the law concerning women's status has been changed, Lovelace says there are still a lot of problems and a long way to go before everything is as it might be. Caroline Ennis, who looks after such things at Tobique, claims that perhaps as many as five hundred women and children will ultimately apply to return to Tobique. But the infrastructure to receive and look after them once they return is inadequate. For instance at a time when the C-31 special housing fund set up by the government had reached the end of its life, 160 names were still on the housing waiting list at Tobique, with no notion of how they would ever be satisfied. And the strains additional numbers place on education, health, and social welfare budgets and resources continue to be exhausting.

Bill C-31 has acknowledged the status of Indian women, but at Tobique at least, nothing much has happened beyond that to work against the prejudice women feel, and to give women a larger say in the community's affairs. The women who occupied the band office, appealed to the United Nations, marched to Ottawa, and wrote a book are still well organized, and that has a political impact. Caroline Ennis says that the women never let the band council get away with any policy "that goes against women." But there are still no women on the band council. Though several have run for election, none has yet been successful. "It's a male-dominated place," says Sandra Lovelace. "Men run the reserve and make the rules." "The man," adds Cora Hofmann, "is dominant and tells his wife how to vote. That's why no women ever get elected."

In Maliseet tradition, the women of the tribe selected the chief. But, according to Caroline Ennis, all that changed with the colonization of North America and the institution of the Indian Act. "I believe that treatment towards women emanates from the Indian Act," she says. "Even though you don't consciously go around saying Indian women aren't worth very much, as long as there was a law written someplace that said 'You don't quite deserve the same respect as even a male Indian,' I think the band councils and Indian men felt they could do whatever they wanted with Indian women. And they could get away with it because if the federal government didn't respect Indian women, why should they? Every society picks on its weakest members, and Indian women are always at the bottom."

Cora Hofmann says that it was the coming of Christianity that changed the male-female relationships in Maliseet communities. The men who were forced to knuckle under in a colonial system became frustrated and started to take out their frustrations on the women and on their families. "Men," she speculates, "treat women badly to get back at how they were treated, and to make them feel superior."

What the women all agree on is that they will have to continue fighting, bit by bit, for what they believe to be their rights. Tobique now hires women on its house-building carpentry crews, but only after Sandra Lovelace approached then federal Employment Minister Flora Macdonald, who in turn insisted on sex based-quotas on federally funded projects. The women are still sceptical of the intentions of the native political organizations, both at the provincial and the national levels; they habitually call them "the men's organizations." Neither the national Assembly of First Nations nor the Union of New Brunswick Indians helped them, they feel, in their struggles toward Bill C-31. The women believe that, at times, these groups in fact worked actively against them. "Women are still second-class citizens," says Caroline Ennis. "The men fear that women, if given a chance, will take over their positions. And the government supports that."

10   Opinions: Georges Erasmus
April 1989

Indians are in the news the day I arrive in Ottawa to meet with Georges Erasmus, the national chief of the Assembly of First Nations. They are so much in the news that my meeting and interview with the leader of the nation-wide body that represents most of Canada's status Indian people seems in jeopardy. When I go for my appointment, he is not in his office but is busily running back and forth to a series of unscheduled, impromptu meetings with his colleagues, with members of Parliament's opposition parties, and, he hopes, with the minister of Indian Affairs. Such is the life of Georges Erasmus, scrambling to put out fires, or, says a member of the federal civil service, to light them.

The issue that commands Erasmus's attention is a hunger strike by a group of native students who are protesting plans the federal government has to put a cap on the money available to pay for native post-secondary education. The Indians claim it is a treaty right; the government claims it is getting too expensive. In 1988, 15,000 native Indian students took advantage of the right, at a cost to the government of $130 million. Ten years before, 3,500 students had cost $9 million. Another government at another time might have bragged about the numbers: "Look how well we are doing in providing advanced education to young native Canadians, preparing them to take their place as productive, educated members of society." The government probably doesn't need to be reminded, that 80 percent of native Indian people are recipients of welfare, while another disproportionately large group inhabit Canada's police stations, courtrooms, remand centres, jails, prisons, probation and parole lists. But in this case the government is resisting, and the native protest has caught on all across the country.

Georges Erasmus came to prominence as leader of the Dene Nation back in the days of the Mackenzie Valley Pipeline Inquiry. Young and articulate, he moved quickly through the ranks of native politics to become chief of the Assembly of First Nations – a group that evolved from the National Indian Brotherhood – in 1983.

I asked Erasmus about the many items on the Indian agenda these days.

Erasmus: The agenda of the First Nations has been left undone for so long. There are many examples of how our agenda continues to be put on the back burner, but I guess the most public one is the constitutional agenda. Here we had a five-year process with First Ministers in Canada, looking at amendments to the Constitution. But as soon as the obligation to consult came to an end two years ago, the prime minister of the day, Mulroney, ended the process.

Regardless of what one looks at – whether it's treaty obligations that in some cases are over a hundred years old, or land entitlement that should have been implemented – many issues are still outstanding. And to make things even worse, there is no process, really, to resolve those old, outstanding questions. From one end of the country to the other, you either have the case of a stalled land claim or else you have pre-Confederation treaties that do not deal with aboriginal title and the land question. Even if you take those issues to court and you win in court, even in the highest court of the land, you still have a federal government that is totally reluctant to deal with you on any of these issues.

Question: The problems at the constitutional conference in Ottawa in 1987 were with the provincial governments as well as the federal government, no?

Erasmus: Yes, but the majority of the responsibility is in the hands of the federal government, because the federal government could go a long way by itself. For instance, in the pre-Confederation treaty situation the federal government is totally reluctant to do anything at all. They don't want to open up that whole area of their responsibility. The approach they take is that it's a closed book, that all the rights of aboriginal people have been superseded by law and that they don't exist anymore. And even when those issues are brought up front and centre, and they are proven wrong by a court coming down on the side of First Nations, the government is still reluctant to act.

In the case of land claims, their policy has been regressive for years. It could have been improved, it could have resolved the question of aboriginal title, it could have resolved the question of self-government for native people decades ago. Instead, they've always had a process of pressuring native people into extinguishing their rights, into abdicating their rights. There's no way that this can be blamed on the provinces. With a minister of Indian Affairs on the side of native peoples, with a prime minister in cabinet who is prepared to move ahead in this area, things could have long ago been cleaned up to such an extent that all that would be left would be some areas where difficult provinces would be slowing things down.

Question: In your view, the constitutional entrenchment of rights is critical, is that correct?

Erasmus: I think it is still the centrepiece action, one that would propel native people out of a situation where so many of our agenda items are outstanding, unfulfilled, and virtually impossible to be implemented. We could deal in the Constitution with the fundamental relationship between First Nations, their governments, their land, and other governments in Canada. And on an equal footing. Any other way of dealing with these issues – whether through legislation or anything else – skirts the issue and does not deal with the primary relationship that can be dealt with through the Constitution.

Question: Do you get any sense that the constitutional matter is on the government's agenda now?

Erasmus: You get mixed signals from this government. If you look at their throne speech they mention that once Meech Lake is resolved the next three items to be dealt with are senate reform, aboriginal rights – including the recognition of aboriginal languages – and fisheries. And what they've done is squeeze in the aboriginal agenda between the senate and fisheries. It's the first sign we've seen from the government that at some point they will deal with this issue again.

But when you look at what they're doing in Meech Lake, you start to see that they're not very serious. They set up a process coming out of the Meech Lake accord that ensures that two First Ministers' meetings will happen every year, one on the economy and one on other issues, which will include fisheries and senate reform and other agenda items. Nowhere did they mention the aboriginal agenda. And the astounding thing was that this Meech Lake accord happened only thirty days after the last First Ministers' meeting on the aboriginal agenda. Here they were setting in place two constitutional meetings in perpetuity and nowhere did they mention that they would deal with the aboriginal agenda. It's obvious that this is an area they are extremely reluctant to deal with.

It is not considered an important item for any of the provinces. Even the most supportive province comes into this problem fairly reluctantly, and it's extremely unfortunate. The federal government should be taking a leadership role in this area, but it would rather deal with almost *anything* else. If you go further into the Meech Lake accord and start looking at some of the other issues involved – the dual character of French and English as founding nations, the distinct society of Quebec, the ways that provinces will be formed in the north, the formula changing from seven provinces to ten provinces, the ways in which provincial governments will be able to opt out of national programs and run their own programs – you start to see that the native people of the country are slipping, we're losing ground. After five years of native people talking to the provinces and the federal government about the important role they should have in this country, you still have First Ministers' meetings putting forth the concept that there are only two founding peoples in Canada, and one of them is not native people. After five years of talking about the distinctiveness of native people you still have a situation where the only distinctive society you have mentioned is the distinct society of Quebec. My Lord! One could have understood that had native people never talked to any of the premiers, had never been involved in a constitutional process that had been televised for the whole country to watch. It's incredibly disheartening.

You ask, do I see any possibility of the government putting constitutional recognition of aboriginal rights on the agenda. It seems to me the only possible way of this happening is if we force the government to deal with our people through amendments to Meech Lake. That has been our strategy. We have encouraged every dissenting voice, whether it has been Frank McKenna or Mrs. Carstairs in Manitoba or Premier Wells of Newfoundland. It seems to be the only way that we might get back on the agenda.

Question: Meech Lake must have really seemed like salt in the wounds coming right on the heels of the failure of the constitutional meeting.

Erasmus: Very much so, not only for native people but for most people in Canada. They are living in one of the wealthiest countries in the world and they continue to see native people on the margin. Many Canadians had hoped that governments would do the right thing during the constitutional talks. The issue was followed by the average Canadian. They tried to figure out what native people actually wanted, and could not figure out

210

why we did not get what we wanted. The polls at the time done by native organizations and other people to see if there was enough support for recognition of native self-government continued to show that over 75 per cent of the Canadian population were in favour of native people having self-government. As a political move it was not a loser. No politician in Canada would be turfed out by recognizing native self-government. They would have been doing what three-quarters of the country wanted them to do.

Question: What inspires you and First Nations people across the country to continue the political struggle when in so many instances you have not won? What inspires you to stay true to your cultural traditions over the long haul?

Erasmus: I'm convinced, and I suspect that most native people are convinced, that we're on the right side of history, whether you're talking about going to our original treaties and trying to get the original spirit and intent implemented, or whether you're talking about what we're doing about protection of the environment and the general questions we've been asking Canadians to look at for the last twenty years in relation to the mega-projects and so forth. I don't think there's been a major issue in this country over the last couple of decades during my political career that native people have been on the wrong side of.

I think we were on the right side of the free trade issue. I think we were on the right side of the proposed pipeline issue in the Mackenzie Valley. I think we were on the right side of the issue of tanking of oil out of the High Arctic, of twin-tracking of the railway. You name it: Lyell Island, clear-cut logging, low-level flights, the proposed military build-up, the nuclear subs. I think we've been on the right side of most battles in this country.

The primary thing we're trying to do is change the basic relationship we have with Canada. We have a situation now where we are virtually living with a dictator, given the relationship we have now with the federal government, with the minister of Indian Affairs. It's a hang-over from colonial days.

It's amazing that a situation can exist where someone can have that kind of power over your life and you have no ability to vote him in or turf him out. You can appoint people to the Department of Indian Affairs who have no inkling of native people and they will decide for you everything that affects your life. It is just incredible that this kind of relationship can still exist.

We are making efforts to change that kind of colonial tie so that native people have self-determination, self-government, and control over their lives. Native people will then be able to have the normal relationship other people of the world have with governmental decision-makers. The average native person will be able to vote in and vote out those who have the power, or have control over government decisions affecting our lives. We want aboriginal government. We want Canada to fulfill the treaty obligations defined in the Royal Proclamation and the treaties. We don't want policies coming down from a benevolent dictator in Ottawa. If we're not lucky we have a cruel master. That kind of colonial, manipulative relationship must end.

Question: It seems to me as I go across the country that what a lot of Canadians, both white and native, do not understand is how self-government or local government can be brought about. Can you identify the necessary steps?

Erasmus: The first thing we need is constitutional process. Also, a number of forums to address the treaty questions. We have numerous treaty situations in this country – some pre-Confederation treaties, some numbered treaties, and so forth. The fulfilling of the original spirit and intent of these treaties would resolve many problems. Implementation across the country would create situations where a land was clearly governed by native people, and the original governmental relationships that were established and recognized by treaty would be implemented. Enactment of policies from the Department of Indian Affairs should stop until native people agree to them.

In the post-secondary education question, we have a very simple way in which government can resolve this. We want them to go back to the old policy. We want them to be involved in a bilateral consultation with us which we will both define, and then we will both agree on changes – native people, the First Nations and government. Then they will change.

For a long time we have wanted the department to shrink in size. It is shrinking, but native people are not directing the way that takes place. In some places we're being forced to protest the way it is taking place. We want some control. It is obvious from things like the LRT Review [the Lands, Revenues and Trust Review] that they are setting up a situation where they're going to be opting out of all kinds of legal responsibilities that the federal government has had since the beginning of our relationship.

Nothing serious can happen until there is constitutional amendment. In that area, we've had a situation where the leadership that should be shown by the federal government has been missing. We have tried since the end of the constitutional talks to do constructive things. We have tried to sit down with government and to work out a number of concrete models that would make it clear to Canadians how the concepts of self-determination and self-government could actually take place. We have not been able to get the government to treat this seriously at all. Instead, they have their own ideas. A municipal model for self-government is what they are looking at, and that would derail the work that has been done by the First Nations across the country in the area of constitutional amendments. They look at other avenues besides constitutional amendment, and then they use the carrot-and-stick approach of providing funding to any First Nation that is prepared to look at the government's version or model.

The position we were taking during the First Ministers' meeting was that native people in this country continue to retain a certain degree of self-determination and self-governmental powers, that the First Nations did not relinquish all of the governmental powers that they had upon early European contact. Government is now using its wealth, its influence, and its administrative power to divide and conquer. They encourage our people to take moneys, to accept delegated authority and the legislative route rather than the approach of the Constitution. Unless they stop this, the frustration of our people will mount. This was made evident by the hunger strikers and the support they received across the country, and the general reaction of leaders, tribal organizations, and chiefs across the country. The government may not realize it, but the level of native people's frustration is getting so high that it doesn't take much to get that kind of reaction.

Question: In Winnipeg there were several hundred people prepared to go to jail on that one issue alone.

Erasmus: There were people who were demonstrating on this issue all across the country. There are people who are still demonstrating. There are people who are prepared to keep demonstrating because we see this as part of the whole. The government is determined to implement Eric Nielsen's report and his recommendations that, over time, obligations, responsibilities, and expenditures be reduced with no serious recognition of treaty obligations. We are starting to wake up to this. More and more our people are seeing this as an amazing threat. It's a threat to our treaties and it's a basic threat to our future. Everybody loses by this policy. The government may be very wise in penny-pinching right now but they are foolish in the long-term view. The best example is that if they are effective in spending less to educate fewer First Nations people, it will mean that fewer of our people will be able to be self-reliant and more of our people will be on social assistance. The government's long-term costs for native people in that area will be much higher than if they did everything possible now to invest in our ability to be formally educated and employable, to pay our own way.

Question: A charge I've encountered in local communities is that the department is more eager to pay for welfare than for economic development. Is that a charge that you would make as well?

Erasmus: Absolutely. If you look at the latest budget, there is an increase in projected expenditures of the Department of Indian Affairs, but a no increase in economic development programs. The level of expenditure – about $70 million a year – is minute. At that rate of expenditure we will never be able to get any kind of major turnaround among native people, we would be just tinkering at the corners. The population rise of our people is twice the Canadian population rate, and the high level of youth amongst our people – over 55 per cent of our people are under twenty-five years old – would not allow us to keep up. To see some significant turnaround we were encouraging a billion-dollar program over five years with expenditures nearing two hundred million a year.

Again, in times of deficit, and looking at how the public should deal with the Canadian debt, we are well aware that we are going to need several decades to get ourselves out from under. The argument we make is that we feel we can be of more assistance when native people are not 90 per cent unemployed. We feel that if the million native people in this country come off welfare, become formally educated, start businesses, become employed, become self-reliant, we will be in a situation where native people will be assisting with the deficit by not drawing on the public purse and by providing their own self-reliant economy.

Question: Many native women have had their difficulties with the government, but many are also critical of what they describe as the "men's organizations" in your politics. The charge is raised that native political organizations don't represent women very well, and didn't when Bill C-31 was under negotiation. How do you respond to that?

Erasmus: I think the reality is that there are less women involved in political life than men, whether you're talking about the general Canadian public or native people. We're seeing more involvement and more native women getting elected, so I presume that things will change over time. There's no question that there's as much male chauvinism amongst native people as there is among other people. No one can say native communities have been so liberated that there is no sexism.

As to the whole C-31 issue, I think it's a lot of nonsense to say that the interests of native women were not taken into consideration. I think we've been paying as native politicians for making a major decision in favor of a positive amendment to the Indian Act that recognizes that, in the past, the government was wrong to take away the rights of native women who were married to non-treaty or non-status people. We went through a very painful internal process to look at whether or not we could support this challenge and on what conditions we would support. It went against our principles at the time, because we were involved in a constitutional process, and we felt that the only way we should be moving forward was on the constitution. At the same time we had the Penner Report, we had the Munro Initiative on self-government, we had the legislative route in front of us.

But we said, because of the injustice that had happened to a huge part of our native community, we would support a change to the Indian Act. We worked with the native women who supported the change to the consternation of other native women's organizations that were supporting those chiefs that didn't support the amendment. In the end we were working very, very closely with them, and on the funding of C-31 we have been working very closely with the native women's organization. We've had a committee to make sure Indian Affairs budgets were increased so our communities weren't worse off because of the increasing population. I think on that whole issue we were eminently correct in everything we have done. When the vote was taken, the majority of the chiefs in this country – they were mostly male – supported it. A very small minority opposed it and Alberta walked out because of it, so I don't know where anyone can get off saying we have not been working properly on native women's issues.

Question: You spoke earlier about the high levels of frustration of native people, and how that's going to mount. What would you predict for the future if the government in Canada fails to implement the self-government option?

Erasmus: I suspect relations would deteriorate to the point where normal business could not occur. The native community is going to become so cynical of government. We are cynical now, but that's nothing compared to what will happen. You'll probably have a situation where native communities develop very radical elements, both within the leadership and also acting outside normal native politics. You're going to see more confrontation and more radical action than happened even in the sixties.

What you have already are radical elements that are coming from among native people. They are challenging leaderships like mine and are saying we're much too soft on government, we're not loud enough, not radical enough, we're not taking drastic enough actions. So I suspect the kind of politics you're going to see is going to be amazingly confrontational, and who knows where that's going to go?

Question: What issues will most command the attention of native leaders over the next five years?

Erasmus: One will be the basic relationship we have with the government. There's no way around it when you consider that they decide policies with or without our involvement, they come out with legislation to change the Indian Act with or without our involvement. If that whole area isn't resolved in the next five years it's going to continue to be a cornerstone issue. Another area is the treaties. The basic relationship we feel we have with this country is through treaties. Closely following that will be aboriginal title and aboriginal rights, whether its fishing rights, the aboriginal right to hunt, the aboriginal right to self-government and so forth.

And I suspect, if you're talking about the next five years, that the constitutional issue will resurface. When the Meech Lake accord comes to its three-year anniversary in the summer of 1990, we will have either the beginning of a native people's agenda, or else you're going to have a situation where the pressure on the government to do something dramatic is going to be so strong that they are not going to be able to keep the lid on.

Question: What is your definition of self-government?

Erasmus: The government and the Canadian people seem to act as if there's some mystery about self-government. For First Nations, we're talking about having the same control over our lives that people have the world round. Since we're living in Canada, we're looking at the extent to which First Nations will be able to exercise their inherent sovereignty and still have the relationship to the Crown that was set up through treaty. In the cases where aboriginal title and aboriginal rights still flourish totally untarnished by treaty, we see a process that should be completely free of the treaty-making process.

In all cases we see First Nations with governments, with tribal justice systems where we are fully governing ourselves. It is not going to be possible for small communities of a few hundred people to do much by themselves, so we see ourselves in larger, extended tribal governments, or nation-type governments if you will, exercising self-determination. We see some good examples in the United States, where tribal governments are recognized to have a large degree of internal sovereignty and have control over Indian country. We can't understand why that does not happen in Canada. If the U.S. government is looking at cost-sharing programs with the states, they recognize tribal governments as the equivalent of states. In environmental clean-up programs, or prevention programs, they don't expect any of the fifty states to be interfering in Indian country.

Here in Canada we're still in the Dark Ages. Canada is looking at new environmental legislation. We go to them and say, "Do what the United States does. Recognize that tribal governments will take care of environmental matters on our lands." When they're considering child-care legislation or day-care legislation, we go to them and request that we be in charge of our own family matters, whether it's child care or other things. Don't set up situations where we have to go through the provinces, because all you're doing is providing them with administrative money. They take, in some cases, something like 85 per cent of federal funds just to administer the 15 per cent that they end up providing to reserves. We argue that, even economically, Canada would be far better off if they cut out the middlemen of provinces and continued to have direct relationships.

Regarding the inquiries into justice, we agree with the Canadian Bar Association recommendation that the native peoples of Canada need their own justice system. The Canadian justice system should be dramatically improved so that native people get more justice. We would set up our system of self-government the same way as is proposed for the Palestinian people. It would mean that different parts of the country would have different things. Traditional systems of government will be used and new modes of government will be set up. In some cases a combination, a hybrid government, would evolve. Twenty and forty communities may come together constituting a level of tribal government, with each community having its own powers. Large single communities might evolve to a level of tribal government similar to those in the United States.

In this country, we will have at least two levels of native government. One is the level of native people as a tribe, and the other is their own community, municipal governments. The whole thing has to centre around recognition of self-determination. The minister of External Affairs can say about the PLO and the Palestinian people that he supports their right to self-determination. At the same time, in relation to the native peoples of Canada, this country is at the U.N. saying they cannot support aboriginal people as peoples in the international sense. They do not support our right to self-determination. They can do it vis à vis the PLO but why can't they use the same kind of terminology vis à vis the native peoples of Canada?

11   Onigaming, Ontario

September is wild rice season. In the shallow bays of Lake of the Woods you can see the beaten-down remains of the natural rice paddies: bent-over yellow straw, chaff floating in the still waters, tracks of canoes through the long grass and the rice stalks. In a good year about 10 per cent of the world's wild rice comes from this Lake of the Woods-Winnipeg River area of northwestern Ontario and neighbouring Manitoba. A good part of that harvest comes from the Indian bands of the area. Many of them still gather the long, meaty kernels in the traditional manner: drifting through the rice paddies in slow moving canoes. The man steers, the woman sits in the bow and uses a tapered stick about a metre in length, called a rice stick, to gently flail the rice so that the grain falls into the open boat. Some of the Indian harvesters have adopted the methods of modern technology; they have acquired pontoon boats mounted with airplane engines and propellers. With these the operation is a much less careful, much less serene endeavour. The boats zoom through the shallows, engines roaring, propellers spinning, sucking the rice into their screens.

1988 was supposed to be a bumper year for rice. All the essential elements were right; it was a dry year so the water was low, and a hot summer had ripened the rice early. But I am told by Chief Norman Copenace that, although it could have added to a thin economy, hardly anyone from his reserve, Onigaming, gathered rice commercially this year. According to Copenace there were two reasons. The harvest in the end wasn't as good as expected because some dirty weather, several days of rain and winds just when the rice was ready, took a great deal of it straight into the water. And a glut of rice still on the market from the year before meant prices would stay low. "Most guys," said Copenace in explanation, "didn't figure it was worth their while."

Though no commerce came from the rice, private picking went on, nonetheless. Wild rice, Louise Shebagegit tells me, is a sacred food. It is one of nature's foods for which the Ojibway offer profuse thanks and is, like tobacco, used in religious ceremonies.

The traditional method of preparing, or curing, the rice is still practised by many people at Onigaming. A thin layer of the green kernels is put in the bottom of a large wash tub. A fire is built and the tub is heated gently while the rice is stirred, usually with a broken canoe paddle until the kernels reach the stage where they are ready to pop, as popping corn would pop. At this point they are pulled from the fire and allowed to cool down. When they have cooled sufficiently, they are placed in a hole dug in the ground that has been lined with canvas. The rice is then danced on. The dancing threshes it, loosening the hulls. By Ojibway tradition only men are allowed to perform this dance on the rice. The rice is then placed back in the pan and tossed into the air so that the wind can winnow away the chaff and the loosened hulls.

No sky gets so blue, no sun so bright, no water so sparkling, as in northwestern Ontario. Here and there along the route of Highway 71 south of Kenora a giant white pine looks ill, yellowing down from its majestic crown. But by and large the forest is rich and green and deep. And the water is clear and cold and deep, held in the clefts of Laurentian Precambrian rock formed four billion years ago. The rocks go deep down and act like a refrigerator. The lakes are iced-in until late April, freeze again in October, and never warm up in any substantial way in between. Some of the water is that of small independent lakes; some is an arm or a bay of the great, sprawling Lake of the Woods, undoubtedly one of the most romantically named lakes in the world.

Occasionally I pass a bay that has been cut off by the highway, isolated, backed up. It turns still and grows lily pads thick as a carpet. I slow and look; sometimes in places like this you can see a moose. I pass another bay and a small flock of pelicans are landing, circling and then flattening down. They are white pelicans, big, clumsy birds that can make you laugh. At another spot I spy a great blue heron, seemingly oblivious but acutely alert as it stands perfectly still. I am driving and I ride through this spectacularly beautiful country caught on the euphoria of the open highway. I meet traffic; between the pulp trucks from Boise Cascade Canada Ltd. in Kenora are cars from Minnesota and half-ton trucks with Iowa plates. Americans are still here fishing; big, sun-burned Americans from Minneapolis and Omaha with their buddies or their wives and their big sons come to Canada to fish.

At a bend in the road I slow, the corner of my eye catches a movement in the deep ditch at the side of the highway. I look in time to see a doe plunge, with exquisite grace and art, from the brush of the ditch into the deep, dark of the woods. At the top of a hill, a blue-and-white sign flashes by, "Sabaskong Indian Reserve." Or, as the people of Sabaskong have begun to call themselves, the Ojibway of Onigaming.

The term Ojibway, Jennifer Brown writes in her essay on the Northern Algonquians in *Native Peoples: The Canadian Experience*, is problematic. "It derives from ocipwe, originally the name that a band north of Sault Ste. Marie gave for themselves in the late 1600s. The same root yielded the variant Chippewa, which has become standardized for those of the same group who eventually found themselves in the United States." Brown writes: "Superficially one may generalize about the ecology and subsistence of these people: all were mainly hunter-gatherers in a cold, wooded environment with winters lasting at least five or six months. Their summer movements were directed mainly along the thousands of lakes, rivers, streams, and the connecting portages that were readily accessible to their light canoes."

223

The Ojibway of Onigaming are part of the Treaty Three Grand Council, twenty-five bands in the Kenora-Dryden-Fort Frances area that all signed their treaty in 1873. In October of every year the elders and tribal officials gather to commemorate the treaty signing. Sometimes they go out to a place called Big Island in Lake of the Woods where the actual signing took place, a location many Ojibway in the Lake of the Woods area consider to be a sort of spiritual home. There, the rusted remains of knives and old flintlock guns still lie in a heap where they were laid down almost 120 years ago as a symbol that the Indians desired peace with the new Canadian government.

The people of Onigaming are true people of the Lake of the Woods. Until the 1920s they lived on a point of land some twenty miles west of where they now reside. But while living there they were hit hard by an influenza epidemic that decimated their numbers. In the face of that catastrophe they were persuaded to move to a spot that would be closer to road transportation and easier medical attention. So they moved to their new reserve on Sabaskong Bay and Crow Lake, where they still live, their houses on the steep terraced hillside straight above the winding highway. They have a sister band at a place called Big Grassy, but the two bands split in 1964.

Sabaskong, or Onigaming, looks pleasant and relaxed in the soft afternoon of autumn. The baseball diamond is the first thing a visitor sees when he pulls in off the highway. There are three sets of small bleachers and a bright-blue fence of vertical boards. A solitary man in brown coveralls rakes the infield, stirring up a small cloud of dust. In front of him a group of a half dozen kids scramble through a makeshift game of scrub. A boy of about eleven swings the bat and knocks a bouncing grounder right past the man in brown coveralls, who continues the motions of dragging his rake across the base paths.

The band office is across the road from the ball diamond and across from two giant pine trees. The road into the reserve is blacktopped, as are all the roads through the reserve, a pleasant contrast to the ruts and dust of the roads of some reserves. The band headquarters is a square, two-storey, brown building with offices up and down. Because of the steep slopes of the landscape, many buildings and homes are split-level with doors on different levels all going straight outside. The police office is also in the band office building, advertised by a red-and-white sign. Atop the roof is a gleaming white satellite television dish being adjusted, at the moment I am observing it, by two young men. If you shift the dish, you can get reception from different places. The band also broadcasts its own programs to the community; televised bingo is a big attraction.

A walk along the roads of Onigaming takes me past scattered houses. Many are quite new. An equal number are in states of either half-repair or half-dilapidation. Because the chief has told me of the house repair program, I suspect the former. Outside one house a man is rummaging around through a yard of topsy turvy furniture, chairs, couches, a washing machine, a wood stove, piles of insulation, lumber; another has stacks of acoustic ceiling tile littering the yard. Yet another house, an older one and abandoned, has a sign in the window, "Closed, please call again." Then there are a couple of very neatly kept dwellings, one with a lawn newly mown and a bird feeder strung in front of a window.

I reach the water of Crow Lake at the end of the community and turn back, up a road that mounts a hill. There, like a new subdivision, are seventeen new homes all painted brown and white, and three fourplex apartments where the school teachers live. The local people call this street "Beverly Hills." On a large map on one of the walls in the band office are shown two alternate plans for future residential developments behind this ridge. I walk down a little trail through the bush, through thick stands of cedars and birch, to another clearing and another collection of houses where there are fish nets drying on boxes.

Though it is a small place by any standard, Onigaming has the feeling of a complete village, with houses, streets, institutional buildings. It is quite sunny and pleasant and serene, not such a bad place to spend your life, I think. What is missing though, I

225

realize suddenly, are commercial buildings. There are no stores. There is no place to stock up on supplies. There is nothing for sale. Onigaming is, I would venture, like too many Indian reserves, an incomplete community. One aspect of community activity, economic exchange, seems to barely happen here. Money does not go back and forth or round and round; it goes through, in one direction.

Good economic practice tries to get some mileage out of money. It tries to make a dollar circulate, tries to make it achieve a sequence of purposes before it leaves the premises. That is not achieved here. Here, money comes in to the community in a variety of ways. Some people earn money from off-reserve jobs, most comes in through the government-supplied band budgets. But money, no matter how it comes in, does not stay to do much more than one job. The teacher does not use her cheque to pay the local storekeeper, who uses the money to pay another local entrepreneur to paint his store, who then uses the money to buy fish from a local fisherman, who then uses the money to buy gasoline from a local supplier, and so on. No. Money at Onigaming, as at many Indian reserves, probably leaves the reserve the same day it arrives there. All commercial activity takes place off the reserve: Indians buying from whites.

What are available on the reserve are services and institutions. A road takes me past the day-care centre and the health clinic (open only when the doctor comes in from Emo, about an hour away). I follow it up to the school. The school is Onigaming's biggest industry. It is comprised of two big corrugated metal buildings, windowless on three sides. They remind me of warehouses and were meant to be temporary when they were built many years ago. But they are still there. A new school is scheduled to be built in two years, the chief tells me. Onigaming is a small reserve, 320 people; half of them are students in the school.

Ten kilometres south of the Onigaming reserve is the tourist community of Nestor Falls. The falls are a three-metre-high pile of rock where the waters from Kakabikitchiwan Lake gush through a channel that leads them into Lake of the Woods. For generations this was a summer fishing camp for the ancestors of the Onigaming Ojibway. Since 1981 it has been designated a site by the Ontario government's Regional Archeologist's Office. In 1988 and 1989 it became a dig site for a team of arch-aeologists assisted by local students. It is a rich dig with a shard of pottery or some such treasure showing up almost every half hour the archeologists are at work. As they work they turn up more and more information. Below the bottle caps and fish hooks from more recent times are pieces which can be dated all the way back to the Laurel culture which thrived between AD 1 and 1,000. The archeologists can show visitors things like a stone scraper, used possibly for scaling fish, and the rim portion from a thousand-year-old clay pot. Some of the frustrations of arch-aeology and the modern world, however, come into play. A guide at the site explained that she expected real rich sources could be found slightly downriver, but that was privately owned land and so they were unable to explore it. The site they are digging has to be explored quickly; they are getting one chance at it before the department of highways moves in and builds ce-ment pads for fireplaces and picnic tables for the pleasure of the travelling public.

Norman Copenace is forty-one years old and is nearing the end of his first two-year term as chief. I meet him first with fifteen or so of his compatriots from the band office as they take their mid-morning coffee break at the Lawg Caybun restaurant on the highway, a couple of miles up from the reserve. Coffee at the Lawg Caybun is a ritual for the people who work at the band office, or in other jobs on the reserve. A relaxed, gentle-looking man with a rather hang-dog face, Norman wears the requisite baseball cap and smokes Export "A" cigarettes. One of his passions is golf and when I join him he and the two other men at his table are telling stories of golf balls lost when playing at the White Moose golf course, a course most of whose fairways border the lakeshore. They replace the balls, they tell me, by buying more from a man who brings used ones into the area from Florida and sells them for $5 a dozen. Later in the fall they plan to travel to an all-Indian-chiefs golf tournament in Manitoba.

After coffee, we go back to the band office. Norman attempts to sum up life at Onigaming for me, and a sort of wistfulness seems to settle down on him. Almost the first thing he tells me is that he has no intention of running again once his term ends. He will stay "involved," as he was involved in the days before he was prevailed upon to become chief. But I get the impression that being chief is a thankless job for which he has lost the stomach.

He ploughs straight into his complaint. "I'm a glorified administrator working on behalf of Indian Affairs," he says. "The nature of the system is that every chief since 1873, when the treaty was signed and the system of band administration was set up by the federal government, has been the same. They [the government] have the power because the power is the money and they control all of that. It's a sad situation, but I'm more responsible to the government than I am to the people."

It's not a happy position to find oneself in, and he wrestles with the question of whether it can change. "Self-government," he says, "would mean being able to get power and get direction from the people. The people would say, 'This is how we want our community to be shaped.' " Currently, though, he doesn't get much of a chance to listen to the people. He describes life as an endless and frustrating round of battles with the bureaucrats. "Last week some Indian Affairs bureaucrats called and asked us what our training needs were. We tried to tell them, and they responded by saying, 'We don't think those are your training needs.' " Copenace raises his hands in a silent "what can you do?" gesture.

The biggest frustration is that they are unable to plan. "We have to wait until April, until dollars are available, before we know what we can do," he says. "We just go from year to year that way. The government never has enough money, so the programs are always Band-Aid programs, just enough to keep our heads above water."

The irritations with the government are familiar ones, repeated over and over like a chorus by every chief and councillor I have met. Copenace, though, also talks about frustration with the people in his community. When he got involved in politics, he says, he wanted to motivate people, he wanted to see movement at the grass roots. It hasn't materialized. People are apathetic. What actions come from the people, he complains, are as likely as not to be misdirected outbursts, pent-up frustrations that find their way into acts of violence or mischief. Vandalism by the kids, he says, eats up a large part of the band's housing repair budget. When he calls a meeting, people don't come. Much of the employment in the community is of the make-work variety with the council as the employer. There are thirty-six jobs in service industries: the school, the band office, welfare and child welfare administration, and another twenty jobs on the housing construction and repair crews. This is almost the total employment in the community of 320 people. "We give jobs to those fifty-six people," says the chief, "and we have the rest screaming like hell at us."

When he is no longer chief, Norman Copenace says he will try to look at it all from a different perspective. "When you have this job you get so wrapped up in the environment you don't have a good rationale to see it with." In his frustration and in the administrative dead ends that he confronts he has conjured up a dramatic fantasy that he nurtures as a sort of catch-all solution for his people. He fantasizes enduring a catastrophe of some unnamed sort, all the Ojibway together; and that being the thing that brings the people together and brings them to a kind of salvation. "I'm for any catastrophes that would unify the people," he says. "I hope that we sink someday. That way we would be forced to get our act together. People have survival instincts. If all the money went dry, the grass roots would have to get involved."

In some abstract way Norman Copenace's life can be seen as an allegory for his people. Crippled, invalided, and impoverished as a boy, he struggled and rose to a certain level. He is still frustrated, but recognizes his progress. Born with a bad left leg, he limped around the community attending school, he claims, only to get a bite to eat from the lunches the school offered. "I grew up on hard biscuits, powdered milk, and cod liver oil," he says. At times his family was so poor Norman would scavenge the dump and the garbage cans at nearby fishing resorts looking for bits of food. If he found a piece of meat he would take it home, his mother would boil it to get rid of the germs, and they would eat it. His father, hunting to provide for the family, frequently crossed paths with the game warden and was put in jail more than once for defying the hunting laws. When Norman was twelve, he was sent to Winnipeg for repairs to his leg. When he returned, he had forgotten how to speak Ojibway and had to work hard "to get my Ojibway tongue in shape again."

When grown, he had to search for work off the reserve, like many other Onigaming members, and like the others, he maintained a house all the while on the reserve. Through the Grand Council of Treaty Three, he got a job as an employment counsellor in Kenora. For a while he worked at the Indian Affairs office in Fort Frances and endured the odd position of living between two worlds. "There were a lot of things I had to do when working for Indian Affairs without wanting to do them. But I wanted to learn. I learned that bureaucrats have a lot of power." He laughs. And he learned frustration. "I wanted to do community development but I found I couldn't do much of that."

Norman Copenace has two children, a boy and a girl. At fourteen and sixteen, their ambitions are standard adolescent ones: one wants to proceed in athletics, the other wants to become a teacher. Copenace's hopes for them are more broadly founded. "I hope they can be contributors to the development of the community, that they can contribute to the earth, both nationally and internationally. I hope they will learn to be good human beings." Will they live here? Will they be able to find their future on the patch of ground and rock and lakeshore between the highway and the Shield? "I'd like to think the economic opportunities will be here for them when they get to the point of making that decision," he answers. "Their roots are here."

If Norman Copenace could do anything to bring his people back to the way they used to be, that would make him happy. "We were like the buffalo, strong and sturdy and free," he says describing his people historically. "Now we are like a cow; we just stand there with a big belly."

Louise Shebagegit is considered a spiritual woman. She has a mimeographed poster on the door to her comfortable bungalow advertising a gathering later in the autumn of the ceremonial Three Fires Society in Lac du Flambeau, Wisconsin. For the full summer and autumn pow wow season, Louise is a traveller and frequently an invited speaker at Indian traditional medicine and spiritual ceremonies all over the Canadian and American midwest. In between, she stays in her house at Onigaming working at her beading, meditating, and welcoming whoever comes to her door seeking spiritual advice. She has a sweat lodge behind her house. A painting on the full length of one of her living-room walls shows two darkened tipis on a spit of land in an orange sunset-fired Lake of the Woods, with wisps of spirit fire streaking toward the heavens and a fierce looking ghost of an eagle fluttering in front of the tipis. The painting, she says, was a gift from some boys in the community whom she had befriended and guided.

Many of those who come to Louise Shebagegit are young people. On the day when I visit, an attractive young couple have come all the way from Winnipeg with gifts of tobacco to have their baby "Indian named."

Louise Shebagegit, who I judge to be about fifty, seems ageless. She wears a print skirt that reaches her ankles, her feet are bare, and her straight black hair is pulled back from a face that is soft and brown and gently turned as modelling putty. She has been working at beading costumes for ceremonial pow wows and shows me some beaded belts, explaining the differences between the symbols of the Ojibway (floral designs) and the Sioux (a sharper, more geometric patterning). She also has a beaded tobacco pouch and deerskin dancer's leggings.

Like so many Indian moralists I have met, Louise starts from deep experiences of pain and trouble. She was an alcoholic, she says, who stopped drinking seventeen years ago and turned all the energy and passion that had been obliterated by drugs straight around and into religious fervour. Over the years she has lost two children, and at one point she gestures across the room and through the big picture window to the waters of the bay. She watched them pull her first husband from the water there, drowned when he was drunk.

Like other Indian spiritual people, and unlike Christian zealots, though, she is not doctrinaire. Anything spiritual seems all right with her. The principal of the school called recently to ask her opinion as to whether it would be all right to say the Lord's Prayer before classes. In Louise's opinion, it was. "That is a way into the spirit," she declares. "Although for me, I don't need to follow those prayers. I can go into the bush and pray with the trees. But it's the same spirit."

Her conversion after alcoholism also opened a generosity within her. She says that over the years since her recovery she has opened her home to three different lost boys. She is, she says, one of the small group of "grannies" that can be found in any Indian community; strong placid women, elders, who keep the spiritual life-light burning and who offer strength and succour to those who need it.

At the end of our conversation Louise Shebagegit turns to me and looks at the notebook I have been holding on my lap. She asks if she can have a look at the notes I have been making. She peruses them for a short moment and then tells me that what I must really know, I will remember. She asks if she can take and destroy the notes.

I meet Peter Kelly, a former chief of the Onigaming band, at a restaurant in Winnipeg. His wife is working on her degree at the

University of Manitoba, and their two children are in French immersion schools in the city. So the Kellys live part of the time in Winnipeg and travel, frequently, four hundred kilometres back and forth between the city and Onigaming.

Peter Kelly has been active in Indian politics for his whole life. From 1972 to 1975 he was the Grand Chief of the Treaty Three Tribal Council; ten years later he was the Ontario region's founding vice-president of the Assembly of First Nations. His brother, Fred, likewise has been an active force in the political world. But when I meet Peter Kelly at a window table of a sunny little bistro restaurant just off Broadway, the street of government and insurance company offices in Winnipeg, it is not politics that he wishes to talk about.

He is a big man, with an impassive face that suggests several possibilities; he is shy, or he is serene, or he is arrogant. He unbuttons his jacket and peels up his T-shirt to show me a row of plastic bandages across the front of his broad chest. It is Monday and he has just returned from a weekend of sun dance ceremonies and the wounds on his chest and on his back are from the piercings of the pointed sticks that are integral to that ceremony. On the weekend to follow, he will leave for Lake of the Woods to participate in wild rice ceremonies and to fast. His seven-year-old son, he says, will accompany him on that fast. It is part of a process that the boy will go through four times on his way to initiation as a medicine man. He is a pipe-carrier now, says Kelly proudly. "He wants to be a medical doctor, an MD. I hope he will be both, an MD and a medicine man."

Peter Kelly has reached the upper echelons of the Midei iwin society, or medicine society. He talks at some length in an attempt to explain to me the sun dance, the shaking tents, dreams, fasts, initiation ceremonies that are the cornerstones of that practice. At middle age he is devoting himself more and more to a life of spirituality and spiritual quest. "I consider myself a warrior," he says. "The sun-dance ceremony, the fasts, are part of the commitment to be the guardian of the land, the environment, the animals."

For Kelly it is all an undertaking of utmost seriousness and importance. It is not the administrative politics he used to participate in, but he feels it directs to the same thing on a different plane; the independence and the identity of his people. "I have a different view of self-government," he says, "than the bureaucrats and the 'white Indians' from down south who borrow their concepts of self-government from the white professors of law." In the way he thinks now, spirituality, the spiritual foundations, the alignment with traditional beliefs, and the understanding of the languages come first. Structures and mechanisms of administration mean nothing if they are not built upon and do not come out of spiritual beliefs. "I have to laugh sometimes," he says, "when I see the people marching off to Ottawa to sit in board rooms discussing Indian self-government and aboriginal rights. Sometimes they aren't even people who can speak the aboriginal languages. How can you attempt to define anything when you can't speak a language?" "The main aboriginal right," he declares, "is the right to have the spiritual experience."

The Ojibway world seems to tremble with an undercurrent of tradition and spirituality. It informs the way they talk and the way they think, and the way they look at the world. It informs their silences. To the non-Ojibway, it is as mysterious and as distant as the shadowy outlines of far-off Lake of the Woods islands. The keepers of this faith and these traditions are the Ojibway elders.

Norman Copenace describes the Ojibway elders as gentle, non-violent people who are sometimes made nervous by the radical or aggressive talk of the younger generation of political leaders. Directness is not their way.

He recalls the style of teaching of his parents, and of the elders when he was a child, a teaching that made liberal use of legend and myth. If he had done something wrong during the day, that evening his parents would tell him a story with an appropriate lesson. The strengths of this method were taken to heart. "If I were to tell you directly, 'Don't do something,' you might resent that," he explains today. "A legend is a way of being told indirectly. You see the bad person in the story as yourself. I would think as a boy, 'Hey, those bad little foxes are like me!' And as a result you clarify and discipline yourself. It is a way of education and discipline."

Historically, the Ojibway were organized politically on a structure of leaders each with specific roles, and each with moral authority in the community. Both Norman and another former chief, Fred Kelly, explain that to me on different occasions. There was the "headman," the "keeper of the drum," the "keeper of the wild rice," and so on. Some of the positions were hereditary, but sometimes the most obvious person would simply rise to the position. The people would recognize an inherent leader and a gesture of consensus would deliver his role to him.

The system of band government instituted by Indian Affairs is not like that, and every Ojibway who spoke to me pointed out that it has few of the strengths of that traditional system. The duty of the politician now is directed more to maintenance of and to the upholding of the relationship with the Indian Affairs administration. The role is not so much one of representing and leading the people, but of pleasing the bosses and keeping everything in order. The people are alienated in such a scheme of things and the leaders are frustrated, and sometimes corrupt. Sometimes leaders cave in and work only for themselves, milking the system for their own and their family's material well-being, thus alienating the people even further and increasing their cynicism. The present system, suggests Norman Copenace, plays on the ego, and ego contradicts the traditional wisdom of the elders. The basic teaching of the elders, says Norman, is that each person is no better and no worse than another. A hierarchical system is at odds with such a culture, and it is difficult to be a chief or leader inside that contradiction. Authority is suspect, those who are in positions of leadership are looked upon as having egos that are too big for their own good, and jealousies emerge. The Ojibway have always questioned if this is really a good way to run things.

The elders built a society, Copenace claims, that was based on harmony with nature, God's laws, and thankfulness to mother earth. These principles were celebrated in a series of ceremonies that took nothing for granted. The sunrise ceremony expressed thanks for the dawning of each new day. The Ojibway people today, believes Copenace, cannot have true self-determination without accounting for these values. The self-determining society would have to be built on an economic base. For Onigaming this might mean acquisition of more land, and more stringent control over and productive use of natural resources. But the new self-governing society also "would have to integrate the values of today with the values of our fathers and mothers."

The unfortunate thing, in Norman Copenace's eyes, is that on the way to creating that new society, the Ojibway stand in severe risk of losing the valuable wisdom of their elders. The elders have watched the world go by and have been frightened out of their traditional counselling and leadership roles, the roles for which they are so sorely needed. "We used to try to nominate elders for the chief and council positions," Copenace tells me. "But they always deferred to younger people. 'We can't speak English,' they would say. 'You do it; you're educated. To deal with the government you need to know how to write, you need to know about budgets.' " So the younger people who knew English and knew how to write and knew about budgets ran for council and ran the reserve. But what they lacked was the wisdom of the elders, the philosophical overview, the ability to speak in parables, the notion of history. The traditional wisdom of the Ojibway elders was thus cut off from the practical day-to-day running of the government. "We don't have many elders as chiefs," says Norman Copenace, "and it's a sad state."

During the time that I was at Onigaming, a judicial committee in Winnipeg was considering the problems of the relationship between Indian people and the justice system. Though it was happening in another province, the northwestern Ontario Ojibway watched the proceedings with great interest, knowing that they could apply the results to their own experiences, which are not at all dissimilar from those of their Manitoba relatives. Norman Copenace says that the Ojibway worry about the court's interpretations of Indian hunting and fishing rights. "The court's interpretations in the past," he says, perhaps recalling the problems his own father had with white hunting laws, "have not been to our advantage. The judicial system has not been culturally sensitive to our needs."

For years, Copenace says, he has been listening to Indian leaders talk about the ineffectiveness of the judicial system. As an example, he tells me that vandalism is a continuing problem on the reserve. The band constable (who works under the jurisdiction of the Ontario Provincial Police) may make an arrest. Or the OPP from Sioux Narrows, sixty kilometres to the north, may make an arrest. From there, everything is disposed of in Kenora, 160 kilometres away, because Onigaming is in the Kenora Judicial District. But by the time a kid who has broken some windows goes through all that process over a period of a few weeks or a few months, the effect has been lost. And the band, who are the complainants, have lost track of it as well. "Back down here," says the chief, "we never hear what happens."

"When we had self-government," he says, referring to some long lost pre-whiteman time, "we had our own methods of dealing with unwanted elements. They were spoken to by respected individuals, examples were set. If you destroyed something, you had to make amends."

It is for the young people that the Ojibway want whatever things it is that they want. The young people seem to be always on the community mind. It is on behalf of the young people that the elders worry.

One day I go to visit Bob Kelly, the manager of the band's education authority, the Onigaming Tribal Education Authority (OTEA). A shy man, given to spare answers to my questions, Kelly nonetheless explains with obvious pride how only three bands in the twenty-five band Treaty Three area administer their own education, and that Onigaming was one of the first to do so. The rest of the reserves either have schools run by Indian Affairs, or they send their children out to provincial public schools.

Before they built their own school, elementary school children from Onigaming went by bus to Sioux Narrows, sixty kilometres away. And high school children went south to Fort Frances or north to Kenora, either to residential schools or to programs that required that they board with families while they attended public schools.

For various reasons, says Kelly, the boarding programs didn't work. "We'd start off with twenty-five high school kids in the fall. By Christmas half of them would be back home, and by spring there'd only be a couple left at school." In 1973 people at Onigaming began to say out loud what they had been thinking for some time: "Why can't we have our own school?" In 1974 they pulled their children out of the school at Sioux Narrows as a protest. By 1975 the first portable classrooms were set up on the reserve and the OTEA was formed. The school authority gets a per-student grant from Indian Affairs that would otherwise go to the public schools that took the Indian children. The school budget is almost a million dollars a year, the biggest single expenditure item by far at Onigaming.

The education authority functions under the jurisdiction of the band council; it administers the budget, hires and fires staff, and so on. The school adheres to Ontario's provincial curriculum but has added things like an Ojibway language program as well as some traditional skills such as trapping, hunting, camping, and wild rice preparation. All of it has added up to making the school their own. The life and traditions and skills of the people are given validity by the school and the people are very proud. When the annual community Christmas feast is held or when the spring graduation exercises are held, the people of Onigaming flock into the school.

Almost half the staff are local, four teachers and four teachers' aides. As well, a couple of the outside teachers have married local people, so they seem destined to stay in Onigaming. The kindergarten teacher is a graduate of the school. "They've licked the problem of school drop-out," says Kelly. The kids stay in school and graduate in great numbers. At no time has the community regretted taking over its school and its own education. It's all been positive in their opinion. The big problem remains, though, a local economy that can't absorb all the people who are being trained even though they want to stay around.

One day I was asked to speak to a high school class in the Onigaming school. I was asked to talk about being a writer to about thirty kids who had gathered in the library. They were a shy group and there was polite attention but not many questions. Most of the teenagers I talked to seemed to have only vague notions of what they wanted to do with their lives after high school. Many said they hoped to go away to college or university, but all imagined that they would then return to Onigaming. Two teenaged boys named Riel and Derek, stayed afterwards and told me they might be interested in becoming writers or journalists. But when I talked to Riel and mentioned the hard work and precarious livelihood writing sometimes offered, he appeared to reconsider. A bright, personable boy, he told me that what he would probably do is get a good education, then come back home. Through the influence of well-connected friends he would then get get a good reserve job, like band manager. He said he did not wish to be chief. "The chief has to take too much heat and risks getting booted out."

What the kids do after their education is the big problem, according to Bob Kelly. The local economy can't seem to absorb them, either on the reserve, or in the whole Lake of the Woods area. Aside from a few provincial government maintenance jobs – highways, natural resources, social services, education, health care, police – the economy of the area is seasonal, based on tourism and forestry. Even if you go to the big towns of the area, Kenora or Fort Frances, you risk being seasonally unemployed as you wait for things to pick up in the busy times of the year. So the problem becomes, what do you do for the kids in school? Do you prepare them and encourage them to leave? Or do you hope that in some brief interim before they graduate something will happen to augment the potential for livelihood locally? The people at the school are not sure which of those paths they follow. But they are certain that they are proud of the fact that they run their own school.

On a Thursday morning the community is abuzz over an article printed on the front page of the Fort Frances *Times*. The previous year, a teacher had worked briefly at the high school but had been dismissed. The newspaper article has been written by his wife. Her article is a reflection, though not a very happy one, on the time she and her husband spent living and working at Onigaming. She is a black woman, born in Zimbabwe, and in the article she declares that Indian reserves are like Third World countries, like her own. But from that point on, she is severely critical of life on Indian reserves and, in particular, of the lack of motivation she says people have to change things. She compares the motivation of Indian students at Onigaming unfavourably with that of students in Africa where, she writes, "education is valued and people are desperate to take over their own affairs." She goes on to describe the people of Onigaming as "essentially bitter. They harbour resentments towards the white man, yellow men, black men, every man."

The article upsets almost everybody at Onigaming. By nine o'clock a copy is taped to the wall inside the entrance of the band office. The carpentry crews having coffee at the Lawg Caybun are passing it around, shaking their heads and clucking. The students in the media class in the high school are running around making photocopies and formulating a reply that they will send down to the newspaper in the hopes that it, too, will get printed on the front page. Riel says the article made him angry. He thinks it unfair and gropes for something to say in response. "The lady never talked to people in the community when she lived here," he says. "She never went out, she just stayed in her house."

I leave Onigaming, but some months later I return. I go to nearby Nestor Falls and check into an upstairs room at the Nestor Falls Motel, across from the float-plane dock. Tourist season is at its height and the highway is busy with cars bearing Manitoba, Minnesota, and Illinois licence plates, hauling big boats, trailers, or big silver airstream campers. Out in the bays I can see boats bobbing in the late afternoon sun: fishermen waiting for wall-eyes. I figure I'll go to the reserve and band office and talk to Norman, see how he is.

A bunch of guys are sitting atop the roof of the day-care centre, they have the roof half torn off and are at work re-shingling it. At the baseball diamond another small crew is working at making some repairs to the blue fence, hammering broken boards back on. I enter the band office and go upstairs to the chief's office, but there is no Norman Copenace. A couple of women tell me that I won't be able to find him there anymore; he is no longer the chief. I call Norman at his house later. "Yeah," he says, "I'm not chief anymore." You've got more free time now, I tell him. "Yeah," he says, "and no more headaches."

The new chief of the Onigaming Ojibway is Katherine Jack. She is a thirty-two-year old wisp of a woman with black eyes, and a voice so quiet that if there is any other distraction nearby, you have to turn your head and listen carefully to hear her. We meet for a conversation over lunch at the restaurant at the motel in Nestor Falls.

Katherine Jack has the determination-charged energy of someone fresh to her office. When I ask her how things are going, she recites a list of things she would like to achieve. In the brief few months since taking over she has given a push, simul-taneously, to almost all the wheels available. Onigaming, like an increasing number of reserves across the country, has begun negotiating a five-year Alternate Funding Agreement with the federal government; the band has laid out a blueprint for eco-nomic development that includes plans for a tourist resort and a mini-mall. The mini-mall, according to Jack, will be populated by local businesses all of which developed their plans during a small business seminar held on the reserve during the winter. They include a laundromat, a hairdresser, a gas bar, a store, and a taxi service. In an effort to create a more participatory style of government, Jack says she has also instituted a system where band members could design the job descriptions of the band staff.

Katherine Jack reiterates the frustration of having to operate in a corporate model so different from the traditional way of the people. In her interpretation of things, the bands were forced by the government to operate in this style because that's how the government likes things. After a season of hearing this complaint, I'm feeling that the government gets scapegoated a bit too easily. Not that there aren't things to blame governments for, but the same brush used over and over starts to lose precision. This observation doesn't make an impression on Jack. When she took a business administration course at the university in Thunder Bay, she says, the instructors theorized similar models and she decided that that must be "because they are all funded by the government." I say, "Don't you think you're a little paranoid about the extent of the government's power and will to do things like that?" She says she doesn't think she is.

When Katherine Jack was young, she was left by her mother with her grandparents and was raised by them. She grew up in Onigaming and worked every tourist season in the nearby camps as a cleaner and chambermaid. When she was eighteen she had a baby. She left for Winnipeg where she got a job in a large hospital. "I was very independent," she says, "and after I had a child, I became very responsible." She lived in Winnipeg for seven years, until her grandmother, back on the reserve, became ill. Her mother came to see her and told her that since her grandmother had raised her, she should repay her by looking after her now that she was an invalid. "That made me feel guilty, so I quit my job and came home."

A couple of years after she came back she was pressed by a number of people on the reserve to take the job of band manager. She was reluctant; she didn't think she had enough education and she was unsure of herself. But she decided to give it a try. "I didn't want to get paid too much because I didn't think I had too much to offer." But she did have a lot of work ahead of her. She describes the band finances as being in a mess. "I spent a lot of my time," she says, "stalling bill collectors." Within two years, however, the band was out of debt and she ran for chief. She was elected chief when she was only twenty-eight years old, and she served from 1985 until 1987, at which time her dying grandfather persuaded her to give it up. She should step back, he told her, and gain more wisdom. In 1989 she ran again. If she is ever out of politics again, she says, she will go and get a degree in business administration. Her quietness is deceptive. She is tough as a cinder, has the stamina for all the meetings, and is adept with terms like "accessing dollars."

"Like every community, we have our squabbles now and then," says Katherine Jack. "But if something happens, every-body sticks together." That, she feels, is Onigaming's greatest strength and asset. She is also proud of the community's young people, who are becoming ever better educated and are eager, she says, about absorbing their culture. The lost generation in terms of culture, according to Jack, are the people who are maybe forty or fifty years old; they were educated in the old Indian schools and "were brainwashed out of their language and taught that their culture was bad medicine." The kids now are not like that.

Before I leave, I pay a last visit to Norman Copenace, now the ex-chief. In the elections in December he declined to run. He took himself completely out of politics; a by-election was held later for a vacancy on the council and he refused nomination for that. Of all the chiefs I met, he is perhaps the most philosophic and, indeed, poetic. And because of that he was perhaps the least well-equipped to function in the bureaucratic world demanded of him. I intend no criticism in that comment, on the contrary I liked him immensely and I found his way of speaking, his style of allegory, the twists and turns of his thinking, and the things he thinks about to be refreshing and instructive. He is reminiscent, perhaps, of the mystic dreamers who were the respected leaders in other times. But you can picture him being a bit at sea in the world of sharp pencils, three-piece suits, pocket calculators,

243

razzle-dazzle consultants, cagey negotiators, airplane rides to Ottawa. One would wish perhaps that our political leaders were all a bit more like Norman.

He sticks close to home now, and is at work building a horseshoe pit behind his house. "I'm getting short of money. Maybe I can win some quarters," he laughs. I get the impression his term in the political arena has worn him out and that he is in need of a long time to recuperate.

Norman is in the process, he tells me, of changing his name. He explains that when he was young his mother dreamed three Ojibway names for him. Now he is writing to the Vital Statistics offices in Toronto to get his name officially changed so that he can use them. One of the names is Awngeweezaz which means, he explains, "I can transform myself," or "One who can transform himself." Another name is Semagemish, or "Warrior." The third name makes him laugh. He says the third name his mother dreamed for him means "moneyman," and he says he doesn't know how his mother happened to dream up that name. But he says that a new name will make him happy. "The name Norman doesn't mean anything. But when I hear those Ojibway names, it brightens me up."

The new names are important because they have to do with culture, and with the language. A problem in native life that has profound ramifications, Norman believes, is that the elders and the young people are unable to communicate. People under twenty-eight years of age can't speak Ojibway; people over sixty or sixty-five often can't speak English. The school language programs might be too little too late. The situation distresses Copenace and makes him sad. And not just for sentimental reasons, but for quite practical reasons. "The English language," he says, "doesn't have much humour. When you talk to someone in Ojibway you lose your narrow-mindedness. It is a very witty language. You look at a bunch of people talking in Ojibway and they're always laughing. You might say, 'What's with these people? They're poor, look at the conditions, but look at them all laughing!' If the younger generation doesn't learn the language, they'll lose all that."

The ramifications are more far-reaching than humour. Language was the vehicle for culture; culture guided the people's actions and thoughts and beliefs. The implications of the culture under duress are all around. "The white men think we are lazy," says Norman. "We are not lazy, but we are not aggressive, not assertive economically. In a way the elders held us back. There are two kinds of economics; the economics of need, and the economics of want. The elders have held us to the economics of need: seek only what we need. If we were aggressive we would seek the economics of want, but then we would lose our souls. Sometimes we forget. Sometimes when I go out to kill something to eat I have a tendency to over-kill because my father is no longer there to scold me. Sometimes I forget to take the tuft from the moose's beard and nail it to the tree as thanksgiving. Sometimes the money comes in. Money is a powerful force for evil. Before we go to the rice harvest the elders bless the rice. But some people, those who want money, sometimes don't wait for the blessing before they hurry off with their mechanical pickers. The elders say, 'Rest the rice,' meaning leave it a while, the birds and the waterfowl need some too. But people don't listen. It's hard to live in the midst of this conflict of the cultures. My kids are more influenced by TV than they are by me. They won't eat my walleyes and my ducks; they want hamburgers. We are losing our closeness to nature. We don't value it. If you value something you take care of it, if you lose that . . . well."

12   Indian Country

That things change is the only constant in history. Nothing that is vital has ever been frozen in time. Time and energy are fluid. Things ebb and they flow. Civilizations rise and they pass. Or they fall. They are not always superceded by other civilizations or cultures that we would consider to be more desirable, but they are superceded nonetheless. Following some cosmic law, some Darwinian imperative of adaptation and survival, societies flourish and then they decline; they live in their world, and then their world changes. They are forced into a migration and they displace others, or they are confronted by migrations from elsewhere. Everything changes.

There are a number of misconceptions about Indian people in North America that seem to be general in people's minds. One is that Indian people are all the same; there is an assumption that regretably still persists that an Indian is an Indian; that a Micmac from Nova Scotia is only marginally different in ethnicity, culture, history, or aspirations from a Haida from the Queen Charlotte Islands or a Navajo from the American Southwest. Another widely held fallacy is the notion that prior to the white man's setting foot on the North American continent, everything was static and had been so for thousands of years. You hear the comment from Indian and White alike, "the native people were living here for thousands of years and doing just fine, and then the whites came and mucked it all up," as if the Europeans were stepping into some pristine Garden of Eden that had held its form undisturbed for countless millennia.

It is true that the arrival of European explorers, adventurers, and settlers was the harbinger of great and rapid, and unfortunately only rarely pleasant changes for the native peoples. But two things are also true. The first is that it was not only life in the Americas that changed in the period from 1500 or 1700 or 1850 to the present, the whole world in that time has been in a turmoil, a turmoil involving vast growth in populations and vast movements in populations.

This has speeded up so that in the modern day, the years since, say, 1945, movements of migrants and refugees are so rapid and so far reaching that it is nearly impossible to keep track of them. The world has been in the process of large convolutions, ever increasing in the speed at which they happen. It can seem sometimes that everything is in turmoil. There have been massive dislocations of peoples and societies. These dislocations in other parts of the world have frequently been the reasons behind the arrivals of one after another wave of immigrants into the Americas. Religious sects have sought refuge from oppression in Russia or Europe; refugees fled wars in Europe and Asia; political escapees left Chile and El Salvador and Turkey to name only three of a hundred places on the globe. In Europe the southerners have been moving north to look for jobs and a better standard of living; in Africa the tribesmen from the plains have been moving to the cities. In London and Paris and Brussels, former colonials from India and Hong Kong and Africa have been arriving seeking work and education and opportunity.

The populations and the societies of the world are in vast flux. And while the tempo at which it is occurring seems dizzying, it is only the speed of change that is different. The movements and migrations and displacements of people have always been, even in North America in times prior to the arrival of the Europeans.

Archaeologists tell us that humans inhabited North America at least fourteen thousand years ago. It is probable that the first human migration across Beringia, the now-disappeared land bridge from Asia, happened some twenty thousand years ago, and perhaps as long as thirty-five thousand years ago. The history of the descendants of those first migrants over the next twenty or thirty thousand years is likewise a history of movement and migration. They moved south and they moved east. Some moved as far south as South America. They moved east as far as the Atlantic coast and Greenland. They moved with the changes of climate, which had a tremendous effect on their food gathering, comfort, and survival. Or they changed as they adapted to those. They moved back and forth as the Ice Age ebbed and flowed.

If they were ever one people, they did not remain so; they became Inuit and Mayan and Cree and Sioux and Inca and Mohawk and Beothuk. They became Thule and Dorset and Laurel and any number of other cultures now extinct. They moved and flourished and declined in consequence of their contact and competition with one another. Barry Lopez in his Pulitzer Prize-winning book, *Arctic Dreams*, writes that the Eskimos or Inuit of the eastern Arctic encountered the European explorers at a transitional time in their culture, when they were in a phase of change, responding to a climactic change that took place between 1650 and 1850 and changed both the type and numbers of animals living in the Arctic. As a consequence, Lopez says, "the hunting traditions, tools and methods had to be swiftly altered for the Eskimos to survive." But because they were in a transitional, adaptive phase, they were at a low point in their culture when they were encountered by the Europeans. The Europeans consequently fixed in their minds an image of the Eskimos as "a backward race," unlike the Aztecs or the Incas who they encountered at the height of their civilizations. But arrival at an earlier time or a later time, and all might have been different.

All changes and must change. It is regrettable, though, when the change represents a disaster rather than an opportunity for a people. It is regrettable when the hand of change is forced by indifference or greed, when it is engineered by a society that claims to be enlightened and compassionate. The change that comes out of that seems tragic and unnecessary.

As I write this, I am in a place called South Indian Lake, two hundred kilometres northwest of Thompson, Manitoba. South Indian Lake is one of a string of tiny communities along Manitoba's Nelson and Churchill rivers, where life was abruptly and permanently changed by the hydro developments of the 1970s and 1980s. The dictum of change arrived suddenly and absolutely in the form of a decree from faraway Winnipeg one day in 1973. And nothing could ever be exactly the same again; nothing in the economy, nothing in the culture, nothing in the lifestyle.

The people of South Indian Lake made their objective peace with the heavy hand of change. They negotiated their compensations. Some found other things to do when the fishing and trapping they had known was no longer possible. But some became lost. They didn't adjust quickly or successfully and were pushed into a migration that might now last for their descendants through a couple of generations. Some took their compensation money and drank it. Some took construction jobs at high wages on the hydro dams and since then have drifted back and forth between wages and subsistence or welfare. Some wandered south to the big cities. A teacher at Oscar Blackburn School in South Indian Lake told me that they advise the children now to get an education in order to prepare themselves to leave the community, their future will not be one of fishing like their ancestors. A woman in the community said bitterly, "The governments and hydro thought all they had to do was give us some money, but money is soon gone."

So it has gone for Indian people for a long time. That Indian people are still, in fact, Indian people is something they have accomplished in the face of great odds. The pressures from the burgeoning society around them to assimilate have been intense, the pressures of sheer poverty should have done them in long ago. Due to some quality – a depth of belief, a patience, a stubborness – Indians, as a people, survived all. And now probably more than at any time since the arrival of the Europeans in North America, Indian people seem sure of who they are and adamant about the reality of their continued existence.

Probably the great turning point in that awareness came in 1969. When the federal government's White Paper proposing to abolish the Indian Act and end special status was published, it spurred a reaction that the government had not dreamed of. The coalescing of Indian consciousness, the search for identity, the gathering power of their political voice from that day on has been phenomenal. But it has not been without hitch. Along that way they have still had to deal with the urge to assimilate; and they had to and continue to deal with the ramifications of their economic impoverishment.

For a long time, the dominant North American society that formed with immigration first from Europe and then from the rest of the world, believed that all immigrants should surrender their cultures and be melted into one. And it believed that, as far as aboriginal peoples were concerned, they should give up and join the culture, too. Even today much government, school, economic, justice system, church and missionary policy holds to this: There is one popular culture in North America, if not the western world, and all must jump in.

In a way, it is difficult to dispute this. Mass communications, travel, the multinational nature of commercial activity, the ways in which styles and tastes and trends in everything from dress to music take off and are instantly everywhere, all make it difficult to maintain a cultural diversity, much less regional or local, ethnic or neighbourhood, differences. To function in the world is, to a degree, to be assimilated by it. But to function in the world knowing who you are and the value of your heritage is much different than being re-formed into something other than what you are. Which is what all talk of assimilation in the past used to imply. A young Indian man in Alberta once said to me, "We resisted giving up our Indianness and being assimilated into the white culture, but we will not have trouble assimilating into the culture of the twenty-first century if we can do so as Indian people." It seems that makes all the difference.

Along with the pressure to assimilate, Indians have also had to cope with the facts of material impoverishment. Poverty, in the material sense, is a very serious fact of life for many Indian people and many native communities. They do not have much money. The word "poverty" is usually used in descriptions accompanied by the adjective "grinding." "Indian people and Indian communities are the victims of grinding poverty." But in my travels, I realized that it is of little help to leave it at that, to say simply, "Indian people are poor and thus need more money." For poverty is only partially the lack of money. It is also and perhaps more significantly the lack of opportunity, the lack of options, the lack of a sense of independence and self-worth, the lack of hope. If you have a sense of who you are, what you can do, your place in the world, the independence to go your own way and look after yourself and your family and your community and to make your contribution to the larger world, you are not poor. Lack of money to such a person is only a set-back. He can make the comment, "I've been broke but I've never been poor."

In this vein, one should not think the Billy family of Cape Mudge, for example, is well-off simply because they have the means to own a half million-dollar boat and spend winter holidays in Hawaii. They are rich because they know who they are and they control, to a measure that still pleases them, their lives and the life of their community. You could also examine the notions of Norman Copenace and the Ojibway about the "economics of need" versus "the economics of want." I would think that young Ojibway Indians, were they to define the wealth of life according to the array of objects that are held out through the commercials on television or in the pages of magazines, might never find happiness or contentment. On the other hand should they succeed in coming to an understanding of how to supply the needs of their lives by living on their land and realizing proudly their ancient role as custodians and protectors of that land, they would be rich indeed.

It seemed to me the more people I talked to and the more places I went and the more people I met, that the poverty Indian people are struggling with is primarily a lack of independence and a lack of opportunity. Yet the public and the media and the government too often identify it simply as a lack of material wealth, as a problem that can be solved through simple money. That is the sort of thinking that caused the government to feel they had done all right by the hunters and trappers and fishermen of South Indian Lake and Norway House and a lengthening list of other places affected by "development," by offering financial compensation. The people were confronted with giving up their independence, their identity, and their sense of who they were through their way of life. Money does not address that poverty. When people talk about self-government, then, the discussion goes round and round. Only those who are not impoverished, who can stand on their own without aid of hand-out, can truly govern themselves. But many Indians argue that only self-government will truly lead them to stand on their own.

There is great evidence that Indian people as a whole are grappling with the spiritual or psychological impoverishment that has burdened them. I should probably not even use the term spiritual impoverishment, for it is likely the spirit has always been strong, elsewise they would not have found the motivation for the current struggle. But one can see case after case around the country of Indian people grappling with the symptoms of spiritual impoverishment, fighting the problems of alcoholism, for example, that in the past brought whole communities to their knees. And on the heels of that, the pressure they are exerting now to insist that they are a people is consistent, relentless, and courageous. It takes the form of re-learning almost-lost languages and cultures, and of resurrecting to places of honour and meaning, spiritual beliefs and practices.

It takes the form of political and administrative action to take charge of local schools and local police forces and local child care. In Manitoba it inspired the courage and the will to oversee a lengthy examination of the relationship of aboriginal people to the courts, jails, and police of the Canadian justice system. It was a lengthy and difficult examination that wouldn't be bought off easily, and wouldn't give up until it had shone a light into every corner and cranny of the troublesome world of native people and the white man's law. In politics it is behind the push for acknowledgement in the Constitution of Canada and for recognition of self-government rights. As this is written, there is still no agreement, expressable in a few sentences about what self-government will mean; the best explanation is that it will and ought to take many forms appropriate to local experience and needs, and that it will come about in many ways, some legislative and some administrative and some constitutional. But what is most important to recognize is that the push for self-government and local control and local independence will not subside. The will and the energy seems to be there to push forever, and that is the will and energy of a people who see themselves less and less as impoverished.

As I returned from journeys that took me to reserve communities and into Indian people's homes and offices and schools and places of work all across the country, I tried to think about the future. Here we are, a country of twenty-seven million people, a half million of whom are status Indians and perhaps another million non-status but who still identify themselves as Indians. Here we are on this continent along with another 250 million people south of the international border, more Indian and Hispanic peoples among them. What will our mixed and common future be?

What will be the culture that evolves to take us into the twenty-first century? Will it be a culture in which national boundaries seem less significant, and in which regional and local differences are respected and cherished? Will it be a culture that seeks to end misery and discomfort, but that understands that our consumer lifestyle and our industrial production cannot continue at the expense of the environment and the natural world? Will it be a culture that thinks differently of ownership of land and of natural resources than we do now?

Will it be a culture whose theology and myths and mysticism seek a different relationship with nature and with non-human life on the planet? Will it be a culture that does not assimilate

253

Indian people, but rather embraces the wisdom and the best parts of their understanding and culture? Already, for example, the environmental protection movement has established alliances with native groups who say, "With all due respect, what you are advocating now is what we have advocated all along." Will this continue to happen?

As Indian peoples remember and rejuvenate their cultures, will North American culture seek to share and to learn? I am saddened to think of the values of mass consumer culture reaching and taking over the children of people like Norman Copenace or Peter Kelly before Norman Copenace and Peter Kelly get a chance to lend their particular cultural wisdom to the rest of us. It makes me sad to think that the urgencies of time might hurtle in such a way that their children will be eating fast food hamburgers grown in the burned-off jungles of Brazil and playing Nintendo games while the pickerel of northwestern Ontario strangle in poisoned waters. This is what people fear for if the mass culture gets to them before they get a chance to influence it.

Might it be possible not only that Indian people re-establish their cultures, but that the rest of us will learn something from them, as well? What lessons of political organization could come from the Mohawks? What notion of the mysterious powers so unfathomable to our rational minds could come from the Kwakiutl? What mysterious learning is to be had from the Indians once they are strong and free and sure enough of themselves to present it?

As I made my travels, not one of the elders or the families or the chiefs or young people I met wanted to withdraw either from North American society or from the current times. All said in their own ways that they must become sure in their culture and in the traditional things that are of value. And they must bring that learning and that wisdom to the running of their own affairs. But if we try, it is possible that in the twenty-first century that learning and that wisdom might go beyond their affairs and benefit all of us.

254